AF323975

THE ADVENTURES OF
DARIUS & DOWNEY

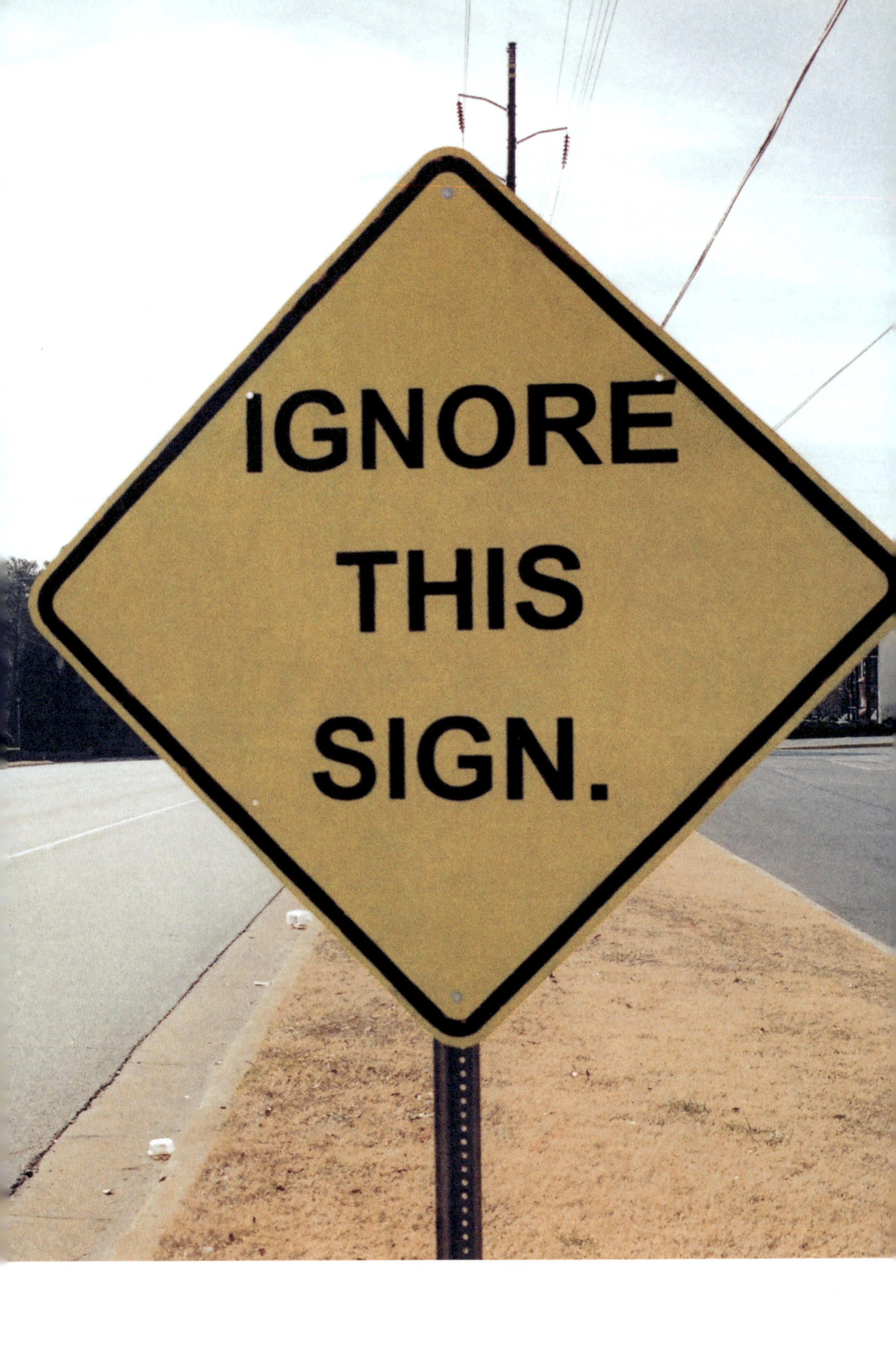
IGNORE
THIS
SIGN.

Leon Reid IV **&** Brad Downey

THE ADVENTURES OF DARIUS & DOWNEY

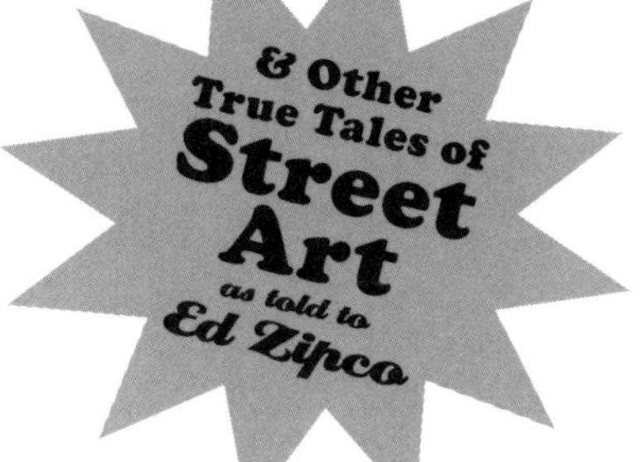

With 79 color illustrations

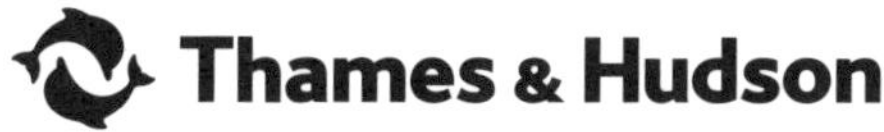

Thames & Hudson

First published in 2008 in hardcover in the United States of America by Thames & Hudson Inc., 500 Fifth Avenue, New York, New York 10110

thamesandhudsonusa.com

Library of Congress Catalog Card Number 2007906879

ISBN 978-0-500-51395-8

Printed and bound in China by Everbest Printing Co. Ltd

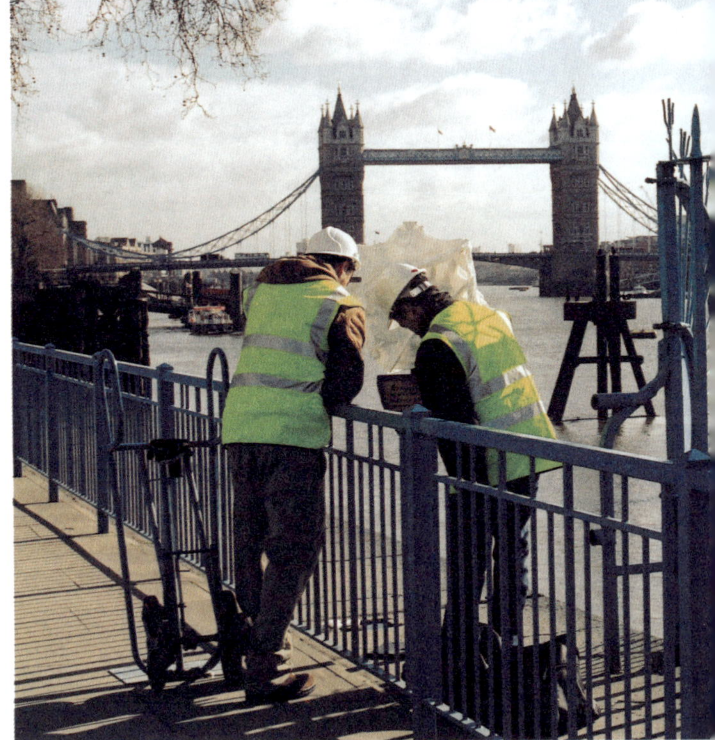

ABOVE Darius and Downey at work in London, 2003. Photo by Eddie Farrell.

PAGE 2 *Ignore This Sign*, Brad Downey, 2004. Marietta, GA. Duration 2 weeks.

Contents

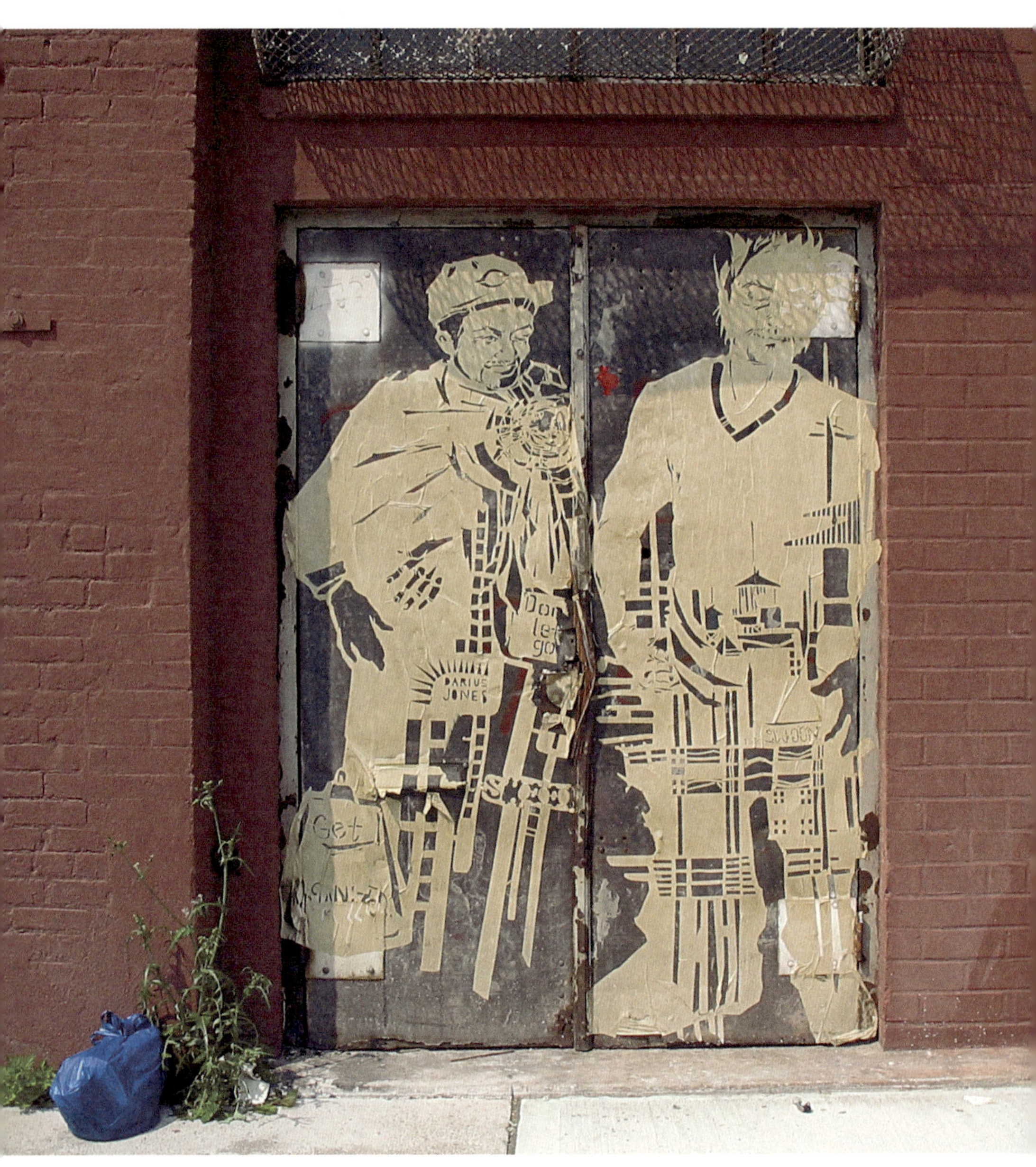

Portrait of Darius and Downey, Swoon, 2003. Brooklyn, NY.

6

FOREWORD
BY SWOON

Darius and Downey never take me out with them on street missions (no one could be less convincing in construction gear), they never take me to paint rooftops (I think they are worried I'll brutally show them up with my skills), and as a rule they won't even tell me where or what a new piece will be until it goes up. Masters of surprise, those bastards. Still, they are two of my greatest creative collaborators — and competition. As compatriot street artists, we are in constant restless dialogue about the nature and meaning of an art form that, in its maverick way, gives itself over completely to the whims of the city. By the looks of the picture I just saw of their latest piece in London, they are kicking my ass in this round.

I met Darius and Downey in 1999, and have watched them evolve from a pair of cheeky get-overs to a rare force for movement and change within the urban art genre, using the city landscape as medium and sounding board. Taking a broad view, their work can be read as something like the evolution of the art of getting over, beginning with a tag and continuing on to something so seemingly distant from that origin that it only remains connected through its existence as an unsanctioned act upon the urban environment.

I had heard that Darius Jones, formerly known as Verbs, grew up writing graffiti in Cincinnati. Inspired by Twist, KAWS, and Phil Frost to push further into the limitless mutations of traditional graffiti, Verbs was a restless mind right out of the gate, and early on began experimenting with the appropriation of bus shelters, advertisements, newspaper boxes, and other basic street furniture.

When I was introduced to his work, he was painting street signs and replacing them on empty poles in Brooklyn. Some with outrageous colors and an obviously painterly feel, some more subtle interlopers. I remember walking down Myrtle

Avenue one day going to use a payphone. By chance I looked up at the overhead sign, which, instead of informing me that it was in fact a phone, bore the name VERBS in perfect payphone script. How many times had I used that payphone before and not even noticed? If it were a snake, it would have bit me.

About this time I would frequently run into Downey with his hands in many pots. He had partnered up with film student Quenell Jones to make what they thought was going to be a two-month investigative portrait of a subject they knew little to nothing about (graffiti), and they asked Verbs if they could follow him. Straight down to business, figuring he could use the help, Verbs had them out on three day-long missions in a row and Downey got pulled solidly into the process.

Having studied fine arts for years, I could see that Downey brought his feeling for color, form, and composition into the obsession. Their two differing areas of know-how joined forces and soon Downey and Verbs were a steady pair, going out together changing street signs and doing roller paintings, with Quenell and his camera bringing up the rear. The film turned from a two-month experiment to a three-year comprehensive view of street art workers all over New York City.

As Revs and Espo had done before them, Darius and Downey went under cover. Downey grew his beard out so that the baby face of a nineteen-year-old art student would better pass for a construction worker.

They studied mannerisms, and acquired uniforms, picking up a Metro Transit Authority vest from a friend who ironically had gotten it through doing community service, and then finding, buying, or stealing construction vests, boots, and hats. Now they could pass for bumbling workers doing a variety of semi-productive tasks both above and below ground.

Their tools were whatever the city would provide: found paint, unoccupied 'No Parking' poles, and fallen-down street signs. They set about recycling the detritus of urban excess and decay, imitating the city's image of work and productivity, and doing it all using public transportation.

One of their most outrageous early endeavors found them in the Canal Street subway station. In plain view, Darius dismantled the Canal Street sign as Quenell and Brad filmed the spectacle. Taking it home with them on the train, Darius asked Downey if he would like to paint the reverse side. Downey accepted and the two repainted it to read: "Downey St., Adorning NYC" on one side and "Verbs St. Oh yes I did!" on the other. They then returned the modified sign to the station via the subway and reinstalled it.

It was a promising start. In my circle, all eyes were on them, waiting to see what would come next, but the momentum was stilted. Verbs, at a personal crossroads, went home for summer to work at a graphic design firm in Cincinnati. Something about performing mindless unrewarding activities all day pushed him toward the realization that he should, in all aspects of his life, be attempting to do something meaningful.

Having already discovered graffiti as a powerful medium with which to communicate to a broad audience, he knew it was the way that he wanted to work, but he now made the decision to drop the egotism and negativity he suspected were a part of his process. Just as he had taken on the persona of Verbs, he transformed himself again. Letting Verbs go completely, he decided to become Darius Jones, a different name, a different mentality. He would use his tools for more than just proclamations of his own presence in the world. He was now Darius Jones, civil servant.

Back in New York, I could see that the pair found renewed

strength in partnership, deciding to sublimate the urge to write a name large and live (and therefore compete with each other) into the practice of working together on one piece, a message or creation that was a kind of a gift from the two of them to the whole city. A sign by the side of the highway blends perfectly with the speed limit signs and exit signals, but this one reads "Don't let go." A giant clipboard forty foot tall appears on the side of a building in the Lower East Side with the cheerful command "Get organized!"

In one conversation with Darius, he told me how he realized there was already so much negativity in the city, especially within the public's perception of graffiti. "Like oh, it's illegal AND it's negative, I'm shocked. Why don't we try to make something that is big and illegal and positive? It's still graffiti but it's not what you thought you were going to find."

Darius and Downey were some of the only people I have ever seen to pull off roller pieces that included imagery. They painted massive gift boxes and cell phones and giant thought bubbles urging drivers on the BQE to "Honk if you love graffiti!" These roller paintings they called "The Booms" because that was the desired affect, you look up and, BOOM! How did that get there?

Pushing further into the conceptual integrity of their shenanigans, the two began to create works that weren't simply additive – not just a painting where there wasn't a painting before – but that became a part of the landscape in such a way that the whole scene makes more sense with the addition. "No Dunking" reads a tiny basketball hoop fixed to the top of a pole outside of the basketball courts on West 4th Street. This piece immediately prompts a reaction from guys waiting to play a pickup game of basketball – within a few days the hoop has been slammed from someone who had to climb up on the phone booth to reach it. A sign across from the NBC station on 59th Street is shaped like a television and reads "Stay Tuned." Members of the Rockefeller Center private security force came over to see if they needed any help during the installation. Seamless.

Looking to sharpen their technique, Darius and Downey bought a hammer drill. They had spent a lot of time and energy recycling the leftover poles and fallen-down parking signs the city seems to leave behind so copiously, but now they wanted to dig a little deeper into their chosen terrain. With this new piece of equipment, with which they could install a freestanding sculpture directly into concrete, it was a whole new ball game.

It was mean and loud and sloppy, and if they had grown comfortable in their previous way of working, they were completely shook again. What's more, freed from the instant context of the street sign, they were forced to reexamine how they could continue creating work that felt like an integral part of its environment. Three or four months of pure screwing up ensued, but tenacity is the other mother of invention.

After graduating from college, and with the completion of the film "Public Discourse," Darius and Downey decided to take on a new challenge in the city of London. They wanted to see how comprehending a whole new place would change their work, and of course, in doing so, to conquer a little bit more of the globe. Within a few months the move did exactly what it was intended to do – it activated a perceptual shift that would take them once again a step further.

Faced with the prospect of trying to fit in anew, of examining the outfits of the British construction workers, of comprehending the new language of street furniture and ordinary symbols, they found themselves deeply examining these kinds of regulatory systems – the signs that direct a large portion of our daily habits, whose mundane ubiquity we internalize and ignore. Like some modern Dadaist rendition of the Madonna and Child theme, a speed limit sign reads 5 (miles per hour) right next to a smaller version of itself that reads 2.5. The little guy is accurate even to the slight angle that the larger sign leans. I know secondhand that people who have been taken to this spot to "See a new piece of street art" often don't comprehend what they are supposed to be seeing, but just stare for a long time looking for the sticker or poster or throwie, until the realization kicks them in the head.

CCTV cameras perched at right angles of a building stare each other down in a ritualistic standoff, or maybe with narcissistic lovers' longing. Street lamps split themselves clean in half, but remain perfectly upright as if nothing unusual has happened, or lean lovingly toward stoic members of their own species. This latest body of work may be my favorite. Years of experience and keen observation of their environments have led Darius and Downey to a phase of street art unlike anything brewing in the current communities. These new pieces are like tiny little monuments questioning reality. The moment you are able to pick out this trespasser as foreign and to question it, you begin to question your whole environment. Everything is suddenly implicated. The change is now within you; it's within your looking.

The Situationists speculated that the most important art to come out of the 20th century would not change the way that we view painting, but would change the way we see the city itself. Having succeeded in doing just that, my boys have a whole new century ahead of them.

Swoon
Brooklyn, NY
9 February 2006

GOOD CHEMISTRY, BAD EXPERIMENT

2000 | Darius and Downey (Leon and Brad), working together for the first time, decide to go big in Brooklyn's Bed-Stuy. Once at their chosen spot, the boys find new dangers in working on such a scale, namely a little friendly competition. Meanwhile Quenell's first time watching the two get up as a team almost ends up being his last.

In the winter of early 2000, Leon, Brad and Quenell were walking down Myrtle Avenue in Clinton Hill Brooklyn, coming back from grabbing some eats over at John's Diner.[†] Once a few cold blocks away, Brad finally shared the idea that had been rattling around in his mind all morning.

"There," he said. "How about there?" Brad was pointing up to the massive white building across the street from the upperclassman Willoughby dorms.

The milky gray sky that stayed overcast for the whole of winter almost absorbed the building's outline, but it was front and center on the block. It was a couple of buildings deep, but taller than the others that sat closer to the avenue, standing high and strong behind them. The entire neighborhood saw the sun hit that building's bright white face and light up the block on a daily basis. This location was not just going to be seen and noticed, it was going to be damn hard to ignore.

Brad had been hanging out with Leon on and off for around a year at this point and filming him as a graffiti artist for a few weeks. Now he was eager to give it a go himself. Most people build up to gigantic acts of vandalism, but that's never really been the way Brad's head worked. With a background in fine arts, what Brad saw when he looked at that massive white wall was a fifty-foot tall, hundred-foot wide canvas. It was primed and ready and he wanted to go big all over it.

The orthodox graffiti world works a little differently. Artists are always building up to something bigger, paying dues, getting respect, and slowly creeping towards the limelight, the big risks. Brad had just pointed at a building like he wanted to own the block, when he didn't have the street cred to rent an apartment. Leon, however, had been working steadily and felt like it was high time to go big and public himself. He'd earned it. Brad sure had done his homework by picking a place out of the local skyline that was pretty much perfect. If he could

---

[†] John's was where you could get a hearty trucker breakfast any day but Sunday for about three dollars. A bargain any way you slice it and a constant, almost a point of pride, in the lives of the more broke half of the Pratt constituency.

figure out the rest of the legwork, Leon was more than happy to go along and add a little legitimacy for the payoff of a strong spot to shine.

They walked closer and inspected the building, looking for a fire escape, a dumpster to scale, some exterior pipes, or maybe an adjacent roof that was lower or that came ready-made with any of the above. Anything pointing upwards in fact. It took about ten seconds to see that this wasn't going to happen easy. Most likely that was the reason why that wall had maintained its virgin white upper section when half of the neighborhood had been coated a hundred times over by graffiti writers painting and repainting walls thirty-two flavors thick for the last three decades.

Leon stared at the ledge of the roof, an easy twenty feet off the ground. "You been thinking any about how? You got a plan on how we're gonna get up there?"

"Well yeah, actually. I know where we can borrow a ladder." Brad was so matter-of-fact he might as well have been shouting down to Leon from the top of the roof already.

Then and even now, borrowing rarely involved asking, and only slightly less rarely involved returning. Brad had been keeping tabs on a two-story ladder that was being used in the construction of the new dorms on campus. Campus security was provided entirely by the Caribbean islands, whose uniformed immigrants cared little to nothing for the comings and goings on around them. A friendly and courteous lot, they were most often seen and not heard. When they were heard, they were impossible to understand. If you went about trying to address them and began spinning your lie, they would drag you down in a verbal quagmire that was the equivalent of a hurricane in quicksand.

But all of this was an amateur's problem; Brad and Quenell had long understood how to circumvent that kind of nonsense. Adopting the guise of "work study" employees from physical plant (the school's

---

Pratt Institute, along with most campuses in America, is willing to hire students who need a little extra money to fill physical labor positions. The college pays them as little as possible and avoids having to deal with local businesses or local employees. It's win/win for the college and, well…the college.

student caretakers) – sporting pissed-off grimaces and clothes covered with paint and grease – the boys simply picked up the valuable two-story extension ladder and walked away with it. No one batted an eye either when they hid the gigantic ladder in the bushes behind the Willoughby dorms, least of all the dorms' security officer, a notoriously heavy sleeper.

Now they had a way up, it was just a matter of getting some materials to work with. Leon was acquainted with a lower basement level where physical plant kept their supplies. Fast as anything, he and Brad had gone down there and lifted a five-gallon bucket of white and a one-gallon of red. Back at Leon's dorm room they started mixing and the white and red turned into a ready-to-pop bubbalicious pink that was just shy of neon. This was way before preppy pink made its debut in hip hop and it became game to rock a soft color. In the year 2000, pink was just pink. But Leon was more than happy to use the color, knowing it would jump off the wall. He would push "VERBS" out there in any shade he could hustle.

Pink or not, Brad didn't want to use the same color as Leon. Even though they were going up together, getting up together, he wanted their work to stand apart. He had a gallon of black and asked Quenell to pick up a bucket of bright yellow on his way back from Manhattan. Brad's grand vision was of a giant golden Brancusi-like head, perched up there with the architecture as its perfect white plinth.

Yellow was the closest he could hope to get to gold on a budget. But even yellow was not to be. All Quenell could find was what he described as "pale yellow." Brad gave the go-ahead, but when he turned up, Quenell's "pale yellow" was in actuality off-white. Or "off-off-white" if you wanted to be generous. On a white wall twenty-two feet up, it just wasn't going to work. The last piece of the puzzle before they were

---

He was shown this stash by Bills, the man who mapped out the NYC graffiti game for Leon, taking the young artist under his wing and showing him the ropes. His first time down on the subway tracks, Leon watched Bills stroll onto the guard beam above the third rail. Leon thought that was it, he was gonna watch his man fry like a convict. Seeing the fear on Leon's face, Bills gave him some of the truest advice he ever heard. "Don't stress. If you don't fuck with the third rail, it won't fuck with you."

launched didn't fit. In the spirit of not losing momentum, Brad conceded to stick to black. The vision was spoiled, but "The Brad" abides.

Around 10:30pm, they got motivated. With Leon's trunk filled with paint buckets, the gigantic ladder, video equipment, and adrenaline, they were equipped and on the move. Once at the spot, they laid the ladder against the wall and, like a found key in an important lock, it hit the ledge of the roof with a clack and rested easy. Quenell stayed on the ground, Leon acted as relay, and Brad was up on the roof in an instant, ready to collect whatever was handed to him.

They moved with quickness and within minutes were all on the roof pulling the ladder up behind them. They began scoping out the surroundings, taking a moment to get their bearings and to observe anyone who could just as easily be observing them. A few buildings away was the parking lot of a White Castle that was teeming with cop cars. Every couple of months it was standard fare for cops to fill the parking lot of said White Castle or the KFC beside it, summoned by reports of robbery or a stabbing. But it being just past midnight, it was more likely just night-shift lunch hour for the local precinct.

Nothing stood out as aware that they were up there, so Brad and Leon put all the paint by the wall while Quenell started looking for angles to shoot and loaded up the camera with tape. But while looking through the viewfinder at Leon, Quenell spotted movement in the background and saw a light go out in an apartment just across the street. He zoomed deep. The image got blurry and more pixelated as he got closer, but he could still tell that someone was there, moving the drapes aside and crouching while looking right back at the three of them.

"Down! All y'all get down!" Quenell whispered harshly.

They took a moment to assess the situation. They had to decide whether to cut and run if the spot was blown, or to ignore the witness, stand back up, and dedicate themselves to the moment. They were dangerously close to the point of no return. If they got caught before the paint was opened, the charges would be far less than getting caught in the act. They opted for a compromise, splitting for the time being, leaving the paint up there. They slid down the ladder, and hid it behind a dumpster at the end of the street. When some time had passed and the neighborhood watch had drifted off to sleep, they'd be back.

The closest place to rest as they ran out the clock was Leon's girl-friend Polina's. Leon gave her a call and the three of them headed over, still full of the weird energy produced by the mixture of adrenaline, fear, and ditching out of a dangerous situation before it becomes do or die. Switching gears into "social hour" was a hard sell, but they made it happen as Polina served up tea and crackers to the shook young criminals. It was surreal, yet the tea and calm company was just what the doctor ordered to ease the tensions clenching their spines.

Choosing Polina's apartment ended up being a stroke of genius, because just as the last of the tension was fading away, and the boys started to settle into the couch that was just a little too comfortable, Polina realized it was around midnight and the apartment became a lot less inviting. The lovely host made it abundantly clear how much less and less welcome the guests were as the minutes ticked by. This subtle push threw the gentlemen right back onto the street and back to business. It was just the kick in the pants they needed to get up there again and actually make it happen.

They retrieved the giant ladder and hustled back up to the roof. All the surrounding buildings were sleeping by then, and it was time to get to work, unheeded by local watchdogs.

This time, however, they didn't pay as much attention when it came to lifting the ladder up behind them. As they tilted it up, the extension (i.e. the lower half of the ladder and their only way off the roof) started sliding out. That metal on metal scraping noise was a gavel falling, it was a cell door slamming, it was a functional escape route closing off. Seized by fear, they pushed their side of the ladder with all their strength down on the ledge, vaulting the other end of the ladder up and catching the tip of the extended section that was still inside the slot with a tiny hooking "tink" sound.

Breathing heavy and with everyone's face paralyzed in a state of suspended fear, with the ladder hanging like a gigantic two-pronged flagpole stretched out a good fifteen feet from the building and almost knocking into a streetlight, just hovering there, they pushed down again, sharply, and the section bounced up and slid deep into the main casing like a gigantic sword being sheathed. The sharp sound of aluminum scraping aluminum, culminating in a loud hollow metal bang as it locked in deep, came as a relief, despite the unnerving volume.

Walking over to the paint and equipment they had set by the wall hours before, they finally got to it. As they stared wide-eyed at the scale alone, it was clear that they were both popping their respective cherries on this great white whale of a wall. Leon had recently gone big in Cincinnati, in the winter of '99, by painting a massive "VERBS" on a decommissioned commuter train car. That gave him the clout to come back to Brooklyn and go big in a very public way. But he had never gone high up like this, had never used an extendable roller on a piece before, and Brad had never "gone" period.

Leon and Brad opened the trunk and started discussing what and where and how they would divide the space between them. Save some throw-ups and tags at eye level, the wall was naked as the day it was born. They could have sliced up that pie a hundred different ways, but at the end of the day, their tools decided for them.

Leon had brought an extension roller that stretched out sixteen feet. Between that and the ladder, he figured that he would be able to get up as high as he wanted on the wall and then some. Brad meanwhile had shown up to do his first big "boom" piece, with aspirations of going as big as the space and his ability allowed, armed with a paint brush. It was laughable, but Brad refused Leon's extra roller, stubbornly determined to stand by his fine art convictions and do things his way.

"You ready Picasso?" Leon started busting Brad's stones then and there, and Quenell and Leon both ride him on it to this day.

According to the limits of their chosen tools, it was agreed that Leon would go above, as high as he could reach with the ladder and pole, and wouldn't go beneath an arbitrary mark on the wall. Everything below the mark would be open terrain for Brad. Nothing was said, but Leon was happy to be going over Brad. The higher you went the better people could see your work, and to go above someone else's work was a sign that you were in charge of the show. It was a position that Leon wasn't used to; the best he had had it was as an equal. It felt good. As the silent observer, Quenell would sit back and watch, capturing the work for the record. Brad and Leon got busy.

Almost immediately Leon started pulling his "V" right down to the divider mark and beyond. Brad held his tongue, not wanting any drama over territory disputes so early into the mission. Leon was trying to go up higher, but the higher you go, the harder you have to push, and the more you have to lean on that ladder and work your arms, shoulder and back. The process was easier, and less likely to run out of steam, if little by little he crept into Brad's area.

If Leon hadn't been full of stubborn pride he might have mentioned how his arms were killing him almost immediately, not yet having the muscle memory to work so vertically. If they had spoken at all, they might have compromised, done something more side by side, less top and bottom. The reality was nothing got said. They just kept working, for better or worse – Leon's better and Brad's worse.

When the "E" in VERBS got spelled out, Brad had a fair idea of how he thought the rest was going to go. His work space was tightened, he had a smaller box to fill, but it was still manageable. He stepped back to see how things were going with Quenell, who was twenty feet away getting a wide shot of the wall and the artists beneath it.

"How's it coming?" asked Brad.

"Oh, you know. How y'all feelin' over there? You keeping warm with all that labor and I'm standing here cold as a motherfucker." Quenell laughed. "No, for real though, looks good, man."

"That V and E came down low out of nowhere. But I'm working it. No biggie," said Brad.

Then, while the two of them watched, Leon got cramped trying to coordinate the ladder with an air conditioner unit on the roof and laid down the ladder. He climbed on the unit, slapped the roller as high as he could reach, and just dragged the thing eight pink feet deep into Brad's space, chopping a third of the height right off. That roller came down like a guillotine and it took Brad's jaw to the floor.

"The fuck?" Brad said to himself.

"Oh shit, boy. Your man there just went way low." Quenell had a penchant for stating the obvious, which at least let you know that you didn't imagine your personal nightmare. "Whatchoo gonna do?"

"What the fuck am I supposed to do? Shit. He just squashed my whole space."

Brad had just had his canvas cut and cut again by someone he thought he could trust, someone who was supposed to be his hookup in the graffiti scene. That guy just smashed his shine without a word of concern or consideration. He was becoming pretty tight with Leon as well as doing a documentary that featured him. Was getting punked on this rooftop worth calling him out, making something out of this, and at the end maybe throwing all that away?

"This sucks." Brad resigned himself to muttering that as his mantra for the rest of the night. As he started walking forward to see what space he could salvage and claim as fast as possible, he immediately stepped in a puddle of ice-cold water, soaking his sock. "This sucks," he muttered again.

As Brad left him and went back to the wall, doing the best that he could with the space that was left, the cold started really getting to Quenell. This was his first winter night spent on a Brooklyn roof. The others had been keeping warm by working feverishly for about two hours, but to sit there and document it didn't work up nearly as much of a sweat. He thought about it for another second and decided it was time to run to Brad's place, grab some warmer clothes, and get back as fast as he could. Leon wasn't using the ladder anymore so he could borrow it to get down without messing with his artistic rhythm.

He walked over to Leon and lifted up the ladder.

"Whoa, man. What you doin with that?" Leon snapped on Quenell.

"I'm just trying to get down real quick to get some layers on. I'm freezing my monkey ass off up here, man," Quenell replied.

"Nah, you should just stay, dude. Cops drive by, spot the ladder and we get popped because you wanted to go pick up some fresher gear? That's stupid."

"Shit. Ok, ok. That's cool," Quenell conceded. "I'm gonna find another way off the roof."

"Shit doo, if you can figure it out, go for it." With that, Leon turned back to the wall.

Quenell walked the perimeter of the rooftop, eventually finding a roll-down gate closing off a parking area. The gate had a chain dropping down to street level. It was about eight feet wide, more than enough space to maneuver down. If he did it right, he could step onto the two-foot-wide cage that the gate was raised into during business hours, grab the chain and climb down. It was some Mission Impossible thinking but Quenell was always an out-of-the-box thinker. He told Brad what he was up to, and Brad threw a dry pair of socks onto the shopping list.

Quenell lowered himself down onto the cage, seven feet below the edge of the roof, turned, reached down, and straight rappelled using the greasy chain. Had he been caught unaware of the grease, his grip would have slipped and that boy would have broken his neck on the ground below. But that didn't happen. Quenell knew that these chains stay heavily greased all year round; the roller gate is the last thing a shop owner is going to let rust. It's a shame that the two artists above didn't take a moment to watch the show, because Quenell slid down that chain without another thought, smiling all the way down.

Brad had missed Quenell's Olympic moment because he was working like a madman trying to claim as much space as possible before another guillotine dropped in for a visit. In the midst of this, Leon had attempted to make amends by offering up the space between the letters, leaving them to Brad's creative devices. This was as much of an olive branch as was available by that point, but it was just enough to keep everyone's spirits up.

Brad did some rough work between the letters, just to map out the space, then went back to finish what he could in the main space below.

As Brad was hurriedly working, Leon stepped back to figure how he was going to shape the "B" and close this big bad pink thing out. It was a windy night, and it was hard to hear a thing while working, but as Leon got further away he suddenly detected a high-pitched sound, a bunch of short sour notes belted out at the top of someone's lungs.

It was Quenell. To get back up, he had grabbed onto the greasy chain holding a thick pile of paper towels in each big mitt of his. Slipping the tips of his sneakers into the slats of the downed roller gate, he had made it onto the cage above. Trouble was, he hadn't made it all the way. An awkward roll had left him half hanging off the ledge. Add to that the fact that as soon as he put his weight on it, the empty cage had started bending away from the wall. It was only a slight bend, but it was enough to shift all of his weight with it and towards the pavement. He was moving slowly, and it wasn't by choice.

Leon got to the edge just in time to see Quenell face to face with an ugly fall that might close his book for good. His eyes were shooting all over the place, looking anywhere and everywhere for salvation. Quenell saw Leon and screamed "Help!"

Leon reached down but there was no way to help him. He was a solid couple of feet lower than Leon could stretch and even if he did, Quenell was double his body weight. Leon would have been pulled to his death, no question.

But that's not what Leon was thinking about. He tried reaching again, then screamed back to Brad, who was completely unaware that his best friend was hanging off the edge of the building and about to fall to his death. Brad couldn't hear a thing; the windy night dropped the volume out of everything. All Leon could think was "I brought him up here. I didn't let him use the ladder. This is my fault." Over and over as Quenell screamed for his help.

Finally Quenell, who was slipping further and further from the wall, had a word pop into his head. Friction. As a last-ditch effort as he started to feel his shoulders turn towards the ground against his will, he pushed the tips of his toes and the edges of his fingertips as far as they could go and he just grazed the edges of the walls on either side of the indented gate.

He felt the friction, almost out of reach, and he shot out his arms and legs again even further and caught some more of it. Even with just the skin on the tips of his fingers, saved by the grooves in his fingerprints themselves, he flexed hard and leaned his weight back against the building, centering himself. He slowly sat up and even as the roll-down cage bent further down towards the pavement, he didn't blink, he was already vertical. He put his hands on the edge of the building and wedged himself into the corner, did a pull-up with the last of his adrenaline, and he was on the roof.

Heading over to Brad with Leon, Quenell was nearly jogging by the time he got over to wall, with Brad still working like crazy beneath it. It had only been a minute or two at most, but it felt like the whole night had been about keeping Quenell's life intact.

"Yo boy, you were almost looking at a dead nigga right here!" Quenell laughed excitedly.

"Hey, hey, hey, hey, hey. Quiet down. You got my socks?" Brad remained unaware, too focused to grasp how perilous the episode had been. Quenell, deflated, handed over the socks and got back to shooting.

It was only as Brad was putting the finishing touches on his piece, as Leon recounted what Quenell had been through, that it began to sink in that his best friend had almost fallen off the building and died. Finally Brad stopped, walked over to Quenell, and looked him over to see if he was all right. He paused to chill with him for a second. His work was near enough done, and the close call was really beginning to affect him.

"So you ok?" Brad asked.

"Yeah nigga, I'm fine. Shit was serious, never been that close to dying before. Shit was fucked up." Quenell responded.

"Well… I'm glad you're ok. You're my best friend, I mean… I'm just glad you're ok." The emotion was genuine.

"I know my nigga, but a nigga like me? I had to think logically to get out of that shit!" Quenell replied. "Friction, baby, friction. I scaled that wall putting my fingers in between bricks 'n shit. I'm your local fucking Spiderman."

As they stood there, looking at the wall on the other side of the roof, and the giant piece that Brad and Leon had done, Brad beamed.

"That's my first piece man. You can even see all the little stuff creeping up between the letters, you know, like behind the 'VERBS'? Looks good," he said.

"Yeah, it does," replied Quenell.

Almost as if he had heard them in the distance, Leon at that moment swept his black paint roller down, filling in the spaces between his letters to create a drop shadow effect. It looked good, but once again and without a word, Leon had erased Brad's work. As olive branches go, that one was short-lived.

"You've got to be kidding me," Brad said under his breath.

"Does he look like he's kidding?" Quenell whispered back.

"This sucks." The mantra was back in full effect.

Brad decided then and there that he was never going to let that happen to him in the future. If it had to be an argument, if it had to be a fight, if it had to be the end of a friendship, he was never going to "sit bitch" again. But for now, watching Leon methodically obliterate over a solid hour's worth of his work, Brad just slowly exhaled, walked over, grabbed his brush off the ground and dipped it in Leon's black paint. For the sake of the work, both Brad and Quenell helped Leon fill in the rest of his letters. They did look better semi 3-D. As a thank-you for the help, Leon made a big fat pink arrow that pointed at the piece and wrote "Downey, Que" on it in black.

On the walk home, Brad laid it out for Leon. From then on out, when they both did something together, they would get equal shine or he wasn't interested. As the experienced one, Leon had felt it was his right to have a fatter piece of the pie, but looking forward to working with Brad and Quenell again, he agreed. They didn't know it then, but that was the birth of Darius and Downey.

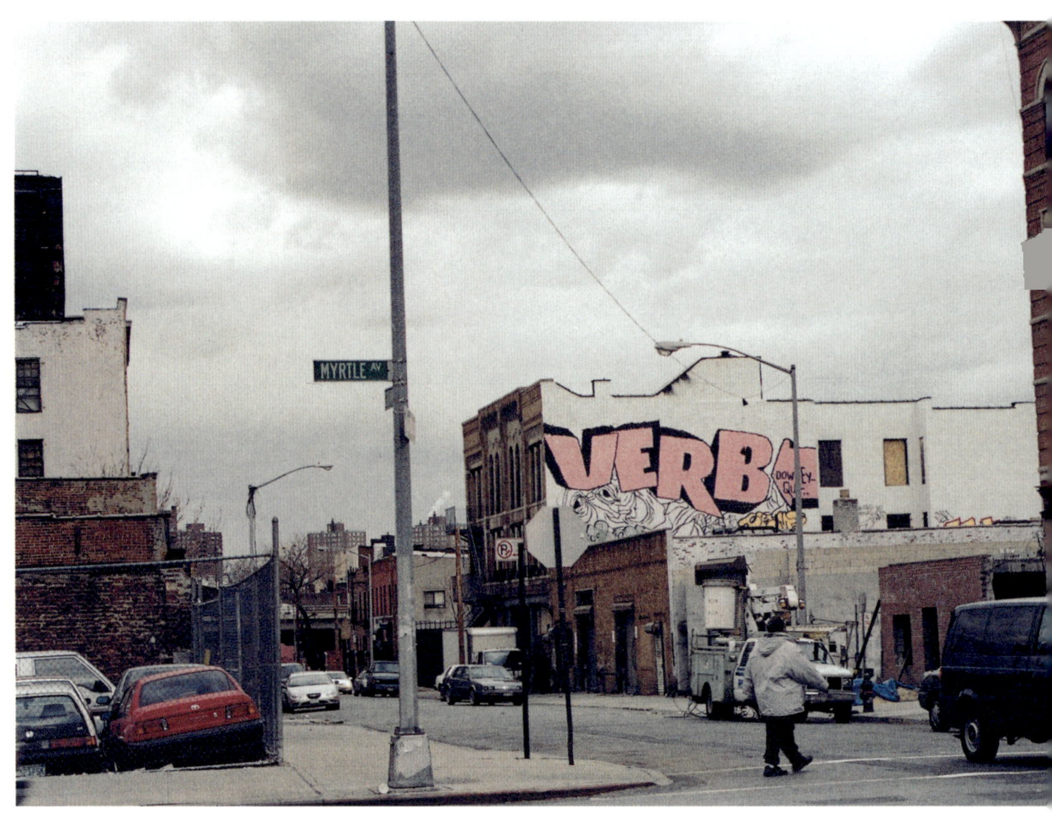

Pink Verbs and Giant Head, Verbs (Leon Reid IV) and
Brad Downey, 2000. Brooklyn, NY. Duration: 7 years
and counting.

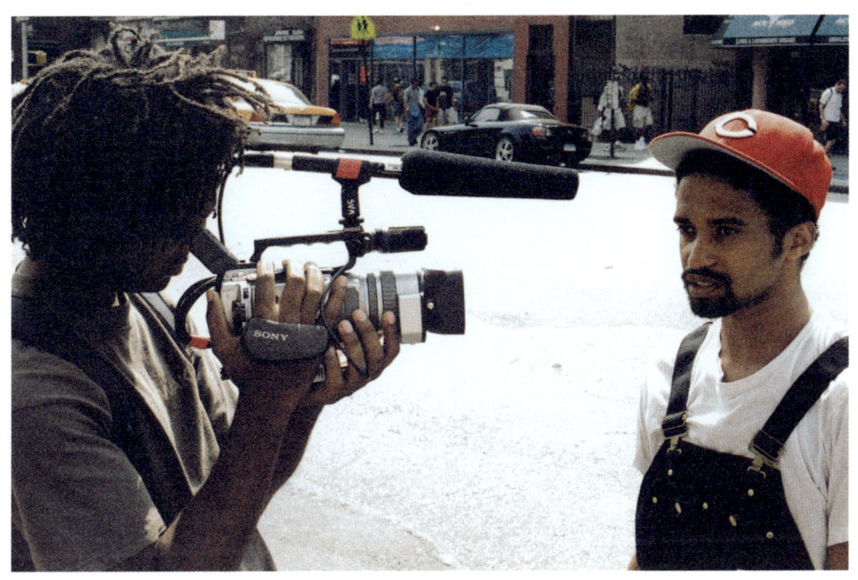

Quenell Jones filming Leon Reid IV for the documentary
"Public Discourse," *c*. 2001–2. New York City, NY.

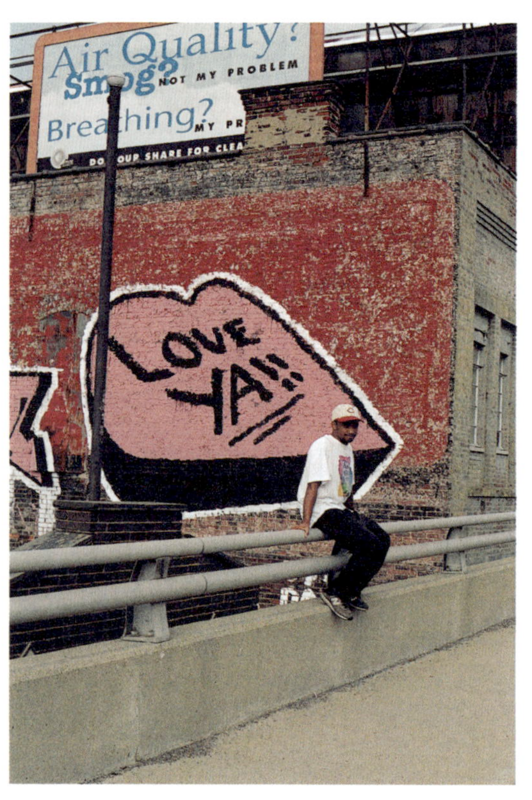

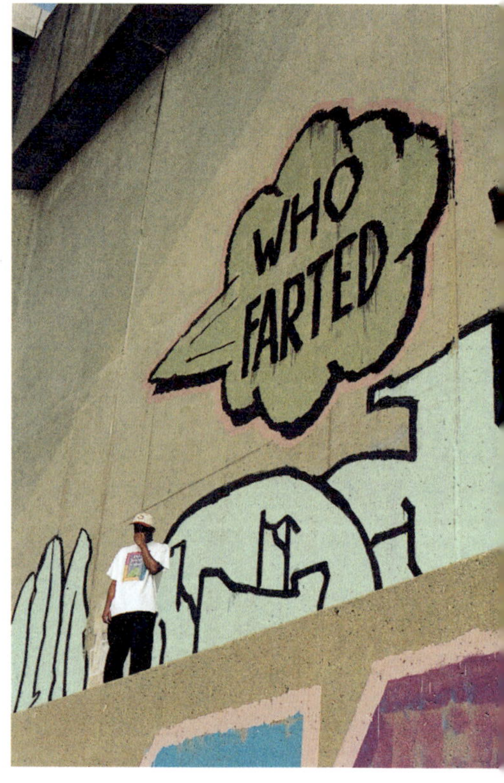

ABOVE *Love Ya!!*, Darius Jones (Leon Reid IV), 2000.
Cincinnati, OH. Duration: 4 years. Photo by Andre Hyland.

RIGHT *Who Farted*, Darius Jones (Leon Reid IV), 2000.
Covington, KY. Duration: 1 year. Photo by Andre Hyland.

OPPOSITE *Get Up Yall!!*, Darius Jones (Leon Reid IV), 2000.
Cincinnati, OH. Duration: 3 months. Photo by Andre Hyland.

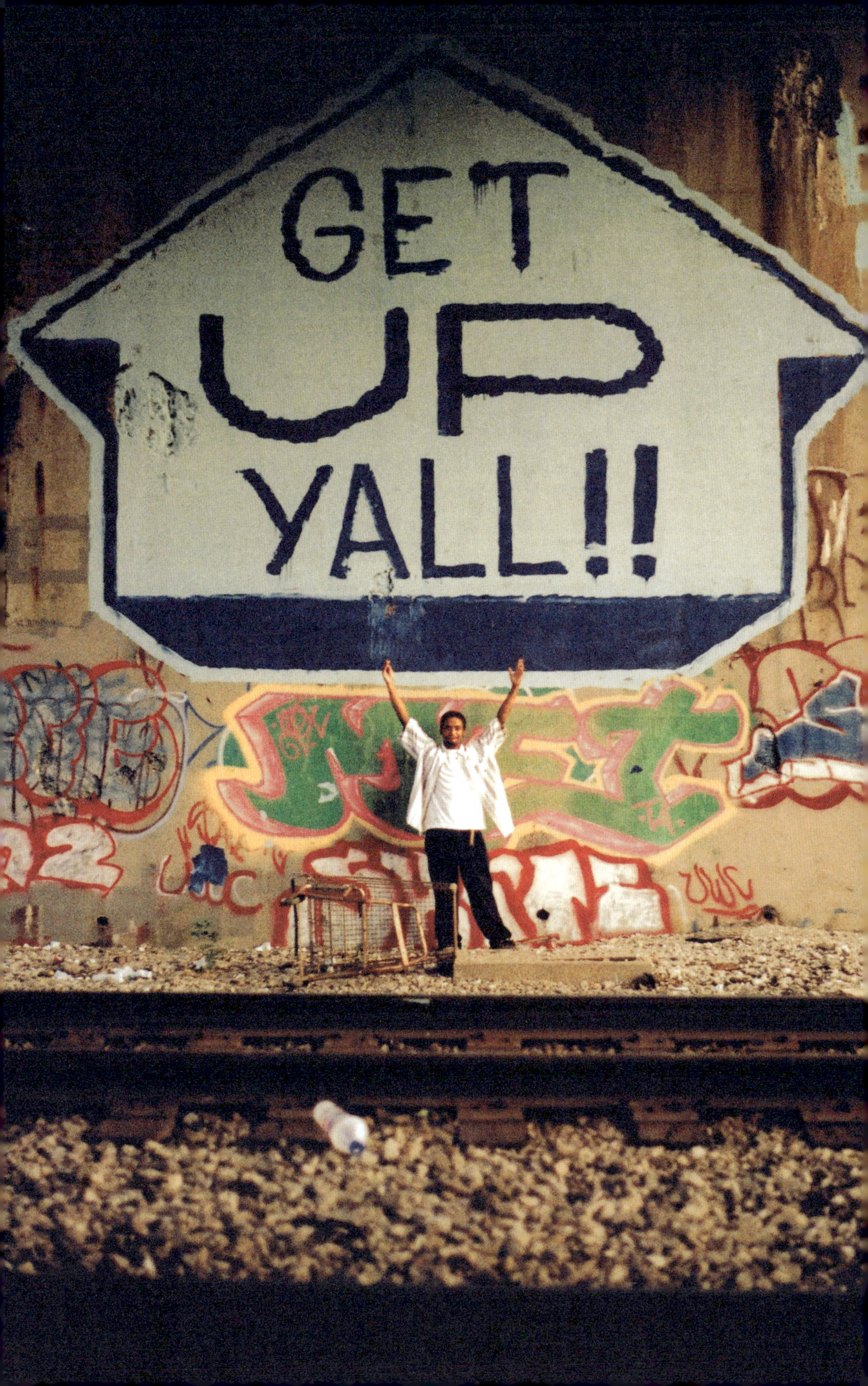

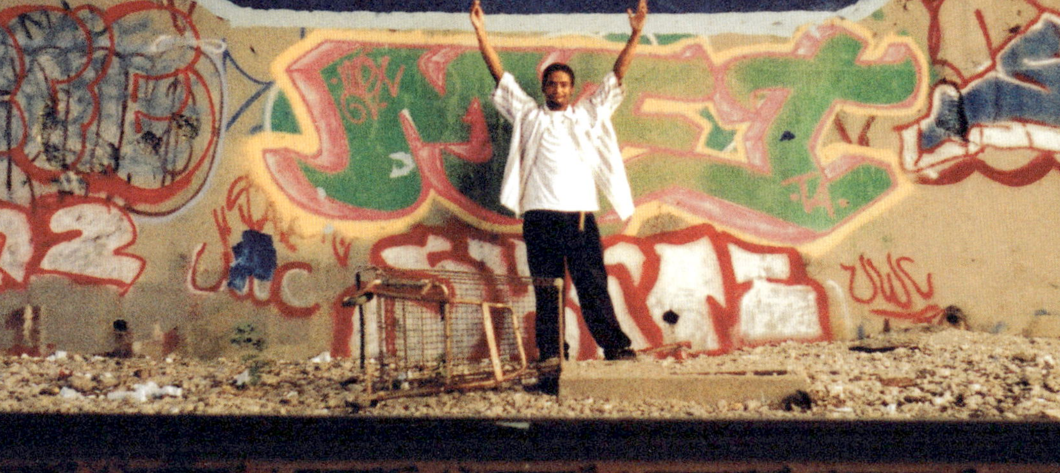

GET
UP
YALL!!

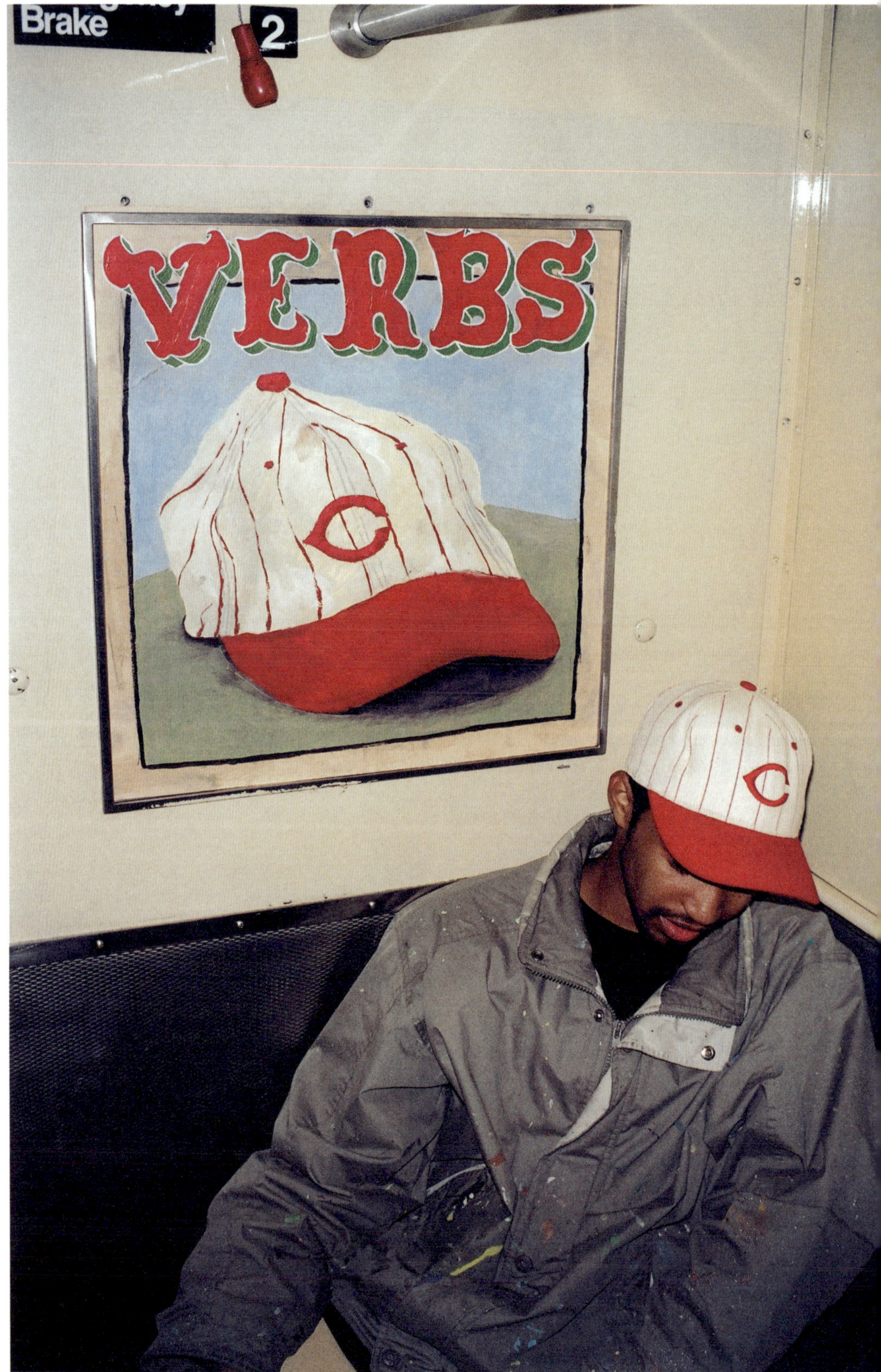
Brake
2
VERBS
C
C

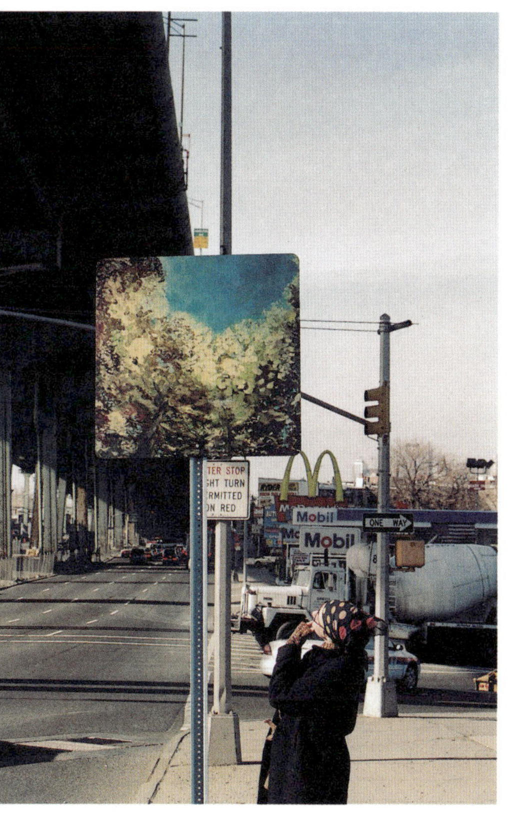 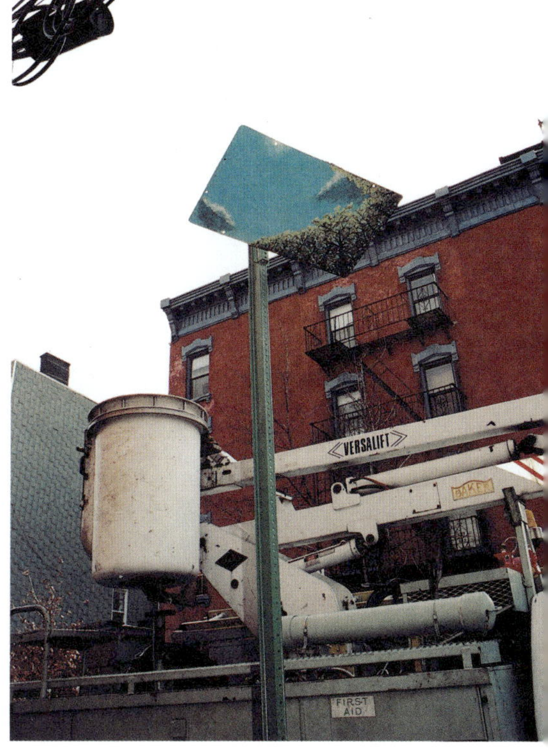

OPPOSITE *Untitled Subway Poster*, Verbs (Leon Reid IV), 1999. New York City, NY. Duration: unknown. Photo by Shevaun Kirschbaum.

ABOVE LEFT *Landscape #2*, Darius Jones (Leon Reid IV), 2002. Brooklyn, NY. Duration: 6 months.

ABOVE RIGHT *Landscape #1*, Darius Jones (Leon Reid IV), 2000. Brooklyn, NY. Duration: 6 years.

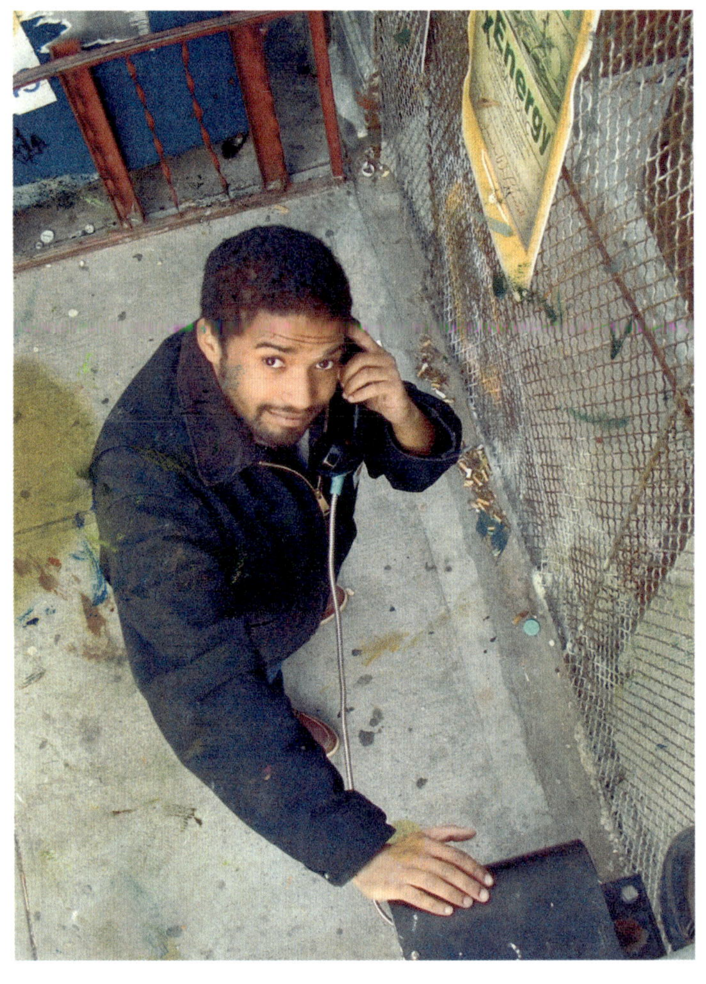

Leon Reid IV posing for portrait. Photo by Josh Benson, 2002.

OPPOSITE *Self-Portrait #2*, Darius Jones (Leon Reid IV), 2002. Brooklyn, NY.
Duration: 8 months.

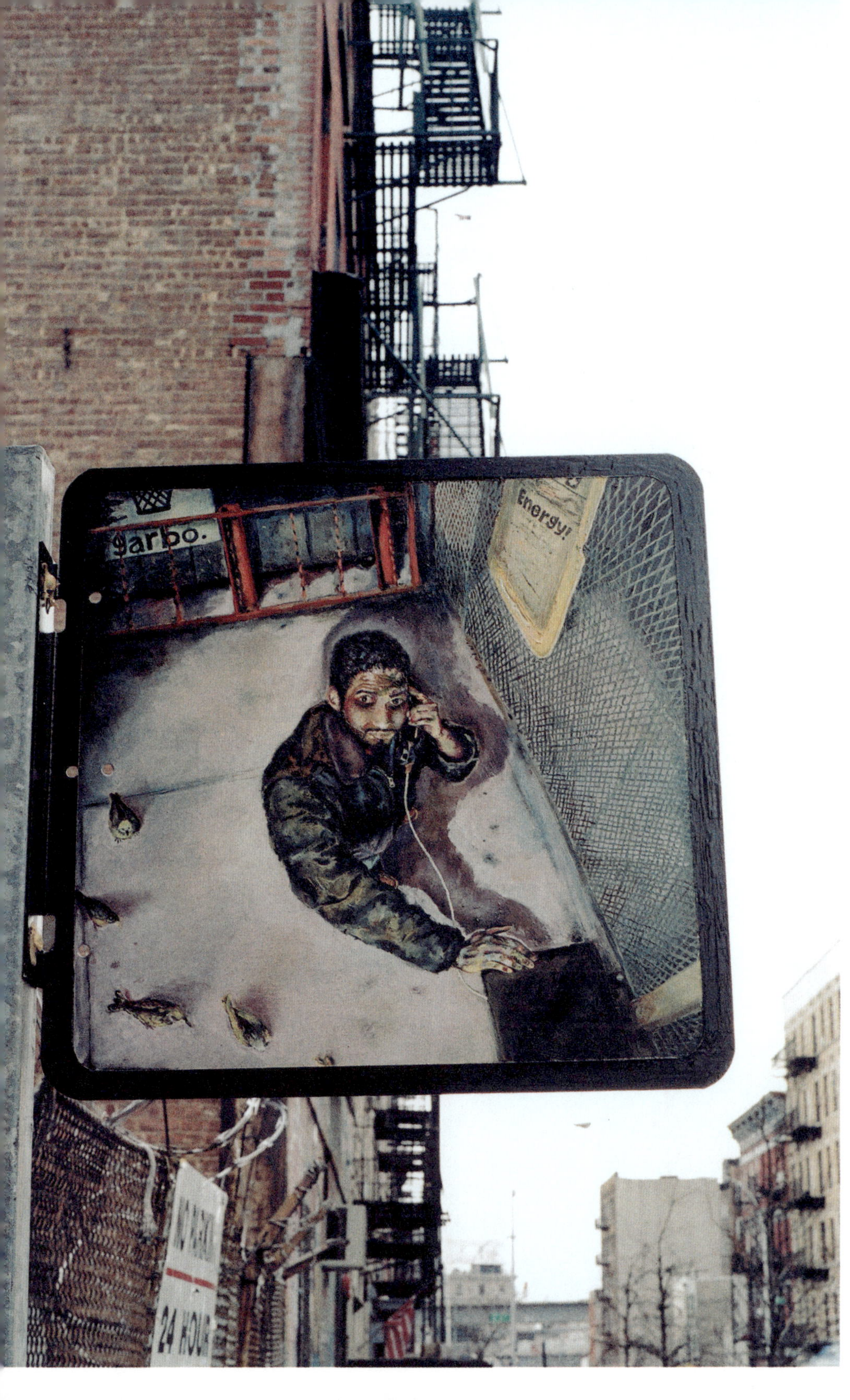

garbo.
Energy!
24 HOUR

EVOLVING COSTUMES

1995–2004 | Leon, the young graffiti writer from Cincinnati still using the name Verbs, goes on an adventure or two with Buddy Lembeck, has an early brush with Espo, and gets his mind blown entirely by Five. Learning that next level thinking is what will allow him to make next level art, Leon puts on a construction suit to make street art for the first time. Back in NYC, Brad and Leon start talking, firstly about Brad and Quenell's street art documentary, then about making street art themselves.

Part 1

In 1995, Leon was fifteen years old and attending the School of Creative and Performing Arts in Cincinnati. That year graffiti, as a form of artistic expression, suddenly swept through the school and exposed young Leon, as well as everyone else, to a world that was infinitely more accessible than what he was being taught in art history class. Not yet able to conceive of how the promise of the art world might even remotely apply to him, wholly without role models in the gallery scene as well as never having even seen a black face in the art history books, Leon felt that finally he had been shown an option. This had some promise.

Together with his friend Joey, aged fourteen, this pair of skinny teenagers, completely new to the game, started getting up the way teenagers do, often. Joey picked the name Meth and Leon decided to write Logic. With that, the two were off and running. Soon, with the end of winter, the fair weather would set both Logic and Meth loose on the streets of Cincinnati.

That spring, Leon did his first full piece, in an active sewer ditch far from the eyes of passersby. He wrote Logic as big as he could, and as soon as he stepped back and looked at his handiwork, he started putting some real thought into coming up with something better. Getting sick of calling himself Meth, Joey was also thinking about renaming himself. Returning from a long road trip, he eventually arrived in Cincinnati as Merz, and a few days later, Leon had made his own transition. It was while watching a music video by The Nonce for their song "I used to sell mix tapes but now I'm an MC" that Leon noticed some fat guy wearing a sweater with VERBS written on the front. With obese hip hop fashion came inspiration. Here was a name Leon could be proud of and he started putting it up for all of Cincinnati to see.

In the following years, the two got more and more into the scene, befriending older graffiti artist Five, amongst others. They spent their days practicing and perfecting their craft, paying dues and getting accepted. The graffiti feudal system treats newcomers like serfs, born to be punked, and Leon and Merz were no exception. But the boys slowly started getting credit for their hard work. Little by little, the two were running and gunning with an older, more prestigious crowd. Merz was finding a warmer reception than Leon, who, although quickly becoming a familiar face, was still kept at arm's length.

Soon enough, Leon found himself going to Scribble Jam[*] to get up a little, in the "way out of the way" far corner spots allotted to him. He understood that acceptance didn't come overnight, but Leon was a bit salty that he didn't get a crack at the choice spots from the start. Still, at the end of the day that wasn't supremely important. Just hanging out in the same room as some of his heroes, getting more respect day by day in their eyes – that was the prize.

It's a brief window in life, when you're old enough to get in the front door, yet young enough that no one expects a thing from you. You're accepted, but invisible. You're closer than you ever thought you could get to the people you admire, yet you might as well be a piece of furniture. An invited fly on the wall.

One day Merz called up Leon to come and hang out at the house of Jason Brunson, co-founder of *Scribble Magazine*. As they entered and sat down on the couch, everyone was geeking out over a photo that was getting passed around and thumb-printed up.

Eventually the photograph made its way to Leon. The picture showed a city sidewalk; people were walking past a store with the massive steel roller gate down. Nothing stood out as significant. The shutters were painted black. Seconds ticked by, but Leon's eyes didn't bug out, his body didn't break into a sweat. He just sat there. Merz took that as a pretty good hint that he wasn't getting it.

---

[*] Scribble Jam is an annual summer event hosting graffiti stars from the East and West Coasts who swoop into "Queen City" and kill it all day long. It's a fun summer thing that showcases the best and brightest from graff-zine fame. It was at one of these events that Leon first saw Espo (Steve Powers). Amongst the catalysts behind Leon's artistic evolution, Espo was a heavy hitter, and seeing him in the flesh, present in the scene, felt right.

"Think big," he whispered, not wanting to draw attention to Leon's trouble, but also not wanting him to miss the big reveal.

"It's Espo's new shit. Check those letters." Merz gestured insistently but vaguely at the image.

Starting to feel the pressure of being the last kid in the room to get the joke, Leon stopped staring and let his eyes do the lazy vision non-focus trick that makes "magic eye" 3-D posters work. He crossed his eyes slightly, holding the picture at arm's length, then brought it closer, nearly touching it to his nose. It was the act of a desperate man, but after repeating this a few times with his back to the group, it clicked. The gates. Those massive black gates in the background. They had white accents cut into the black squares.

"Oh, shit," said Leon. His jaw dropped.

The whole gate itself was the piece. There was no little tag to find, hidden in the photograph. It was just "E" "S" "P" "O". Espo just crushed the entire storefront. Now Leon could see what the commotion was about, and could have seen it from across the room. There were no longer any people in the picture or a street or a sidewalk, even the giant metal roller gate was gone. It was as if Espo had written "ESPO" on contact lenses that Leon would be wearing for the rest of the day.

Merz quickly broke it down to Leon, as it had been broken down to him.

"He goes and buffs the whole roller gate white and then cuts the letters out in black. He does it in the middle of the day, he just dresses like the storeowner or Super or whatever and just paints them in the day. Can you believe this?" Merz was having trouble containing his excitement.

Leon was speechless, but the boy was beaming. In that instant, everything had changed for Leon. This was the reinvention of the wheel, it was Mickey Mouse taking the head off his costume because it's too hot out, it was the world made round. This was more than thinking outside the box, it was thinking outside the Rubik's Cube.

In short, the way Espo was working blew Leon's mind. Going out in the daytime, in a costume of sorts: here was an alternative to simply putting his name up bigger and bigger, and in harder-to-get places, to earn acceptance. This all was groundbreaking to learn and it absolutely seemed the way to go. Leon had been trying to rise through the ranks and gain respect the traditional way for the last few years. Watching it happen so easily for Merz, who was more personable and outgoing than he could ever be, made Leon eager to try something different.

Around this time, graffiti magazine *12oz Prophet* had exposed the world to the current work of Twist and Kaws, who were showcasing their posters in bus shelters. The photographs showed the posters fully installed, large as life, like the advertising for a summer blockbuster. Leon couldn't figure out the "Where" or the "How" but he and everyone else knew the "What" and especially the "Who." And that was most certainly the "Why."

Thinking that he might stand out more if he went a less traditional route, Leon decided he would give the day shift a go. But he wasn't yet sure how to go about it. Everything came into focus when talking to Cincinnati graffiti champs Five and Optik, who were doing street signs and installing them throughout Coryville and Clifton Heights. Five took Leon aside, and being as stand-up as possible, shared a secret with the eager youngster.

"Look under the bottom of the poster case," he said, pulling on a roach and passing it to Leon. Leon passed it right back without as much as a puff, to which Five happily hit it again and kept walking.

The next day Leon walked to a bus shelter with a measuring tape and looked closely at the poster inside. Tracing his fingers along the bottom of the case he felt two flat-head screws and suddenly he knew exactly how to pop the case. Writing down the measurements of the giant poster, Leon smiled to himself and started hustling home.

That was it. All it took was that first helping hand. As soon as Leon was told "Go and try to figure it out," a whole new world began to open up before him. It wasn't about being a member of a secret club. Anything he could look at and set his mind to, he would eventually figure out. It wouldn't be the best way at first, but he would learn bit by bit, all by his lonesome if needed. Five had taught a man to fish.

Leon spent the better part of the following week painting a piece of paper that was cut to poster size. Sitting at home, the day before he had scheduled his solo mission, he started coming up with his costume. Taking a white button-down shirt, a pair of his father's dress pants, his swankiest shoes, and a borrowed pair of prescription glasses, he assembled an outfit that completely transformed him into someone else. Not someone official, mind you, just not Leon. He was masquerading, very convincingly he thought, as Clark Kent.

The next day, Leon put the glasses in his pocket and drove to his chosen location. Parking several blocks away, he got out of the car and put on the glasses. Now in full costume, Leon breathed a little easier, but was, for all intents and purposes, blind.

He stumbled his way towards the bus shelter with his poster rolled up under his arm and the screwdriver in his pocket. After a block, he gave in and lowered the glasses to the tip of his nose, restoring his vision, while keeping the disguise intact.

When he reached the bus shelter he quickly twisted the screws loose and yanked the poster down. As the heavy stock paper rolled itself up, Leon reached up and inserted his own poster. Without checking if it was in straight – it wasn't – he pushed the case shut again and started screwing the screws back in with the poster at his feet. As he tightened the second and final screw, he heard a voice.

"Leon?" His friend Seb was standing there above him, looking down, looking confused.

"Oh!" Leon jumped to his feet and started stuttering. "H-Hey. Um, what's up man?"

"Why are you dressed like that? You wear glasses?" Seb was looking at his friend uncomfortably, unsure if he had walked in on something private.

Leon put the poster under his arm, "Um, no. The thing of it is…."

Seb, focusing solely on the screwdriver still in Leon's hand, interrupted. "No man, don't worry about it…. You look busy. I'll catch up with you later." And with that, he spun 180 degrees and quickly walked to the store down the street. Leon stood there watching as Seb walked right back out, impossibly fast, with a slice of watermelon. Seb then looked in Leon's direction and stared at him, slowly walking backwards until he blended in with the human traffic on the sidewalk, and was gone.

Leon turned back to the poster and saw it was slightly uneven,[*] but definitely hanging securely. Silently counting his blessings that his friend Seb wasn't a local police officer, Leon kept the glasses on the tip of his nose all the way to his car. Once safely inside, he undid the top three buttons of his dress shirt, took the glasses off forever, and exhaled a breath that he felt like he had been holding since he touched that first screw.

With his first experiment a moderate success, Leon began taking note of what he had learned. His costume was a good attempt, but a misstep. The object wasn't simply to not look like himself, it was to look like someone who was supposed to be doing what he wanted to do. The ideal costume would make him invisible.

---

[*] As an OCD perfectionist, this bothered Leon. Even today, the image remains crystal clear in his mind, and he recalls precisely how crooked it was.

Part 2

Merz, a traditionalist, wasn't interested in Leon's new agenda. He was happy with his success as a graffiti writer, and felt that was where he belonged. Leon always enjoyed working as part of a team, so now he finally decided to bring his best friend into the scene. Andre and Leon had been inseparable since kindergarten, but after Andre's family recently moved outside the city limits, the two were now districted to different high schools. Something like that would usually put a strain on a close friendship, but for these two it simply meant that they each got the best of both worlds. It was only a matter of time until whatever one of them was into was shared with the other.

Leon had introduced Andre to graffiti before, but Andre wasn't interested in coming up with a graffiti name, his thing being to spray-paint bizarre illustrative shapes and body parts alongside tags of name after name after name. As Leon started putting some real thought into his costume, he realized that Andre, who had been videotaping himself doing sketch comedy for years, was an expert. Invited to collaborate, Andre jumped at the chance. He decided to work under the name Buddy Lembeck, and with that, Leon had found himself his first real partner in innovative crime.

The two of them spent the next few months of the summer of '98 putting up sign after reappropriated sign, creating their costume bit by bit, and gaining confidence by the yard. Soon both were wearing gray and navy jumpsuits with work boots. One day, while waiting for Leon to pick him up, Andre walked through the family garage and saw a hardhat that belonged to his city planner father, bearing the official seal of the city. Walking out of the house looking a hundred times more legitimate, he tipped his hat to Leon, whose smile in response was as big as his face could manage.

At the end of summer, Leon left for college, heading straight to Brooklyn. He took the first semester there, as most will, just to get acclimated. Getting familiar with the comings and goings of a new city takes a little time and a bit of guidance. Stepping on someone's toes and getting beat down is the easiest part of coming to a new city, and if someone doesn't tell you what the cops are used to, you could be the freshest catch of the day.

By second semester, Leon had tapped into the grapevine enough to find Pratt's graffiti scene, and after becoming fast friends with graffiti writer Bills, he started getting taught the ropes of bombing the Big Apple. The generous way that Bills shared the city's secrets without making him prove himself time and again always stuck with Leon, and cemented his belief in the "don't just tell, teach" school of thought.

While running through the streets of Brooklyn one night, Bills taught Leon the true secret to success in graffiti or anything else worth doing – confidence. That became the most important part of the costume Leon would wear for the next decade of his life. If he didn't act with confidence, people would see right through whatever disguise he chose. "Cops are like dogs," Bills explained. "They can smell fear."

During spring break of 1999, Leon headed back to Cincinnati eager to tell Andre of his adventures in the city. After decompressing for a few days, they agreed to go on a mission to remove some signs. As a favor to the two, Five agreed to come along as lookout.

Picking Andre up from school that day, nothing seemed to be going right. They were in a rush, having to get Andre back in time for his class in the late afternoon, and were ill-prepared at best, with one hardhat between them, jeans instead of jumpsuits, a toolbox for a stepladder, and nothing to tie up Andre's shoulder-length hair.

With the three in the car, they sped towards where the signs were posted, parking a few zigzagged blocks away. Walking over, Five worked on his limp, going for the "wounded hobo veteran" look, eventually splitting off and slowly pacing back and forth before settling down on a stoop across and down at the other end of the street. Both Andre and Leon looked far from their most professional, and they knew it. Figuring it was better to work fast than to cancel the mission, they turned the toolbox on its side, stepped up, and started unscrewing the first of two signs on the post.

With one sign finally down after a ten-minute struggle, and still two to go, the team didn't exactly exude confidence, but they kept their resolve and continued onto the next sign. With Five out of sight, Leon and Andre had no contact with the lookout and were left to spot the white car pulling up out of the distance themselves. As it got closer, the crest of the city council became clearly visible on its passenger door. But still the two decided to try their best to ignore the car, hoping the driver would run into a building to drop something off.

Instead, the driver, a mustached man in his late forties, pulled over and walked right up to the two.

"What the hell do you think you're doing?" he questioned angrily. Their luck was bad. Here was one of the few people who knew enough to know that Leon and Andre were, most likely, stealing from the city.

The two turned to face him and Andre was the first to offer up an answer. "We're part of the City Arts Program. We were told to take these signs down."

City Arts was a real program and although the two weren't in any way affiliated with it, Andre's quick thinking gave them a semi-legitimate excuse for what they were doing. The man opened his notebook and quickly started writing down everything they said.

"What are your names?" the city official asked.

"Scott Mutter," Andre replied.

"And you?" he pointed at Leon.

Leon paused then stuttered out, "Joseph Costas."🏴

"Let me see your IDs. Get 'em out," he demanded.

Andre, quicker to respond, apologized. "I'm sorry, we left them in the truck."

🏴 Leon was trying to remember, and use, the name of famous sportscaster Bob Costas. Luckily, he didn't, because it would have gotten them hemmed up on the spot. "What's your name?" "Oh I'm famous announcer Harry Carry. Oh and Cubs win! Cubs win!"

"That's a load of…"

"Do you want us to put the sign back up?" Leon countered, before the man could call Andre a liar.

"Yes!" he shouted.

And with that, Leon passed the sign back up to Andre, who screwed it back on as fast as he could while Leon tried to pacify the official. "We'll grab our IDs from the truck and be right back. Then we'll call in to the City Arts office so we can figure out the mix-up together, all right?"

"Yeah, fine…" replied the now confused official.

With the sign up, Leon and Andre left him by the side of the road. As soon as they were about a block away, they started sprinting to the car. Once there, they had started the engine and were about to exit the scene when the back door opened and Five jumped in.

"You were gonna leave me?" he asked.

"Where were you? Lookout my ass!" Andre replied.

"I was too far away, he just pulled up out of nowhere, there was no way to let you know what was coming. A civi-four-door? It wasn't like a police cruiser you can see ten blocks away, that's just a regular car with a sticker on the side. Blame someone else."

"Like who?" Andre asked.

"Like someone who cares," Five replied.

Five was right, there wasn't anything that could have been done. They walked into the situation unprepared and got busted. They were lucky that it was just a civil servant, who knew they were up to something, but at least didn't carry a gun. If it had been a cop, they'd be handcuffed by now. Lesson learned, Leon dropped Five off, and got Andre back to school just in time for class.

Returning to Brooklyn, Leon was itchy to get back into the swing of things, and in April started rounding troops up to be proper lookouts. Needing to switch up his routine a little, and still somewhat shook by his bust in Cincinnati, he decided to go at night, sans costume, to install his latest piece. Finding two friends, Pat and Kevin, who were down for the cause, Leon wrapped up a sign that he recently acquired and painted, and around midnight they headed to Manhattan.

With his two lookouts in place, Leon set about his standard procedure for putting up a new sign on a naked pole. First he would paint the pole itself a new color, this time brown, then he would paint the outline of a signal square at the base, to further alert people to the fact that there was something different about the pole. Then, once the paint was dry, he would quickly slide bolts through the sign and the pole, tightening the nuts as hard as he could. When the sign was secure, he would fill in the square, pull up the masking tape he had used to mark it off, and unwrap the sign.

He heard the screech of tires literally as he finished pulling off the wrapping and unveiling the piece to the world. By the time he turned his head, two cops had already grabbed one of his lookouts, and were hammering away at his psyche, getting him to give up inside of a few seconds that he was there to do graffiti.

The police systematically made their way to Leon, and now a few feet away, and smelling the wet paint in the air, the shorter, fatter, more aggressive of the two got started.

"Ok smart guy, where's the graffiti?" he asked.

"What graffiti?" Leon responded, silently thrilled with himself, that he hadn't just written Verbs in giant 3-D letters on a wall.

"Stop wasting my time, I can smell it. Your boy gave you up. Now where is it?" he demanded.

Leon just stood there silently, with a bucket of green paint at his feet.

"Oh wow, Joe, look at that," the taller thinner cop said to the fat one while motioning to the sign above Leon. "What is that, a baton?"

It was. Leon's sign showed a police issue nightstick with a paintbrush on the tip, reading "Night Regulation."

"Oh, that's something. That's the SB24 Baton. That's what they'd give you in the late seventies when you got out of the academy. I've got one in my locker," the fat one replied. "Kid, you know that's the SB24?"

Leon shrugged his bluff along. "Yes sir."

"That's somethin'," the officer repeated, and looking at his partner said, "The kid did his research."

The fatter officer then turned back to Leon. "You got ID?"

"Yes sir," Leon replied as he handed over his out-of-state license and his student ID. "I'm an art student in Brooklyn."

The cop all but ignored him, looking at the sign again. "You know, he really nailed the thing. That's crazy." Then he looked at the ID, wrote down Leon's name on a pad of paper, and handed it back. "Listen kid, come back tomorrow and take it down. If you don't, I'm gonna come get you at your school. I come here tomorrow and it's gone, you and me are good. Sound fair?"

"Yes sir." Leon was rightfully thankful.

The cops drove off leaving Leon and his friends jittery and confused for the long subway ride back to Brooklyn. Leon never came back for the sign. He could recognize an idle threat, a mere formality from one of New York's finest art lovers.

Part 3

A few weeks after the incident with the police, while hanging out at the apartment of friend and fellow graffiti writer Bisc, Leon came across a New York City Transit Authority vest sitting on a pile of laundry.

"Oh wow, where d'you get this?" he asked.

"I don't know, I've had it forever. I guess I stole it," Bisc replied. "You want it?"◆

"You serious? Well yeah, I can just have it? Thank you man."

The costume was getting more official by the day, and with the school year coming to a close, Leon packed the vest in with the rest of his gear and headed back to Cincinnati for the summer of 1999.

Once back and with his costume the most complete it had ever been, he started prepping himself for a solo mission. It would be the real test of everything he had learned up to this point. All the layers of confidence he had been stacking back to back would be put into effect, and his new vest to boot.

He set out around noon, fully in costume, and parked a few blocks away from where he had spotted an unused or "naked" street pole. He looked at himself in the reflection of the driver's side window. He had his hardhat on, and tilting his head down slightly, his face disappeared into its shadow. The orange vest was a nice touch; it was an additional bit of color to attract the eye and deflect any curiosity to see his face.

All in all, the costume fit well. Carrying a bucket of paint and his sign, finished and wrapped in newspaper, with a paintbrush and tape

---

◆ The thing about young people in New York is that if you put something unique or strange, basically anything at all, in front of them and blink for more than a second, it's gone. With the moral quiet with which you might reappropriate a newspaper out of a hotel lobby, a New Yorker would steal a manhole cover if they could lift it. Things such as traffic cones, cell phones, a stranger's address book, or a fireman's Dalmatian are walked away with on nearly a daily basis. The less immediate value it has to the thief, the easier or more happily they will, without bout of conscience, pick said item up and disappear with it, until it can be of use. Or until someone comes over, notices, and wants it, at which point they either give it away without a thought, or perhaps, if broke, they will sell it. Such is the only true act of recycling in NYC.

in one pocket and a wrench in the other, he turned from the car and approached the pole with confidence. His costume was doing the trick; it gave that added bit of gravity to his step, the sense of having a "job to do." The sidewalk was empty, it being now just after most people's lunch hour, but even if people had been rushing by him, he felt he wouldn't have broken a sweat.

Once at the pole, he laid down the sign and got to work. First he took the spray can and steadily painted the street pole teal. Then, while it dried, he taped off the square below it and painted this yellow. Waiting for the painted pole to dry, he stood up for a few moments and watched the traffic whip by. He was at the corner of an intersection and when the streetlight turned red, cars would line up, and occasionally people would look in his direction.

When a woman driving a gray station wagon turned to look directly at him, he felt a line of sweat run down the back of his neck in the afternoon heat. But he didn't flinch. Gradually he realized the woman was looking right through him. At any other time it might be disturbing to be reduced to the status of an object in the eyes of a fellow human being. But for Leon, as the woman accelerated away, her obliviousness to his presence was a sure sign that what he was doing was working.

With the pole now dry, he slipped the bolts through and tightened the nuts down, securing the sign in place. Then he leaned down to pull up the masking tape. Balling up the tape and stuffing it in his pocket, he rose to unveil the sign. And at that precise moment, stopped at the red light not fifteen feet away, was a police officer in uniform, in an unmarked car.

Leon stood up straight and reached back into his pocket. The police officer was looking directly ahead, but started slowly turning his head in Leon's direction. Leon pulled his hand out of his pocket, now holding the wrench, and went back to loosening and retightening the already secure nuts and bolts on the sign that was covered in newspaper. The police officer looked directly at Leon now, and Leon felt his stomach tighten with every second the light stayed red. Finally with the bolts retightened, Leon stood still and let his eyes meet the police officer's. The officer, like the woman before him, was staring right through him. As the light turned green and he slowly pulled away, Leon felt his right knee buckle slightly.

With the green light promising another forty-five seconds of uninterrupted freedom, Leon quickly peeled the newspaper off the sign, revealing the fresh Verbs painting to the streets and public of Cincinnati, and began picking up his things. The walk back to the car took what felt like seconds rather than minutes. Not wasting another instant on his reflection, Leon threw the hardhat and vest onto the back seat and revved the engine.

The uniform, the costume, the confidence: all had worked while staring dead into the eyes of the Law. Absolutely invisible under the most difficult test-run he could imagine, Leon was confident that he was now, finally, onto something that would allow him to do nearly anything he wanted.

Bringing his newly honed technique back with him to Brooklyn in the fall of 1999, Leon was ready to work. After a few months, he met Brad, and through Brad, Quenell.[⏹] Brad's artistic interests were all over the page. Never wanting to limit himself to one medium over another, he was interested in animation, film, fine arts, design. Always excited to collaborate and wanting to work with Quenell specifically, the two decided to make a film.

Brad heard about Leon's technique, and, thinking that it would make for interesting material, approached him in the winter of 1999 to

[⏹] Brad and Quenell were fast friends from the minute they were waiting on line to register for classes. Both recently from Atlanta, Georgia, they bonded instantly over their shared quick, bombastic sense of humor as well as Brad being one of the few people who could understand Quenell's thick ATL accent. (That accent, and Quenell's good looks made him possibly the worst wingman on the face of the earth, if you shared tastes in women.) Eventually, both Brad and Quenell switched programs, Brad changing his major to film and Quenell his college to SVA, so their third year in college effectively became their second sophomore year. Now happy where they had landed, they were interested in working together on a project. That project became the film "Public Discourse," an internationally successful documentary on graffiti and street art.

ask if he was interested in being filmed. Brad quickly found himself immersed in the aspects of the art form that were hard to dismiss. He knew that it was not only about new ideas, but about new places to present ideas. What Leon was tapping into and offering up was the ability to convey messages on a scale as yet unavailable to Brad, as well as the chance to positively effect the environment without needing permission or spending untold amounts of money.

Brad soon found himself working alongside Leon, eventually donning a costume himself. Having worked in the past as a construction worker, and familiar with dealing with police from a childhood spent skateboarding, Brad took well to the process and strategy Leon presented.

Leon remembered exactly how it felt to be new to the scene, how hard it was to learn the ropes and secrets. He also remembered Five and Bills and how their generosity and tutelage had opened his eyes. So he willingly took Brad under his wing. He shared all of his years of experience, all the trials and errors, never making Brad pay his dues to nearly the degree expected of him earlier in his own graffiti career. Not to say that Leon didn't occasionally take advantage of Brad's inexperience, but he was always happy to be in the role of the teacher, giving Brad the benefit of all his years of hits and misses. That said, Leon isn't known for his patience, so it was lucky that Brad proved a quick study. Thanks to the mixture of his background and Leon's crib sheet, he was up to speed soon enough.

The two men, very different people indeed, worked well together, challenging each other and pushing towards bigger and better things. To make the uniform his own, and to add to the overall visual authenticity, Brad started growing a beard, having observed that most construction workers had some amount of facial hair. Leon already had a goatee and looked fifteen years older with it, but Brad, fresh-faced without it, blended and acclimated much more easily with even the bit of scruff that appeared almost overnight.

But eventually, having worn the costume more times than either could count, and having reached optimum levels of confidence, the matter of facial hair came to feel like no more than an unnecessary security blanket. The final evolution for the city worker uniform was when Brad and Leon (and Quenell) left the States to get master's degrees abroad. Upon their arrival in England, both Leon and Brad felt foolish for packing the orange disguise when seeing, on their very first walk through the city, construction workers dressed in their bright official lemon yellow vests.

Learning to observe and adapt to any environment was the final lesson in creating costumes. Not merely a matter of color, there were new mannerisms, new neighborhoods, new procedures, and new terms to learn. As well as a new accent to master. (Which, for the record, neither of them ever did.)

OMAR/SWATCH

2000–2001 | Leon and Brad, while walking around with close friend J.C., encounter the notorious street art hustler Omar selling stolen art work on a Manhattan street corner. When Omar is confronted for selling one of Leon's pieces, things take a turn for the worse, with death threats suddenly thrown into the equation. In the midst of all the shouting, Leon and Brad meet and gain a little support from Rate and Zyre, two fantastic NYC writers.

While in Cincinnati, during the late fall of 2000, Leon finally heard word through the graffiti grapevine how to add a little staying power to the signpost work he, and now Brad, were putting up. The word was epoxy. That's the high-strength glue sold in its own little chemistry set, two tubes filled with chemicals that, when mixed in equal amounts, make liquid cement. If crazy glue is used to build a working model airplane, epoxy is what's used when building a working model space shuttle. The freshly tipped technique gave Leon the confidence to put up his new sign on the high traffic corner of Broadway and Houston in Manhattan. It was as if he was parking the car he had built with his own two hands in the middle of the Bronx, that's how much he trusted his new security system.

Collaborating with fellow writer Anti, Leon dedicated the piece to Amadou Diallo, the unarmed black gentleman who was shot dead by the NYPD's Street Crime Unit in February of the previous year as he reached for his wallet.[*] In the weeks following this tragedy there were unending protests, marches that flooded the streets and shut down any street-level transportation throughout entire Brooklyn neighborhoods, and a very real fear of a reckless and ultra-violent NYPD. Leon's piece was a Night Regulation sign, and had VERBS spelled out with a handgun, a bull's-eye and the number 50, after the old cop show *Hawaii Five-o*. A word bubble read "Hey! We saw you doing it." It looked slick.

With his newly discovered finishing move, Leon was confident that this piece would last theoretically forever, or at least longer than any previous attempts at street permanence. He was also gassed to have it up in a prime location, having recently spotted a naked street pole in the cross-street that defined the corners of SoHo, the East Village and the Lower East Side.

Quenell joined Leon for the installation, watching the process at a distance and filming on Brad's 8mm. This was the first time that Quenell

[*] Forty-one shots were fired by the four officers on the scene, including one who appeared to his colleagues to have been shot, but in actuality had tripped on the curb. Seeing a downed officer set off the others all the more. Diallo was hit nineteen times. The "Street Crime Unit" has since been disbanded.

had run solo with Leon on a daytime mission, seeing him fully in disguise, and Leon was feeling the pressure to be faster, slicker, and more professional than ever. He wanted to show him just how good good could get.

The only thing that let him down was the inevitable physical side-effect of adrenaline and anxiety: slight hand tremors. Leon could hide this in the bigger gestures – pushing the bolts through the signpost, pulling the socket wrench down to get the nuts as tight as he could; even drawing the chalk outline of a homicide around the base of the post went smooth as silk. It was only when he started mixing the chemical compound on a ripped piece of thick cardboard to create his über-glue that it became apparent that his hands were shaking like a lifetime alcoholic dealing with the morning DTs.

Leon was embarrassed that he wasn't coming off to Quenell as the consummate professional, the unshakeable master of his craft. But when he looked up, he realized that Quenell wasn't even looking at him, much less his nervous twitch. Quenell was much more concerned with his combined tasks of filming while keeping an eye out for the police and not getting arrested. In his preoccupation with artistic perfection, Leon had forgotten about the fear that lives in the hearts of men. Being arrested or murdered by the people hired to "Protect and Serve" was a very relevant fear at that time for young black males on the streets of New York City.

But the installation was completed without incident, and they jumped on the train back to Brooklyn, both thinking about the upcoming winter break from school and making plans for the spring. Leon's thoughts drifted easily from how good it would feel to have a break from the city, to how free it felt to be able to leave, secure in the knowledge that the creation he just set loose into the world would be safe and sound in his absence.

Returning from Cincinnati a few weeks later, Leon diagonally crossed Houston and Lafayette to the opposite corner, coming up on his spot. His corner. After dodging taxi drivers and other motorists, and briskly turning up Broadway, he looked up and couldn't breathe. It was gone.

The pseudo-permanent installation and Leon's heart had both been ripped out of their rightful place and Leon felt the earth beneath him fall away, just slightly. The new epoxy technique, the 11th commandment that got sent down the mountain, had just gotten debunked. Once again, Leon was left without belief in perfection.

A month later, Leon and Brad were walking around with J.C., a friend from Pittsburgh, through Chinatown and the Lower East Side. Brad was videotaping them talking about graffiti, throwing up tags, showing off a little for the camera. They came upon a big yellow "Case2" tag that Leon and J.C. both threw up smaller tags around, all happy to discover another piece by someone they respected. Case2 was the charismatic one-armed graffiti writer from the film "Style Wars," and a fresh spray tag of his was something none of them had expected to come across that day.

As they walked west on Houston, passing Broadway, Leon couldn't help feeling bitter, being in the neighborhood of his stolen work. His artwork, dedicated to an innocent man who was murdered, had been killed itself.

Walking up to the Puck Building, they came upon signs for the "Outsider Art Fair," presenting work by artists not formally trained and, for the most part, not part of the traditional gallery "art scene." In front of the building, separated from the show by twenty or so feet of iron gate, brick wall, double-paned and triple-curtained windows, and a veil of legitimacy, was a booth on the sidewalk.

Co-opting the signs, advertising and foot traffic, this booth identified itself proudly as "Outside the Outsider Art Fair." It was manned by a sturdy New Yorker who looked to be in his mid-thirties. As Leon, Brad, and J.C. stepped up, their eyes popped out of their heads at all that the booth had to offer. It was wall-to-wall street art. Brad watched as an assistant in the background quickly sold a Bast painting on wood, while the man in charge was interviewed about his contribution to the fair. Brad lowered his video camera to waist level and flipped it onto record.

"I'm Outside the Outsider Art Fair! They don't have any of the most outsider art on earth in there. It's crazy! Tell me, what art is more outside than graffiti? It lives outside, it breathes outside! That's where this stuff is born, on the street. Tell me, what's more outside than the street? This booth is Outside the Outsider Art Fair. That's how real this shit is!"

As Brad, Leon, and J.C. watched him wrap up his interview, Leon and Brad scanned the three panels behind the booth, each one some eight feet tall by five feet wide. They saw a few recognizable names up there. A lot of Bast's paintings on wood hung around, seemingly for sale, and the guy was unrolling a Kaws poster before them. Then Brad's eyes drifted over to one of the panels and he looked over at Leon.

"Yo Leon, isn't that yours?" Brad asked.

"Oh man, it is…" Leon's heartbeat just paused. Right there in plain daylight was his baby. The Amadou Diallo piece. It lived.

That wasn't the only one of his Lindbergh babies that was there; the guy had a few of Leon's signs hanging on the panels. But it made his heart race to see this one intact, not destroyed by a civil servant's indifference, or carelessly thrown in a garbage compacter, or – nightmare scenario – kept in an evidence locker as part of a growing stack of his work that would eventually be logged into the court records as evidence articles A through Z and back. Here it was, right in front of him, saved from the ravages of the System.

"Yo man, that's mine. I write Verbs," said Leon.

"Oh shit man, you do beautiful work. I'm Omar. I write Swatch," the guy running the booth replied as he threw him a pound. "You know some woman just came up, like an hour ago, pulled out two fifties for that sign. I told her she was crazy, it was worth way more than that. For real man, you've made some art here. That's the most beautiful piece I've seen on the street in a long time."

Leon was beaming. He was getting some real recognition; his work was respected by a stranger and a name in the game at that.

"Who are your boys?" asked Omar.

"Brad Downey," answered Brad.

"I've seen your stuff," Omar quickly replied. "You've been doing that work that looks a bit like Phil Frost."

"…Yeah." Brad was floored. It was true, he was one of the only people besides Phil Frost to be doing image-based and figural work. But this was only for the past three weeks, and Omar already knew about it. This cat knew what was going on, he was keeping a real eye out for new work. Just then Omar's eye caught Brad's video camera.

He tensed up. "Yo, shut that camera off."

"It is off," Brad lied.

"Yeah well it looks…." Omar saw J.C. pick up a smaller sign on the table and got distracted. "What about you? What's your name?" Omar motioned at J.C.

"J.C." he replied.

"Yeah I know you too. You guys wanna see some really special stuff?" Omar opened up his catalog of work that was too good to just have lying around in a booth. As they were looking through the photographs of everything this graffiti collector had gotten his hands on, Leon was slowly coming down from the initial high of discovering that his baby was saved from oblivion and taking on board the fact that someone else was raising it now.

"I take a really good photograph of everything while it's still up, in the context and location of where it was before I took it. I document everything. Then I take it down and store the biggest and best pieces in my warehouse." Omar bragged on. "I've got a little of everything and everyone. I've got Keith Haring, Jean-Michel Basquiat, Revs, Bast, Twist, KAWS… you name him, I've got a piece in my collection. That shit's valuable."

That was when the reality of the situation washed over Leon. Not only did Omar steal something he worked so hard on, but he was selling it on the black market. That's not the future he had planned for his art. Leon didn't want it hanging anywhere but where he put it. The work was for the street, that specific street that Leon risked his neck and his freedom on. He accepted that the police or the city might eventually remove it. That's just the high cost of living. Landlords repaint buildings; the city authorities reassert their monopoly over the streets. That's the name of the game. What he wasn't ready to concede to was this new, capitalistic threat to his art.

Every street artist makes a decision at the outset. They don't make art in the hope that it may hang in a gallery that 1% of the city goes to. They give their creations for free to the whole city, putting them out there for an entire neighborhood to walk by and see. Now Leon's piece had been stolen from where it had been successfully installed in order to be sold to someone who would hang it in his or her living room where 0.0000001% of the city could see it. It was exponentially more selfish, and even harder to take from someone who was in the scene himself.

Omar claimed to have been writing SWATCH all over New York City subway cars since the late 1970s. His name was known in the scene. What he was into now seemed like a huge disconnect from the graffiti hometown hero he should have been. He was selling out his art form.

Leon was boiling over, but he couldn't just snap on the guy and attack. Omar was twice his size, and had two guys behind him assisting and about another six sitting in a van on the corner. Leon stayed cool and switched tactics.

"How did you get it down?" Leon asked. "I used epoxy, that's supposed to be impossible to get off."

"Nothing is impossible to get off. I can twist off epoxy in an instant," Omar smirked.

"What if we used concrete? I heard concrete works pretty well," Brad asked, still secretly videotaping Omar from the hip.

Omar laughed. "Concrete's easier than epoxy. I just whack it with a hammer and that shit crumbles away. If you want your work to last a little longer, make my job a little harder, I'll tell you right now: bend the bolts. Use the six-inch ones, and once you've gotten the nuts as tight as you can, take a hammer and bend them bolts down. Do it as close to the nuts as you can. I can still cut the bolts, but it's not gonna be easy."

This was a big moment for Brad and Leon: security advice from the most aggressive thief/collector of street art next to the NYPD Vandal Squad itself.

"Damn," Brad said. "That sounds like it would work."

"I can still get it if I want it," Omar replied. "It just won't be easy. If you don't want me to take it, don't put it out on the street, period."

"Or else you'll steal it and sell it?" said J.C. "How you gonna do that without giving a cut to the artist?"

"I would never sell something this good," Omar snapped. "I would never sell it."

Omar looked over at Brad and noticed the camera again. "Yo I'm serious, shut that camera off."

"Because Leon's standing right here, you wouldn't sell it," J.C. shot back. "That's bullshit. You oughtta just give him his work."

Just as things started to heat up, two guys walked up to the booth and started looking at the signs.

"Yo, once you put it out on the street, it's not yours anymore. You want that shit to stay yours your whole life, keep it in your bedroom," Omar scoffed. "As soon as you put it out on the street, it's not up to you what happens to it anymore. I've been doing this shit forever; you little tourist art school newjacks got no idea. I'm from the Bronx. We invented this shit."

"How you gonna tell me that the sign I made ain't mine?" Leon asked, pointing at the sign in question.

Looking at the piece everyone was arguing about, the taller of the two onlookers asked, "Hey man, you write Verbs?"

"Yeah. That's mine."

"That's cool, I've seen your stuff around. I write Rate. This is Zyre. What are you guys getting all heated about?" he asked.

"This guy steals graffiti and sells it. That's what's got us all heated." J.C. answered for Leon.

"I've been writing SWATCH on the trains before you could even bust nuts and you're gonna tell me what I can and can't do with graffiti?" Omar was getting angry.

Rate couldn't get his head around what he had walked into. Omar/Swatch was someone who had been in it from the start and Rate was amped to meet him. But here it looked like he was ripping his own scene off and selling it to anyone with cash. This hometown hero had suddenly turned to feast on his own culture. And now, confronted by one of the younger kids who was following in his footsteps, Omar was threatened enough to get loud, and worse, was dissing the scene itself, saying it's a sucker move to put that stuff out there to begin with. None of it made sense, and just as fast as that, he was involved.

With Rate and Zyre blending in with Brad, Leon, and J.C., suddenly things seemed like they might rapidly escalate towards a fight, and Omar wanted to flex a little bit to show what these youngbloods were in for. They were about to have to fight a grown man.

"Yo, if we were in the yard right now…." Omar took off his denim jacket, getting ready to bring it to a physical level.

"What are you talking about? We're on the sidewalk. In *Manhattan*." Rate laughed. "This is weak, man, you should just give him his shit back."

As they were talking, Omar's van on the corner was starting to empty out and fill in behind Brad, Leon, and the rest. Suddenly there were a lot of guys around the boys ready to back up whatever play Omar was about to spark off.

Rate kept talking. "That's weak that you took something he worked on to put out there for people to see for free, and you took it so you could sell it."

"Yo I'm from the Bronx, and if you want to try and start some shit at my booth, I'm gonna fuck you up," Omar said as he came closer, stepping around the booth.

While Omar was getting loud, Brad kept filming, and Leon leaned over and just picked up the Amadou Diallo sign. It felt good just to feel that flat weight and to look close at the brush strokes of something that just an hour ago was a mixture of memory and imagination.

Omar snatched it out of his hand and threw it on the concrete sidewalk. Then he stomped his foot down on it and put his face in Leon's.

"You want this shit, you're gonna have to take it from me! It's mine!

This shit isn't yours anymore. I'm from the Bronx and you're gonna have to whip my ass if you want this so bad."

At that point it was do or die, and no question about it, if Leon had picked "do," he would have gotten the hell knocked out of him. Leon backed up.

"No one's trying to fight you man." He took a step back. "We're going."

"Get going," Omar prodded. "I'm not trying to have my whole day be about this shit."

Everyone started to walk away from the booth and split further east towards Ludlow Street.

As they got about twenty feet away, Brad yelled out to Omar, "I'm putting something big up soon. Don't take it."

"Don't put it on the street and I won't take it," Omar sneered.

Brad paused mid-step. "No. Seriously."

"I'm serious as a heart attack," Omar screamed back.

With that, Brad caught up with Leon and J.C. and the three of them took off, filled with anger and the adrenaline-laced energy that comes from getting so close to violence you can taste it. The anonymous collector of street art now had a face. They knew he wasn't the only one doing it, but he was the only one they had seen so far. And he was damn good at it. High tempered, and seasoned by decades of running in both sides of the street art game, putting it up and just as stealthily tearing it down, Omar was someone that wasn't going to go away.

That night, Leon was consoled by Polina that every artist needed an enemy, a counterpoint, someone to work against. But Leon could see nothing positive in having Omar exist in his life. He was a physical manifestation of the death of his hard work, forever on the horizon, feasting on his labors like a jackal. In the days that followed, Leon vented in the ways available to him, and what was very available was going out and doing a few quick throw-ups with the short and sweet messages "OMAR PIMPS GRAFF" and "SWATCH DON'T KNOW THE TIME."

Brad, however, was less convinced that Omar was entirely in the wrong. He respected the collection that Omar was building and saw that the eventual retrospective that he could curate for New York City graffiti would most likely be unparalleled in sheer scope. It sounded like he was doing his collecting with respect to the work, photographing it in context, and preserving it as best he could, which is far better than anyone else was offering when removing the art work from where it was installed. Brad even attempted to correspond with Omar to set up an interview for his documentary. This didn't go so well. Veiled and unveiled, specific and unspecific death threats got sent Brad's way, via electronic paper trail.◖

The one thing Leon and Brad could agree on was that now, knowing someone out there was thinking about how to take their work down just as hard as they were thinking about fixing it up, they had to constantly be finding better ways to keep it there. When he calmed down, Leon figured he had paid a reasonable price to learn a valuable lesson about those bolts. If it gets put up, they would now take the time to make it harder for Omar, or any Omar wannabe, to take it down again. No more freebies.

◖ Immediately following the encounter with Omar, a serious argument had got started on the graffiti message board of choice at the time, Tagmag.com. Leon opted to craft a statement, sign it, and post his piece there in one blow rather than get caught up in the battle of words that was sparking off and promising to land people in the hospital.

Appended by: Verbs.
Appended on: Tue Feb 1 17:11:57 MST 2000
This is my first time viewing this site. My man informed me today about the list of responses posted about the occourance on saturday...I'm not upset that I don't have my work in my room today because it belongs on the street, not in anyone's hands, not on anyones selling rack not above anyones couch not even in my house. I do my work for it to reach the public. Are you with me Omar, Rye.....? Let me ask you a couple of questions. Do you guys write graffiti? If yes then the nature of your work is not to be sold. Do you install artwork in the framework of the city? If so then the nature of your work is not to be posessed? And if you truley have been producing for ten years then you should know this better than I! ...But I understand you guys gotta make money somehow but why pollute your own artform?

Appended by: OMAR IN DA HOUSE
URL: www.oldskoolwritersmakemoney.com
Appended on: Tue Feb 1 12:19:19 MST 2000
...IF YOU THINK THAT THIS IS A HAPPY WORLD WHERE ALL THE STREET ART STAYS UP FOREVER, THEN WHERE THE FUCK IS ALL THE ART!!! YOU SHOULD BE FUCKING THANKING ME, I DOCUMENT THE ART BETTER THAN ANYONE, I PRESERVE THE ART BETTER THAN ANYONE, AND IF I SOLD YOUR WORK I CERTAINLY WOULD NOT SAY THAT THIS PAINTING IS BY SOME NEWJACK TOY FROM CINCINNATI WHO DOES NOT KNOW ANYTHING ABOUT STREET ART, OBVIOUSLY STILL LIVES WITH MOMMY BECAUSE HE HAS THESE FEEL-GOOD IDEAS ABOUT GRAFF AND MAKING LOOT...

Brad's overtures to Omar via email met a similar response:

> Subject: documentary
> Date: Sat, 5 Feb 2000 15:33:22 -0800 (PST)
Omar,
I was documenting the conversation between you and verbs. I mentioned wanting to talk to you for the documentary. Me and my partner Quenell are interested in getting together with you to listen to your ideas. I would appreciate it if you would call me at my place in Brooklyn leave a message if im not there. My name is Brad and my number is (718) 687-5750.
Brad

i would be happy to discuss anything regarding my activities, and would like to know more information about your project, frankly im kind of pissed that a half hour after that happened, theres a post on tagmag.com saying that im selling stolen stuff and must be on heroin,,,there's not that many suspects and i will place my hand around the neck of the person who did it and squeeze very hard... and what is the subject of your documentary,,,verbz? he's no street art expert and i dont see how you can compile a worthwhile depiction of street installation art by walking around the street in Feb2000, shits been going on for years and there's many more players in the game...
Omar

> Subject: Re: documentary
> Date: Sun, 6 Feb 2000 20:55:38 -0800 (PST)
Omar,
Thank you for responding to the E-mail. I am not involved in graffitti in any traditional way and I am not in any way involved with the post on tagmag. My project roots from my intrest in fine arts and documentary film making. I am a film student and fine artist. My partner is the same. We plan to work on this project for two years. I asure you that Verbs is not the only street artist we are folowing but he is one of them. I also am aware of all the street instalation artist that I don't have yet. I find your instalation work interesting and also your art of collecting. You are the only street installer with such a large collection that I know of. We would like to interview you and talk about your instalation process and your collecting process. I would appreciate it if I could talk to you in person or on the phone.
-Brad

> Subject: touching base again
> Date: Sat, 2 Mar 2002 09:20:34 -0800 (PST)
OMAR,
I have not E mailed you in a while and would like to touch base again. I am still working on my film. I have over 75 hours of interviews with street artist. I would still like to have a sit down interview with you. If you would like to. let me know and we can set up a place to meet one day when you and I are both free.
Thanks Downey

> Date: Sat, 02 Mar 2002 13:24:14 -0500
> Subject: Re: touching base again
i would need to know what you want do and what questions you will ask. and would need to see what you have done so far, in terms of how its being put together as of right now, any footage you took of me in front of the outsider art fair is off limits to use, if you use any footage of me or have anybody in your video speak bad of me then you will be held accountable, are you sure you want to continue persuing this path it wont be laywers contacting you if im unhappy feel free to work with kids and punks from other cities but im not the one to fuck over or think that you can get away with editorial freedom, freespeech, fuck him its my movie etc. i am not to be subject matter unless i consent and we are not talking about legallities im talking illegalities of which im perfectly capable of accomplishing i would suggest you think about what you may be setting yourself up for before you put yourself in a situation you cant get yourself out of

EXPERIMENTS IN HELL

2000–2001 | Brad, unable to afford his college bills, is summarily kicked out and has to return to Atlanta. There, in the midst of drunkenly lashing out, he has an artistic epiphany that keeps impacting him for years to come. Upon his return to New York City, a foolhardy adventure with Ben Grimm lands him in jail for the first time. All in all, Brad learns an important lesson – partly thanks to a teenaged boy with Down Syndrome and a keen sense of civic duty.

Brad was more than ready for summer. His sophomore year at Pratt was coming to a close and he was eager for a few hot New York City months. The summers in Brooklyn are good ones: the heat puts everyone on the streets, house parties happen on a daily basis, and until the annual late June heat wave hits there is a pretty amazing lust for life in the air. In addition to all that, before the end of this particular summer, young Brad would finally be turning 21.[*]

In the past few months, Brad had not only gotten a good foothold in the graffiti world, putting up the massive *Pink Verbs + Giant Head* piece with Leon as well as an impressive stack of signs all over Manhattan and Brooklyn, but he had adapted fully to the city, both geographically and socially. Between the documentary he'd been focusing more and more on over the last year and the vast arena of street art, Brad had no shortage of creative outlets and an open summer to pursue them to the best of his ability. With the same idealized fervor of a twelve-year-old boy dreaming of summer vacation and its promise of unparalleled freedom, Brad saw the city nearly brimming over with possibilities.

As a last-minute formality, Brad decided to get an idea of what his next year would look like at Pratt. Attaining this information was absurdly complicated and bureaucratic, and he visited three different offices before finally being directed by a janitor to the secretary who dispensed schedules for the upcoming year.

He found himself in front of a forty-foot counter that ran the width of the room, blockading the smaller desks and work areas behind it like an old fashioned post office. This massive countertop created an impression of authority and efficiency and was very effective at keeping fit-prone students at a safe distance.

After five minutes of standing at the counter, Brad eventually attracted one of the receptionists and asked where he could get his upcoming schedule. He was reoriented with a raised finger towards the

[*] The legal drinking age in NYC and the rest of America, and the last hassle of youth to fall away. As a man who could legally buy his own for BYOB events, Brad's summer was primed to be a hazily memorable one.

back of a line hugging the entirety of the left wall. The long progression of students led to an elderly, bald, male administrator who manned, fully on autopilot, an apparently even older printer. One by one, the young artists would hand the man their student IDs, take the paper that was spat out, and head wordlessly back towards the door.

The long listless line led right back out into the hot afternoon sun. Taking his place at the end of it, Brad tanned his neck and checked his watch. As his friends were lounging on the courtyard lawn, drinking brown-bagged beers and eating deli sandwiches from Hyun's corner bodega, Brad was standing in line for information he didn't really care about. But with the summer stretching endlessly ahead, he resigned himself to the wait and stayed put, watching one student after another reemerge into the daylight at inexplicably long intervals, each one bearing a simple six-line block of information printed out on a wide-striped green and off-white piece of paper: Teacher Name, Room Number, Weekday, Time In, and Time Out.

But when Brad finally got to the head of the line forty-five minutes later and handed his ID over, all that came out of the printer was a bill. When he asked the liver-spotted gentleman why, he was met with a shrug and a hand pointing at the receptionist Brad had started with. Without even looking at the paper she wrote a room number down on a Post-It note, handed it over, and walked away.

This time Brad made his way to the Bursar's office and a face-to-face session with a woman whose job it was to provide advice and council for the young student in crisis.

"Drop out," she said. "If you don't have the money to pay for college… you must drop out."

"That's it?" Brad asked, stunned. "The only option at this point is to drop out of college?"

"People often use the word option when there isn't actually a choice," she replied, deadpan and disinterested. "You don't have four thousand dollars to hand the cash officer downstairs, do you? That's the minimum payment to even put you back on the books and save your spot in the classes you registered for. Without that… well, do you have the money?"

"No."

"Well then Bradley, there's no option. You just dropped out. Now, if you'll excuse me, I have a long line of students to help behind you."

"That's it?" he asked.

"That's it," she replied.

Brad walked out of the office shell-shocked. He knew that his parents had fallen on hard times, but he didn't know that for the last six months they had stopped paying the portion of his loan bills that they had taken upon themselves to handle. The only option he had was to take a temporary leave of absence, go back home to Atlanta, and get a job. He could live there for free, save up the money, and eventually get his life back on track. As the woman had said, the word option implies choice, but he only had one road before him… Brad was heading home.

In an instant, not only had he lost a great deal of his freedom and autonomy, but he was brought face to face with the troubles that his family had been going through – troubles of which, up to now, he had only heard bits and pieces.

Brad's father had been in the Marines throughout his childhood, and with that, Brad had a typical military childhood growing up near different bases for a few years at a time and then moving again. The Marines had given them a good life, trained Brad's father to be a pilot, and always kept them financially comfortable.

Good with people and possessing a strong mind for business, his father eventually got involved with real estate and had done very well for himself. He was a man who prided himself on always, no matter what, obeying the letter of the law. The trouble is, when dealing in great sums of money, other people are all too willing to play dirty to take what's been earned honestly. Brad's father had had all the profits of his hard work stolen from him through backroom deals and dirty pool. By the time Brad came home, his family was barely scraping by, and he had to cinch his belt as tight as it could get and pitch in.

Finding gainful employment in Atlanta while bearing foot-long dreadlocks wasn't the easiest thing to accomplish, but eventually Brad found work as a waiter in a lousy Tex-Mex restaurant. Two weeks later, he started splitting his paychecks evenly between a savings account for college tuition and his family's emergency reserve. It wasn't much money, but it was appreciated.

Brad had for some years found friendship, guidance, and support in his father's friend "The Judge." The first real patron of Brad's art, right back from when he was fifteen, the Judge had steadily bought work and financially supported his craft throughout its development. When Brad came down to Atlanta this time, he found that the Judge had great plans for him, providing contacts and paving a road into the super wealthy homes of Georgia's conservative Republican Party set. But when Brad excitedly showed him photographs of the artwork that he had been putting up all over New York, the Judge did not hold back with what he thought. This was immature, a dangerous road, and if he were to continue in any way on this path, things between them would be different in the future.

It was a classic invitation to sell his soul for success, and it was one of the most difficult decisions Brad ever had to make. In the midst of his family going through bankruptcy, he had to choose between a future of financial stability offered by a longtime friend, a man who had supported him from the start, and a world of expression that he found himself infinitely more in tune with. It was where he felt free, and where he felt his art would actually interact with, and be available to, the audience he wanted to reach.

Brad chose the harder road of street art, and the Judge withdrew his support. Both were saddened at this turn of events, and all at once, Brad felt another option crash down before him.

Brad's time in Atlanta was feeling like more and more of a dead-end. The money wasn't coming fast enough, and he was drowning in his day-to-day routine. He was treading water in the name of getting ahead, and the anxiety that generated was pulling him deeper into depression.

Thankfully, Brad soon found ways to pass the time and still believe he was doing something of value. He found a Kinko's that was managed absently, and started printing out gigantic photocopies of his drawings, building a stockpile for his eventual return to NYC. Printing out large-scale copies normally costs between twenty and fifty dollars a time, depending if you go black and white or color. That's an easy way to break the bank. But Brad noticed that it was all rung up on the honor system, which as a destitute artist was music to his penniless ears.

Soon he was going to Kinko's every night after work and would print twenty or thirty posters and pay for one, maybe two on days that he felt guilty for getting over on a billion-dollar international corporation. With time, word spread to friends back in NYC and he was doing favors across country. Inside of a month he was printing out countless posters a week and mailing them back up to New York. He supplied Adorn and Matt Hollister (known at the time as Ben Grimm) as well as turning out a healthy amount for himself.

One Saturday night, while drunk and lying in the back of a friend's pickup as they drove to a house party, Brad glimpsed a gas station out of the corner of his eye. The giant red neon letters forming the word SHELL were momentarily cropped so that Brad only saw the huge word "HELL" suspended above him. He was jarred sober. Suddenly he felt a spark of interest he hadn't experienced in months. Between waking up and helping around the house in the morning, going to work, ripping off the copy center, and drinking beer until he passed out, Brad was long numbed by his routine. Finally something had grabbed his attention and he could feel his brain begin to work again.

After a solid month of talking himself out of doing it, Brad stopped pretending it was a debate and got prepared. One night around midnight, he took a metal mallet out of his father's toolbox and an extendable ladder out of the garage, and he commandeered his mother's minivan for the rest of the night. Driving over to the gas station, he already felt the guilt sinking in. He could see the damaged ceiling of the minivan, which he had ruined one afternoon while moving some of his art. It was a testament to him being a burden, him taking advantage, not taking responsibility, making his parents' life harder. Looking at it now, and knowing that he was borrowing the van in order to commit a deliberate act of vandalism, stung deep. But his mind was set.

He pulled up across the street from the Shell station and parked on the side of the road. It was still open at 2am. He shut off the engine, sat there and reflected upon what he was about to do. A half an hour passed. He thought about what it would do to his parents if he got arrested, using their vehicle to commit a crime. He thought about what he was doing here in Atlanta – working for barely more than minimum wage, stealing from Kinko's on a nightly basis, amassing a vast array of street signs, drinking too much, and now out at two in the morning waiting patiently to smash out a light at a gas station…

Suddenly the main lights switched off at the station. The white halogen bulbs that lit the pumps, the street corner, the shop inside, were all extinguished. The only thing that lit the street at all was the word "SHELL" in dark red neon, floating ominously twenty feet off the ground, tinting Brad's eyes bloodshot. The gas attendant pulled out of the parking lot, not wasting a second's thought on the minivan parked across the street.

As the attendant sped off into the distance, Brad moved his head back slightly, letting the edge of the driver's side door crop the light as he remembered it. In the night sky above him, the letters H-E-L-L spelled out in the color of blood spoke volumes. Brad got out of the car and pulled out the ladder.

Brad was far more shook out in the silence of suburbia than he ever was in the city. In a metropolis, there is so much background noise that you could jackhammer into the concrete in the middle of the day and no one would blink. In the quiet nights of a small town, all you had to do

To cover his bases Brad had stretched a wool beanie over the license plate in case there were cameras at the gas station. He didn't wear anything over his face, thinking that would be an instant indicator of guilt if someone drove by and saw him up on the ladder with the hammer. The logic wasn't fantastic, but there it is.

was raise your voice or slam a car door and someone would be checking what "all that racket" was. Any passerby who spotted the ladder would have pulled over out of nothing more than curiosity and busted him redhanded.

Brad climbed the ladder and inspected the neon lettering up close. He had gotten this far but still wasn't sure if they were single lights, or if they were connected like strings of Christmas tree lights. If smashing one made them all go out, then he really would be engaged in mindless vandalism. Looking closer, it did seem that each letter had an independent power source, so he decided to take his chances.

He pulled on pink rubber dishwashing gloves borrowed from his mother's kitchen to protect himself from electrocution, took a breath, and swung the metal hammer, whacking the letter "S" hard on its side. The lights inside flicked quickly on and off about ten times, finally remaining on. Past the point of hesitation, Brad smashed the side again, this time with everything he had. No more flickering, the light just went dead. In the partial red light of the remaining letters Brad was finally making good in his own personal Hell.

He quickly got down, packed the ladder into the back of the minivan and looked at his illuminated handiwork. Thinking that they might fix it first thing in the morning, Brad got back out of the van and climbed the grassy hill behind. He sat there for a while and stared back at what he had created. Suspended high above him in the dark of the unlit street, the word HELL floated lonesome and surreal in the sky, the only light source for miles.

At first all Brad had wanted to do was recreate a trick of the eye, but now he realized that he had uncovered something much more than that. Possibilities began to suggest themselves and ideas to fly. Here was subtraction as a tool, used to recontextualize, to transform, to give new meaning to what was left behind in the altered environment. His thoughts were still murky at best, but here was a new way to interact with street furniture, not just to add and change and mutate, but to cut away, to sculpt through subtraction.

With this epiphany, things were looking up for Brad. The months had been racing by, even if it didn't feel like it, and by the time he had finally adjusted to life back in Atlanta it was December. With Pratt's tuition all paid up, and due back in class mid-January, he decided to spend the rest of his stay with his family enjoying the holidays.

Driving home one day, Brad's father suddenly started furiously cursing at the road.

"Of all the stupid shit! What moron decided this road needed to change?"

The road from the shopping mall, which connected directly to the street Brad's family lived on, had been blocked off from the turning lane. Now, thanks to the freshly painted double yellow line, he would have to drive halfway around the enormous mall and pull a U-turn to get to his house.

"If it ain't broke, don't fix it! God damn! This is going to add five minutes of driving each way, every time I leave the house!" he protested. "You want to do me a favor?" He turned to Brad. "You paint an arrow on the road, where that turn used to be, I'll give you a hundred bucks."

"Consider it done," replied Brad.

His father smirked and they laughed at the idea of going out at night to fix every stupid mistake city planners made.

That night, without telling his father, Brad went out to do just that. He taped off an arrow, painted it, and placed either side of it a couple of traffic cones he found nearby to protect the paint while it dried. By morning the cones had magically retreated back where they came from, and there were a couple of faint tire tracks through the paint, but the eight-foot white arrow looked as official as could be.

When his father saw the arrow, he couldn't believe it. He pulled over on the side of the road and called Faye, his wife and Brad's mother.

"I was just kidding. We were joking around last night, and before I woke up it was done." He was telling Brad's mother about it while feeling a strange combination of pride and disbelief. "I guess I owe Brad a hundred dollars." Brad took the money, and wished his father Merry Christmas.

Before Brad knew it, the calendar read January and he was packing for the trip back to Brooklyn. With hundreds of posters and a dozen large, freshly altered street signs that were far easier to steal and work on in Atlanta, Brad realized how much work he had ready to put up once he touched down. He stuffed everything into his giant portfolio case, checked it with the rest of his luggage, and ordered a handful of tiny whiskey bottles from a stewardess for the quick flight back.

Brooklyn took Brad back to its wintry yet welcoming bosom. It was strange at first, being so out of the loop, the awkwardness of seeing old acquaintances and explaining over and over again why he'd been M.I.A. for the better part of a year. He was never sure if they really cared to hear it, or if he cared enough to tell the same story for the hundredth time. However, he was up and running soon enough. The winter house parties were somehow hotter than the parties he left behind in the summer. With so many people crammed into a tiny apartment, the radiator and hundred-person body heat combined their powers to toast you when you walked in, winter-geared up, fresh out of the cold. It felt good.

After getting acclimated, Brad was itching to put up some of the work he had done down south, so he reached out to Matt Hollister to go on a mission. Over the better part of a day, they went through Brooklyn and into Manhattan putting up wheat-paste poster after poster. Once in the Lower East Side, they really started carpet-bombing buildings with posters. Brad was eager to get his fresh work up and feeling somewhat bulletproof following the success of his minor exploits in Atlanta, and before they knew it they had put up over a hundred posters, covering block after block from the LES to the East Village.

What neither Brad nor Matt knew was that they were being followed. As they were pasting up an absurd number of posters, a teenager with Down Syndrome was trailing them on his BMX bike and taking Polaroids of everything they did. Every fifteen minutes or so, the handicapped kid called the cops with an update on where Brad and Hollister were and what they were up to.

As the two artists were bombarding the Lower East Side of Manhattan, blissfully unaware of the handicapped gumshoe on their tail, the police were driving up and down every street in a twenty-block radius looking for two white males in their early twenties, their arms full of posters and paste.

As he was pasting a poster over the glass door that led to the offices of the Village Voice, Brad heard a blaring "woop-weep!" scream up behind him.

The cops cut the siren, stepped out of the car, and approached the two.

"What the hell do you think you're doing kid? Don't you know you're breaking the law? You're putting shit up in the middle of the day!"

Brad was stone cold busted and had to think fast. "This is illegal? I didn't know that. I'm from Atlanta." Brad handed his Georgia Driver's License over to the cop. "I see posters up all over, I thought it was ok. Wait, look," Brad pulled the still wet poster and it peeled down easily. "See, it comes right off," he said brightly.

The cop handed the license back to Brad and said, "Well I guess if you pull it down, it's not such a big deal…."

Suddenly someone rode up to them. "Finally! Here is the evidence I collected!" proclaimed the out-of-breath and overexcited teenager as he jumped off his bike. He handed a four-inch brick of Polaroids to the other police officer. The photos documented every poster they had put up for the last three hours. Out came the handcuffs.

They put Matt in the squad car first. As they were pushing Brad's head down so it wouldn't hit the top of the door, he couldn't help but reflect on what had happened. This was the first time he had ever been busted doing street art, and it was not only because he came back to the city cocky. This was karma. He had used his artistic/criminal talent for non-artistic work and personal gain. As he considered giving back the hundred dollars to his dad, a gnat flew directly into his eye. Already handcuffed, and no one willing to do him any favors, he just grinned and bore it. He was going to have to take his karmic licks; no negotiating was going to get him out of this.

It being after 5pm when they got picked up and brought to booking, they had to spend the night in the holding cell and see the judge in the morning. They were given baloney sandwiches, which they eventually used as pillows, and killed the clock as fast as they could.[7] The next day, after being fined a hundred dollars each – which confirmed Brad's karmic theory – the two headed back to Brooklyn. After a sobering dose of reality, Brad was home.

[7] Brad killed time freestyling with some guys who were jailed on minor marijuana busts, while Matt laid down and took a nap, getting woken up an hour later by a black guy who whispered in his ear "Yo, I'm Slim Shady, the real Slim Shady." Matt, being blond, skinny, and white, took a lot of teasing, while his partner in crime, just as white with ridiculous dreadlocks, was making all kinds of friends in the cipher.

THE BIRTH AND CONFIRMATION OF DARIUS (AND DOWNEY)

2000–2001 | With Brad in Atlanta, Leon has an epiphany of his own while in Cincinnati and changes the name he goes by from Verbs to Darius Jones. At the same time he and Buddy Lembeck get famous on a local level thanks to an interview with Fox News and some quick thinking. Upon Leon's return to Brooklyn, he and Brad agree to officially combine their artistic powers and ambitions for the greater good.

During the summer of 2000, Leon had gotten an internship at a Cincinnati-based graphic design firm, and with that, he had more confined free time than he knew what to do with.[†] Being by nature nearly as retrospective as he is introspective, Leon spent most of that time thinking and rethinking about the previous year. One thing that stuck out beyond all else was the conflict he had been having with one of his teachers, one of the few that cared enough to get involved. That is, he cared enough to call Leon out as "artistically stunted" and "short-sighted" on a nigh weekly basis.

The continual argument was over the work Leon had been bringing into class, which was primarily "Verbs" written repeatedly in different innovative and visually explosive ways on street signs. His teacher was trying to break him of the habit.

"Why don't you try something different, just once?" his teacher finally asked, in front of the entire class. Tired of trying to reach Leon in their after-class talks, he was bringing this conversation front and center.

"This *is* different. This is a different way to write Verbs," Leon replied, feeling slightly proud to be standing up for himself and what he believed in in front of his peers.

"That's the same thing you said last week when we talked after class. You're in art school. Try something new. Why is this name so important to you? Experiment with new things," his teacher pleaded.

"This was an experiment. I never did it like this before. It's new to me...." Leon was feeling boxed in. He had been putting his all into writing Verbs for the last five years, and the reception had always been warm, but suddenly his teacher was telling him that what he was doing was wrong and he should stop. It wasn't going to happen. Not then at least, not simply because he was told to.

[†] Internships as a rule being exercises in honing one's meditative skills to the point that upon sitting down, one focuses on the speck of nothingness one amounts to in the universe/business world, only to soon realize that it's a quarter to quitting time.

"Why are you even in college? You should just go home to Cincinnati, and do this in your basement. You'd be learning about as much down there, by yourself, and it wouldn't cost you twenty thousand dollars a year." The teacher had stopped commenting on the piece in question and now was heatedly talking to Leon about Leon.

"Well, hold on now…" Leon muttered.

"No you hold on, Leon. Your tuition is paying my mortgage, which is fine with me, but trust me, you're not learning a thing here. You're fighting me every step of the way, refusing to learn anything." The professor took a breath and looked at Leon with pity. "So tell me, do you like it in Brooklyn so much that you'll pay college tuition just to have an excuse to be here? Do you like it enough to be in debt for the rest of your life?" With that, the bell put the dot under his question mark and the professor lowered himself into the seat behind his desk.

Leon had more to say, but the room was already clearing out. He walked up to the professor's desk and they looked at each other for a moment, then without another word Leon turned and left the classroom.

The following week, Leon brought in another sign that said Verbs. It went up on the wall for critique and came down at the end of class, without either of them wasting a word on the subject. With that last, tired, stalemate classroom experience, the semester was over.

While sitting in his cubicle in Cincinnati, Leon's magnetic tape memory replayed that afternoon again and again, hitting auto-rewind every time the bell rang. Away from the judgmental eyes of his fellow students, he really let his professor's words sink in. Embarrassment came flooding back and he could feel his face getting warm. What he was doing with himself, with his art? Why was his name so important? He had been doing it for five years straight and couldn't stop just because one man had issues with it. But was stubbornness going to keep him a fifteen-year-old boy in an ever-aging body, never maturing, because doing something new would devalue his past? Suddenly, unquestionably, Leon knew it was time for a change.

What exactly the change would be, he wasn't sure of yet. Working so close with Brad these last few months, and seeing someone so confidently put his birth name all over town, he couldn't help but feel that perhaps an alias was irrelevant. But that wasn't enough of a change. He had such a bad taste in his mouth over the humiliation he suffered in class that he wanted to get names in general away from what he was up to. Maybe he should just make his work an anonymous gift to the city? This was as far on the other end of the spectrum as he could get, and it seemed like the right move.

With that, Leon set about making signs that he felt would grab the attention of passersby and make a positive impact. This would be an altruistic departure from the selfish feeling he was starting to associate with the act of putting his name up. It was time to offer something more substantial to the community. This was a(n) (r)evolution in his thinking.

Before he could second-guess it, he had already put up four signs. One said "READ," in one of the most illiterate, poverty-stricken neighborhoods in Cincinnati, while others proclaimed "YOU CAAN DO IT!" and "DON'T LET GO." Signing none of them, he started to feel that this was a way to connect with people and to give something back – a smile, a laugh, a positive word of encouragement in a part of town that only had advertisements and prohibitions in public view. Leon was starting to see the real power and possible impact of his medium, and it had nothing to do with getting his name up.

Proud of his new work, Leon called up Brad in Atlanta to discuss what he was up to.

"I'm going to drop Verbs and start making work without signing it," Leon explained.

"Why don't you just add a first or last name to Verbs? Like Leon Verbs, or Verbs Reid?" Brad asked.

"Because I want to keep it separate. I'm done with Verbs. That was a different part of my life and I don't want to mix the two," Leon replied, without a hint of debate on his voice. The decision was made.

"…Ok, well then why not sign Leon Reid under it?" Brad asked.

"Because I don't want the police showing up at my mother's house every time I do a piece. I don't want to sign my address and zip code under it," Leon laughed. "I'm just not into that."

"The police never came to my mom's house… but whatever. Just keep thinking about it," Brad replied as they ended the conversation.

Leon pushed his finger down on the cradle to his landline cubicle phone, and without even putting down the receiver called Andre to check his thoughts on the subject.

"Why not just use Darius, like you told that reporter?" Andre shot back when Leon asked him the same question. "I've used Buddy Lembeck as a pen name for years now."

In the summer of '96, Leon was interviewed in a local paper and had his picture taken in front of a fresh burner. Asked by the reporter what his real name was, Leon wasn't going to read her the name off his birth certificate any more than he was going to sign the graffiti with his Social Security number. No one was going to believe he was christened under the name Verbs, so instead he blurted out "Darius Jones," and the name was born.

"That way you can sign it with something that sounds like a real name, and also keep yourself separate from Verbs. That works, right?" Andre asked.

"Yeah… Yeah it does," Leon answered.

Reminded of what he had thought of as a single-serving, throwaway alias, Leon took it up again and from then on started exclusively working under Darius Jones. Like a hermit crab that had outgrown its old shell, he had no reason to look back; he just had to reintroduce himself to a lot of people who knew him as Verbs and Verbs alone.

That summer, with Andre painting his massive characters beside him, Leon did giant rollers of slogans that maintained the same positivity, from "LOVE YA!" and "WHY NOT?," to the twenty-five-foot boom "WHO FARTED?" next to the Ohio River and well in range of its notorious stench.

The following winter, Leon was in Cincinnati again and he and Andre came up with a fun idea. Keeping in the same tongue-in-cheek vein, they decided to start putting slogans on the highway overpasses.

Over the next two freezing weeks, one-liners like "GIRLS FART," "HOME DEPOT GOT PAINT," and "CHRIS SABO DIED FOR OUR SINS" started popping up down the highway overpasses, much to the delight of schoolbound children and wage slaves on the morning commute. Here were inside jokes that every local Cincinnatian could share, from lobbing a softball diss to a local overweight weatherman – "PAT BERRY SAT ON ME" – to the universal gross-out "I MADE OUT WITH MARGE SCHOTT," Marge being the very wealthy, very racist, gravel-throated, prune-faced owner of the Cincinnati Reds, and the last lady anyone would brag on. In time they went slightly deeper with their commentary – "VANILLA ICE = COLIN POWELL" was one – but they always kept it fun.

They were silly; they were finger food for the masses; they were the amusing non-offensive graffiti that you find in men's room stalls, one-liners that provide light reading while otherwise occupied.

The response was near immediate. People were loving what they were reading. It was easy to grasp; there was zero learning curve. If you lived in Cincinnati, and traveled on the highway at all, you had seen the work and it was fun to talk about around the water cooler as well as in the playground. As the number one peddlers of water cooler content, local radio DJs started dedicating time to it within about four days. Catching their work being discussed one day on the Willy Cunningham Show on 700 WLW, Leon and Andre called in and offered to talk about it on the air.

After acing a Q & A session hastily designed to weed out imposters, Cunningham's producer gave Leon and Andre the benefit of the doubt and put them on with a three-second censor delay. They had gotten the green light to talk for three to five minutes about what they had been up to. Charming as ever, the two soon turned that into an hour and forty-five minutes, eating up the better part of the show.

Towards the end, during a commercial break, the radio show took a call from a producer at Fox 19 News wanting to interview Leon and Andre for the local news. It was agreed that they would meet at a Chuck E. Cheese's in the suburbs of Cincinnati and do the interview, but only if they were allowed to disguise their identities. Fox offered to blur their faces, but the boys had their own idea.

When the reporter and cameraman showed up at the children's playground themed pizzeria, they saw them instantly. The two dapper gentlemen were sitting next to an empty box of pizza, wearing paper bags on their heads and ill-fitting Salvation Army suits spotted with white paint. After some muffled introductions, they walked outside and on that snowy night, the two boys stood in front of Chuck E. Cheese's and got a little more famous. As bag heads, anyways.

With that, Christmas break was coming to an end and Leon, like Brad, was due back in Brooklyn. He had a new name, a new game plan, and a renewed dedication to his craft, having seen how many more people he could reach if he chose to put his message into words.

At the end of January 2001, with Leon back from Cincinnati and Brad back from Georgia, the two decided it was time to combine everything they had learned in their time apart and go big. And this time the credit would be to Darius and Downey.

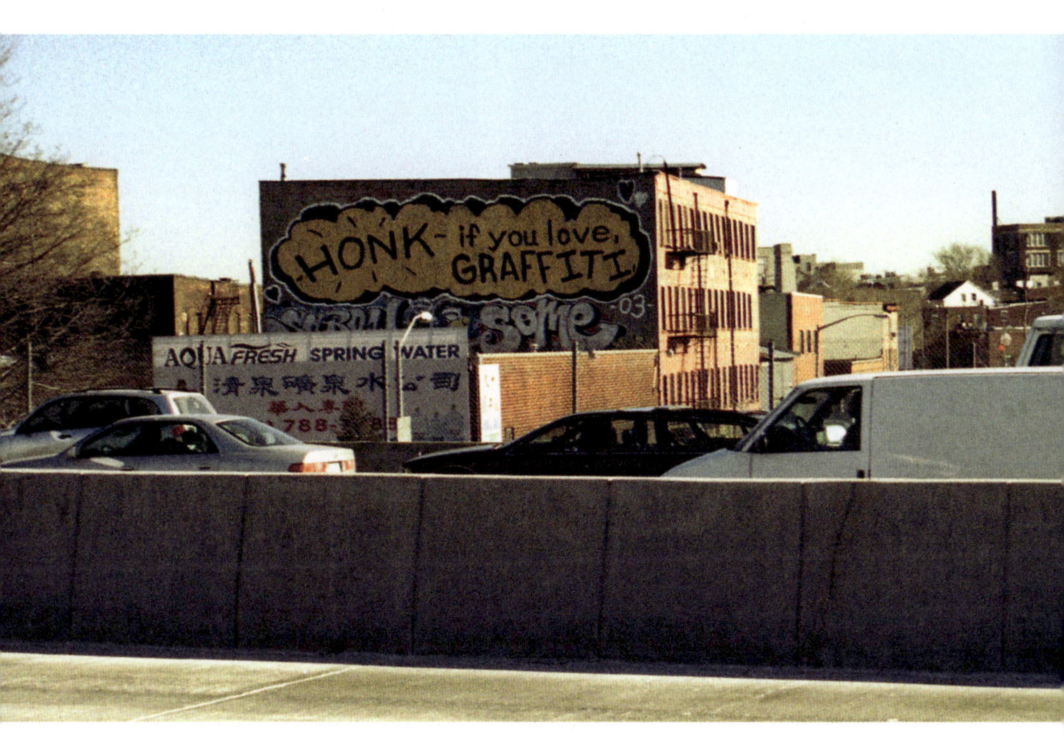

Honk if You Love Graffiti, Darius and Downey, 2003.
Slogan by Buddy Lembeck (Andre Hyland). Brooklyn, NY.
Duration: 1 month.

hell

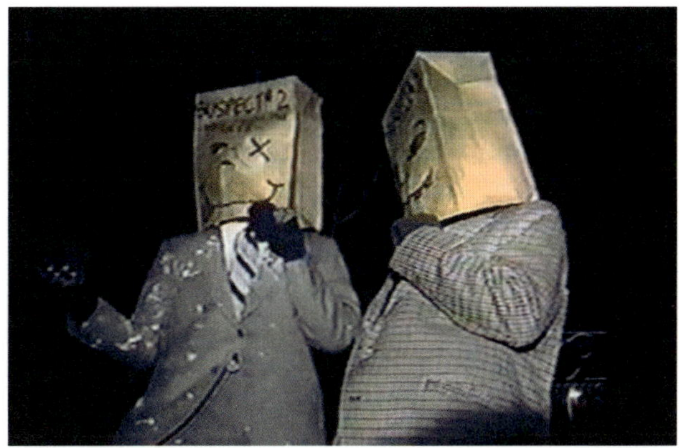

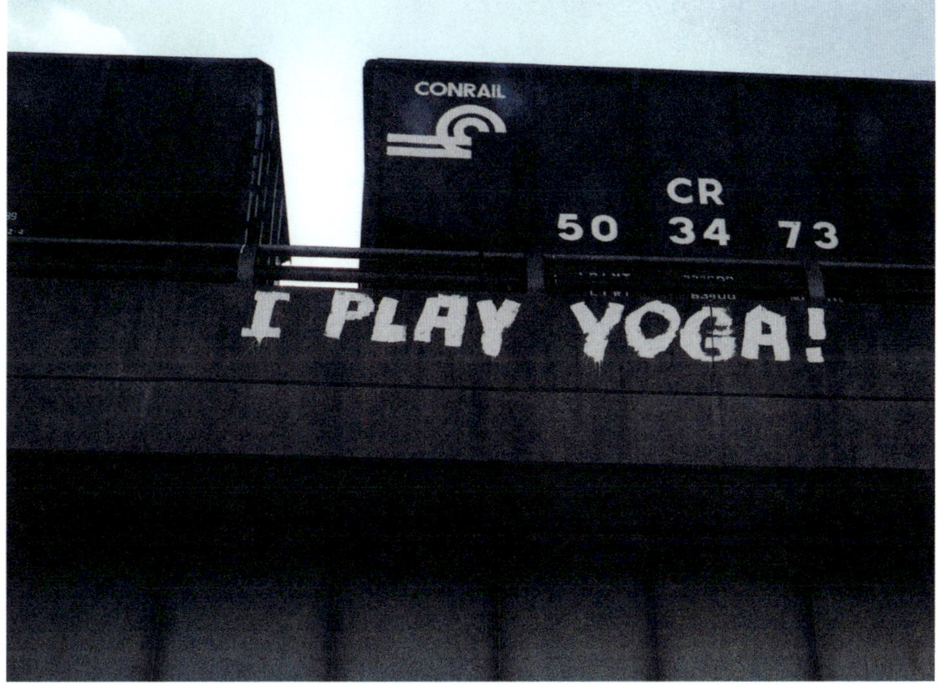

OPPOSITE *sHELL*, Brad Downey, 1999. Atlanta, GA. Duration: unknown.

TOP Leon Reid IV and Andre Hyland in a video still from the Fox 19 News, 2001.

ABOVE *I Play Yoga*, Buddy Lembeck (Andre Hyland) and Darius Jones (Leon Reid IV), 2001. Cincinnati, OH. Duration: 4 years. Photo by Andre Hyland.

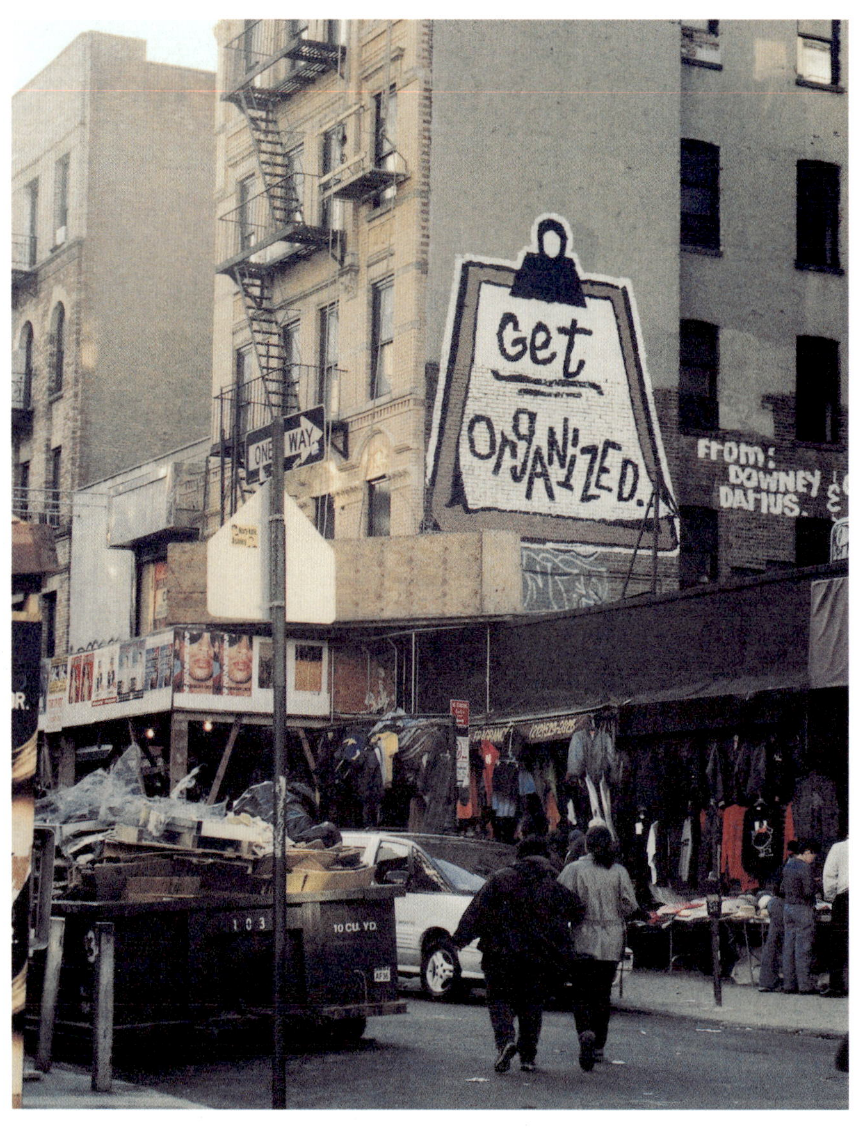

Get Organized, Darius and Downey, 2001. New York City, NY. Duration: 2 years.

OPPOSITE *The Gift*, Darius and Downey, 2001. New York City, NY. Duration: 2 months.

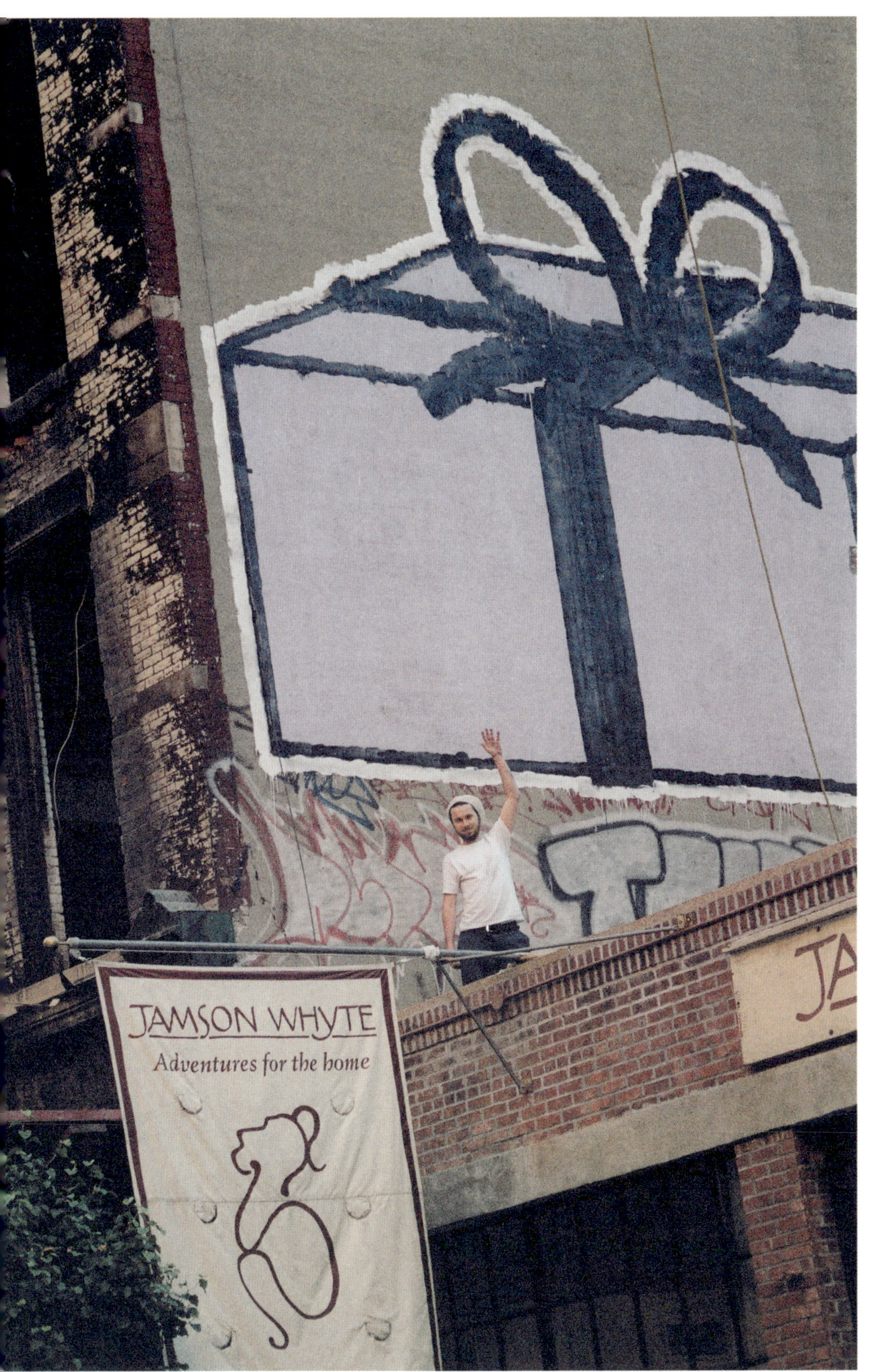
JAMSON WHYTE
Adventures for the home
JA

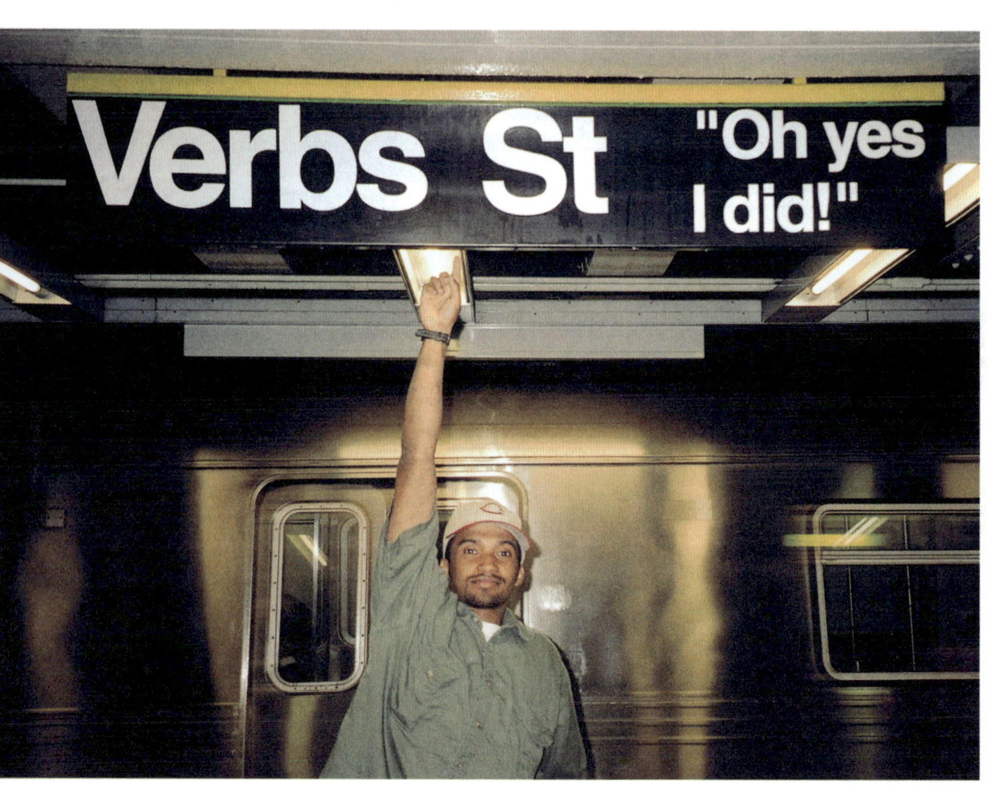
Verbs St
"Oh yes
I did!"

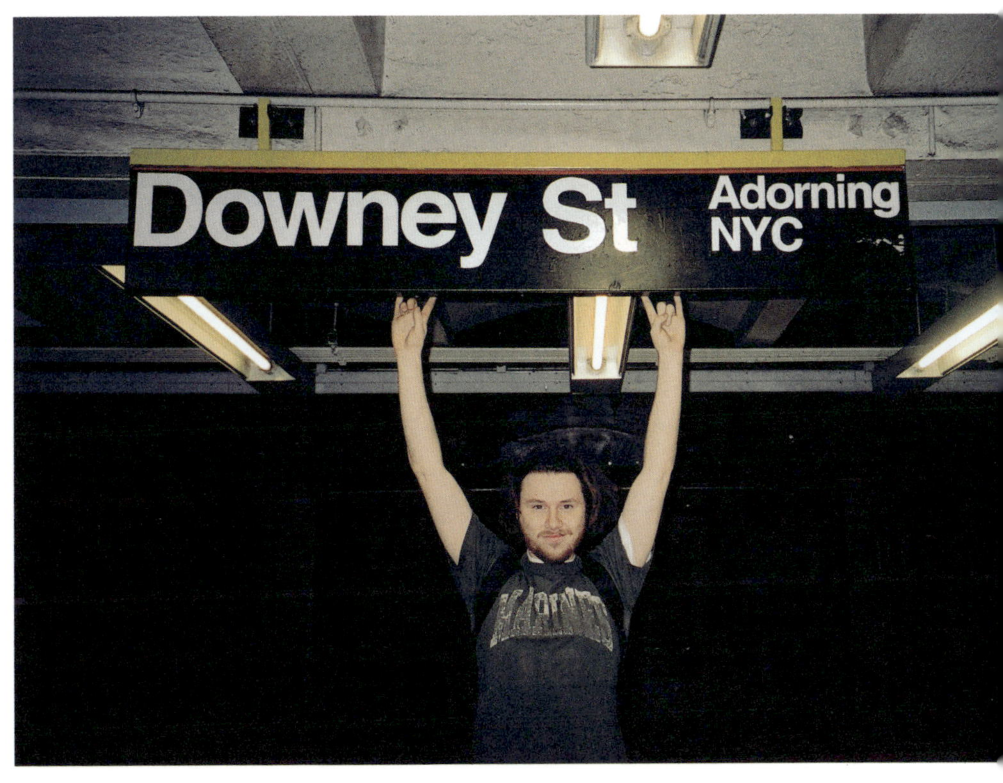

Verbs St./Downey St. (front and back), Verbs (Leon Reid IV) and
Brad Downey, 2000. New York City, NY. Duration: 3 weeks.

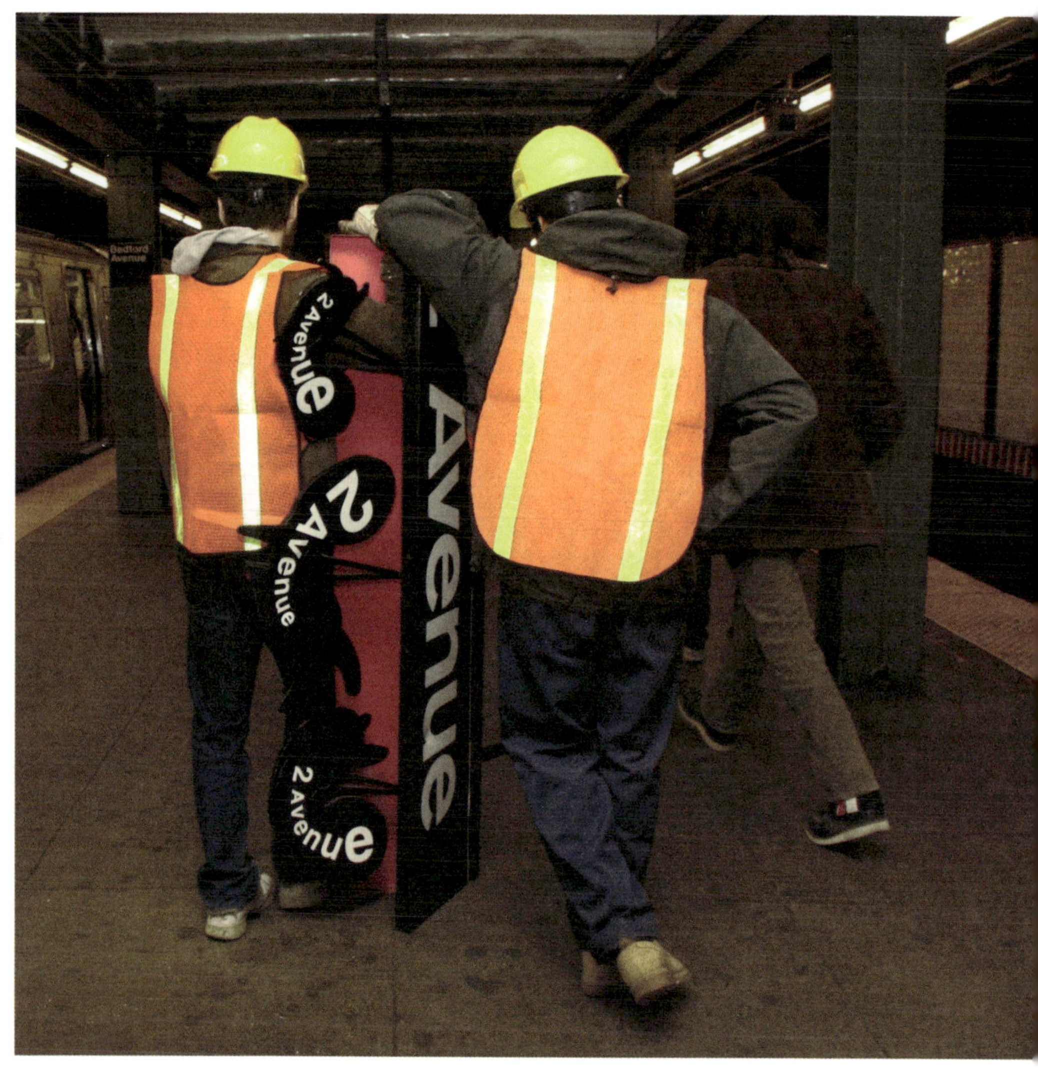
Bedford
Avenue
2 Avenue
2 Avenue
2 Avenue
Avenue

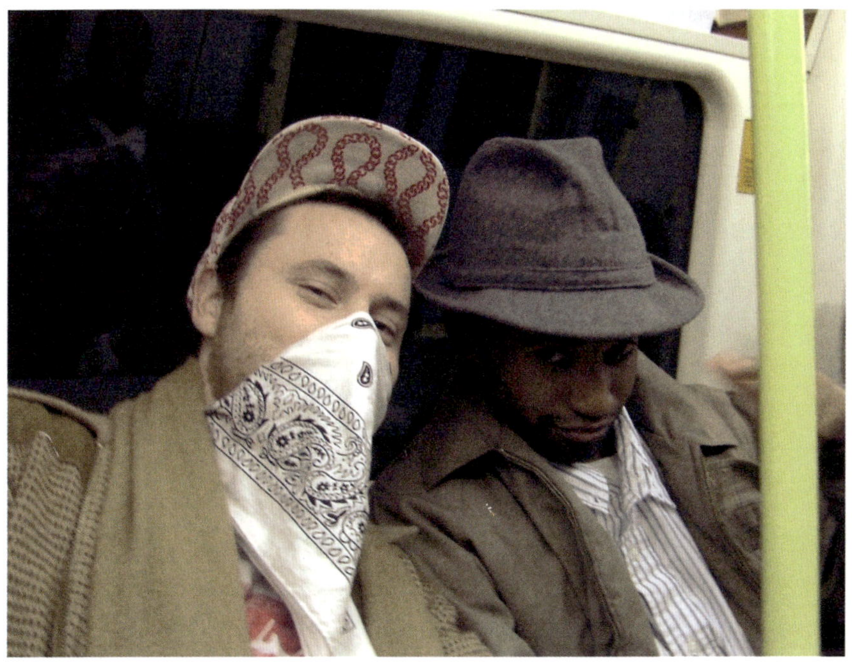

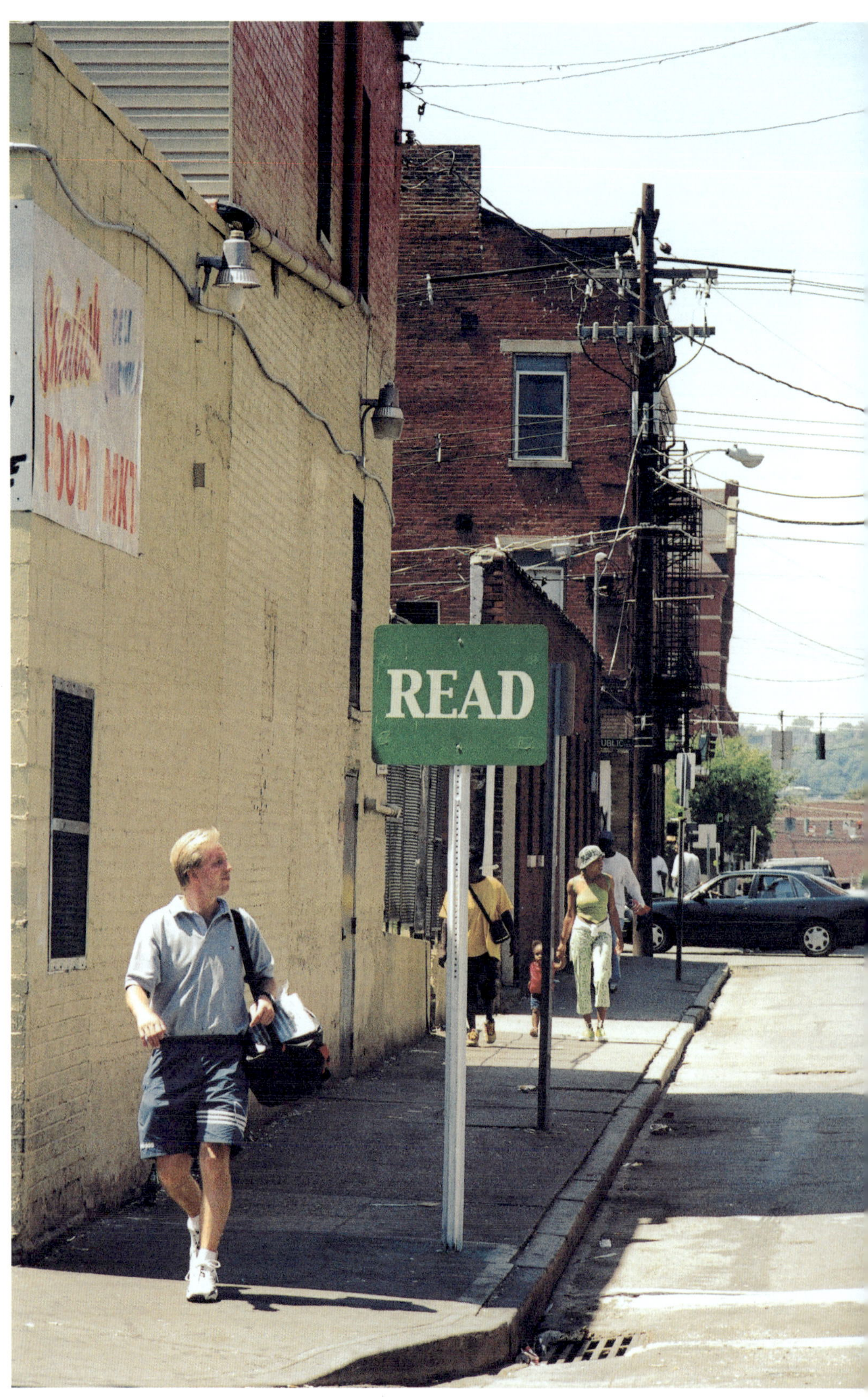

READ
FOOD MKT

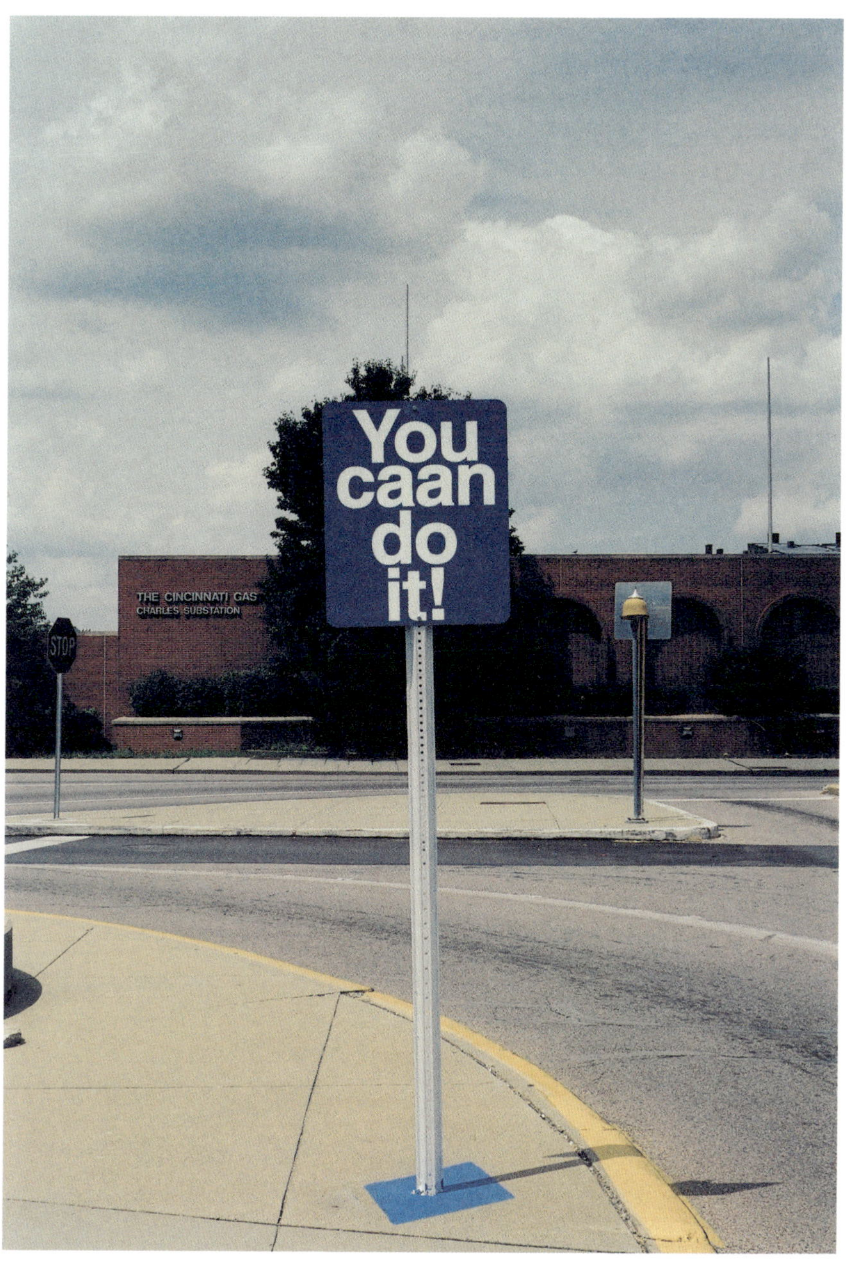

OPPOSITE *Read*, 2000. Darius Jones (Leon Reid IV). Cincinnati, OH. Duration: 9 months.

ABOVE *You Caan Do It*, 2000. Darius Jones (Leon Reid IV). Cincinnati, OH. Duration: 4 months.

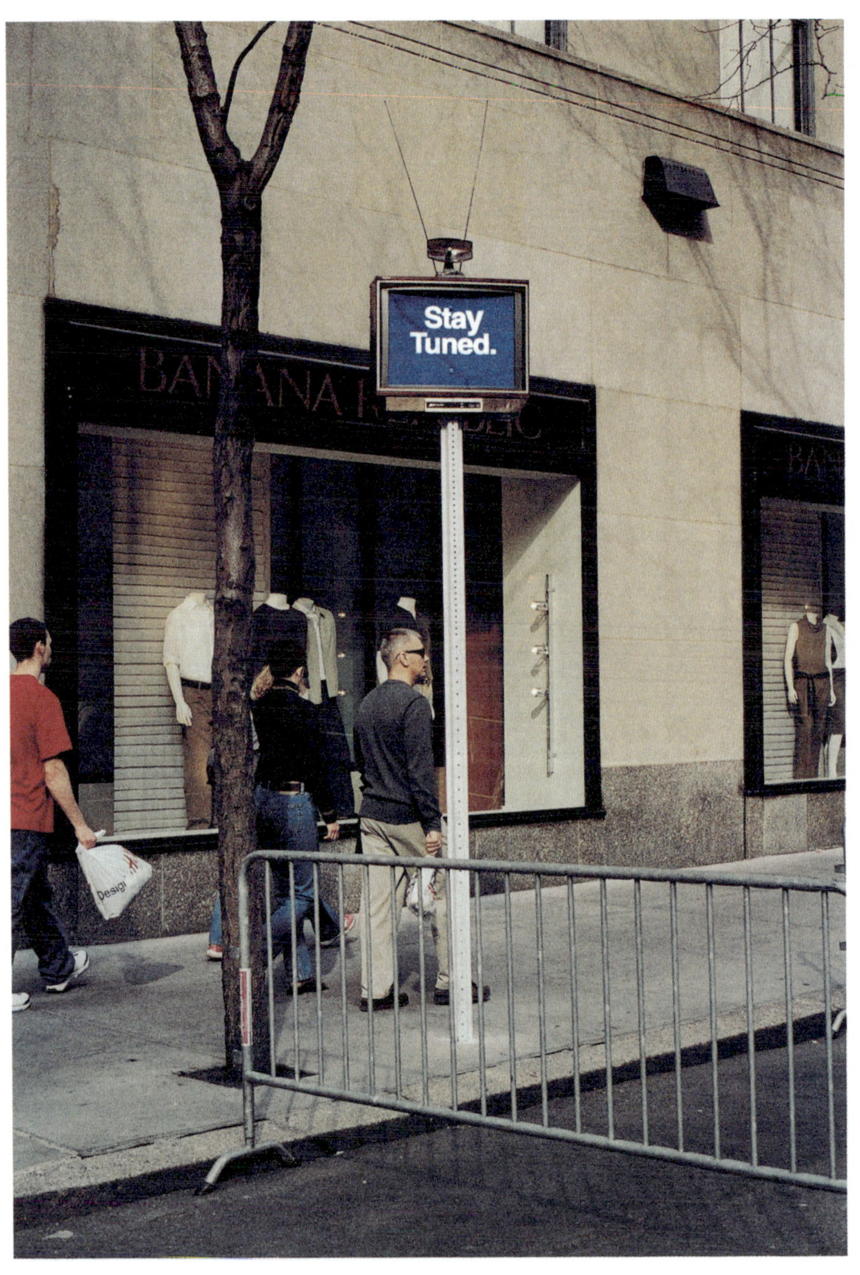

Stay Tuned, Darius and Downey, 2001. New York City, NY. Duration: 6 weeks.

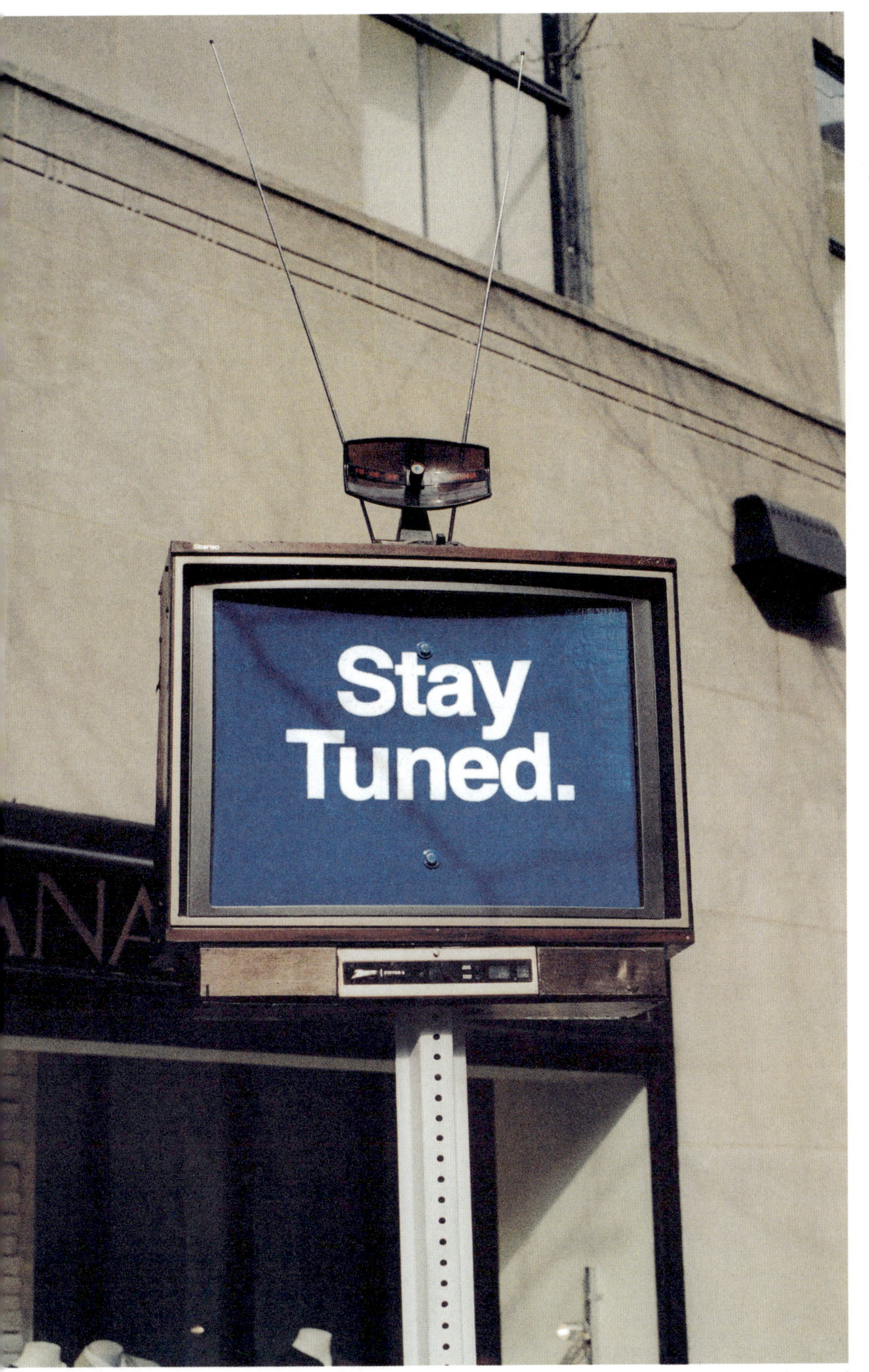
Stay
Tuned.

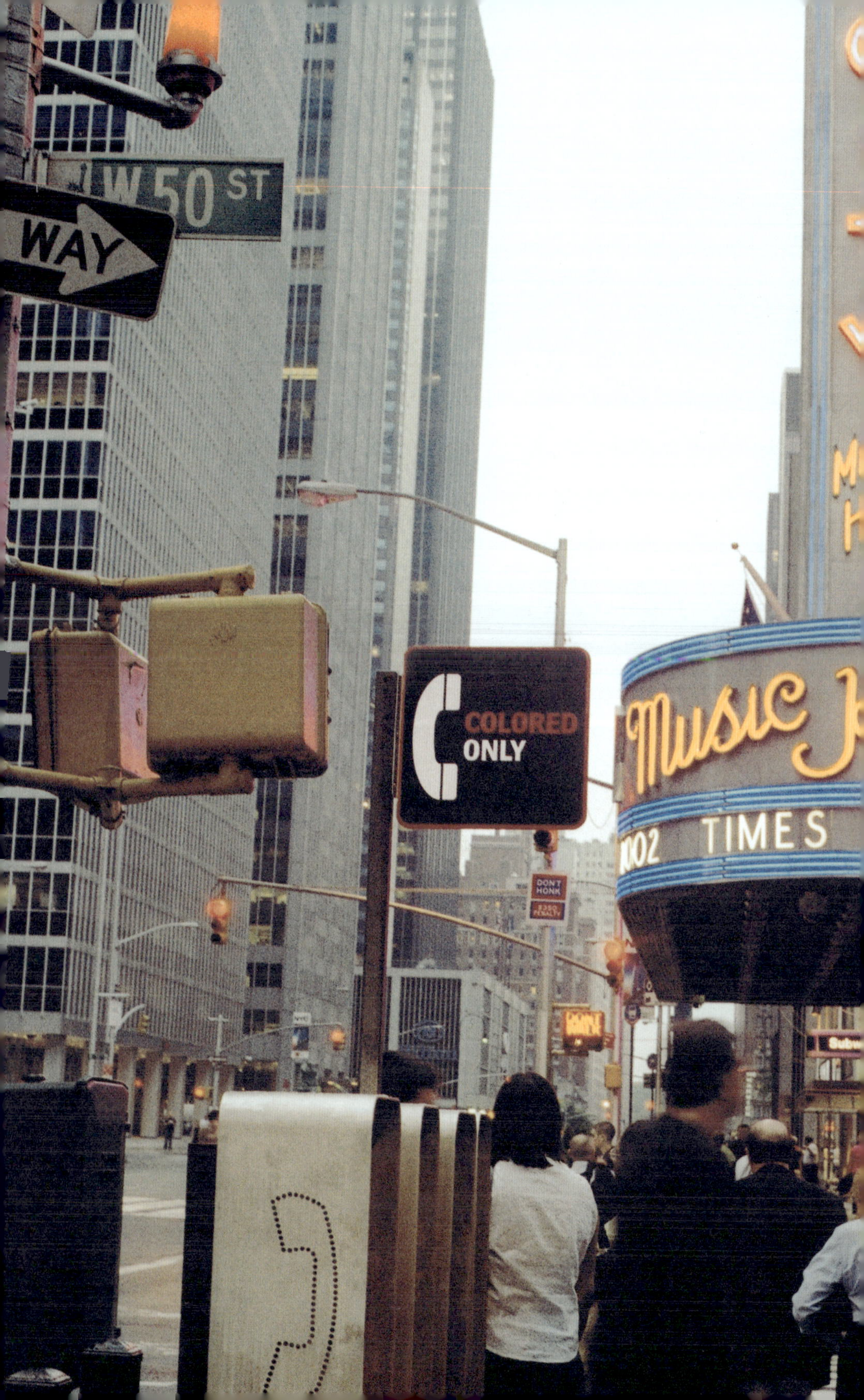

WAY
W 50 ST
COLORED ONLY
Music H
1002 TIMES
DON'T HONK $350 PENALTY

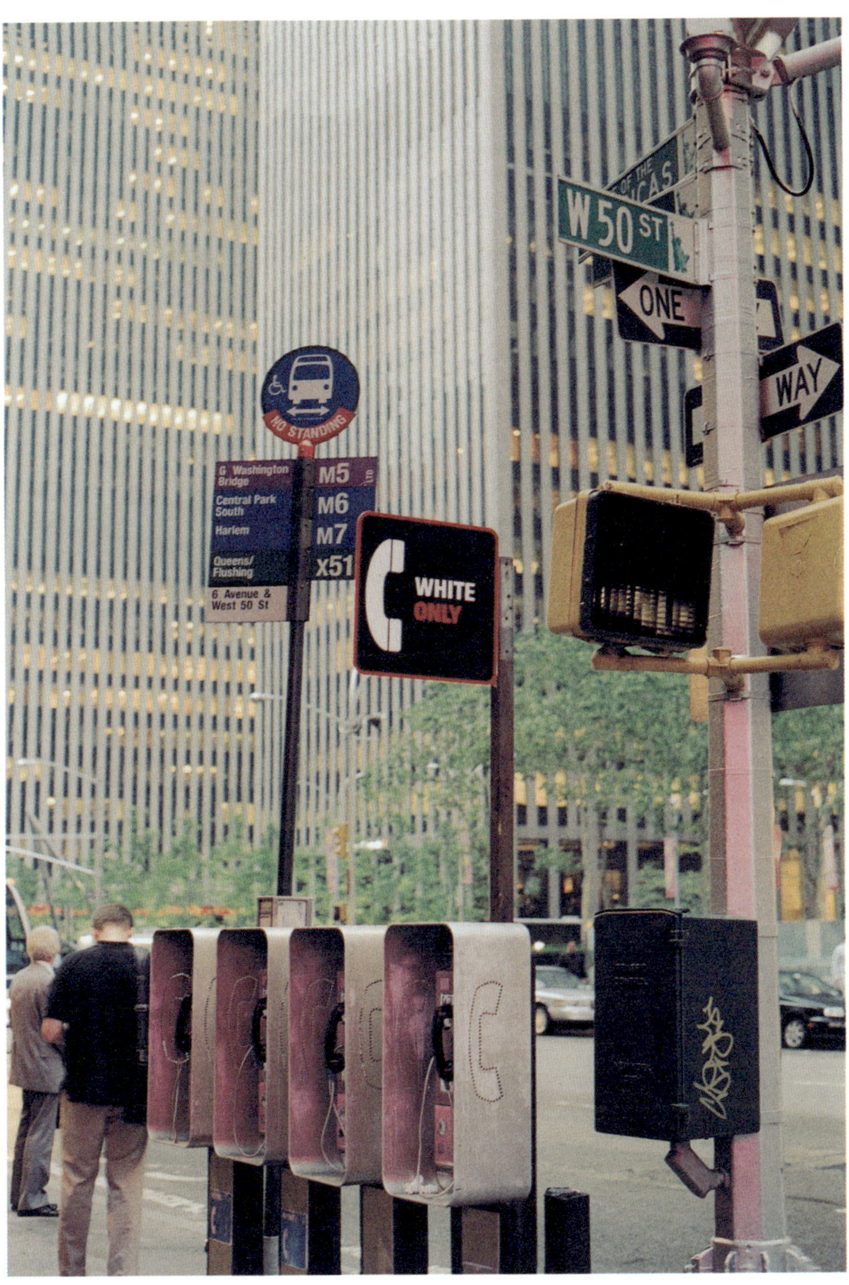

White Only/Colored Only (front and back), Darius Jones (Leon Reid IV),
2002. New York City, NY. Duration: 12 hours.

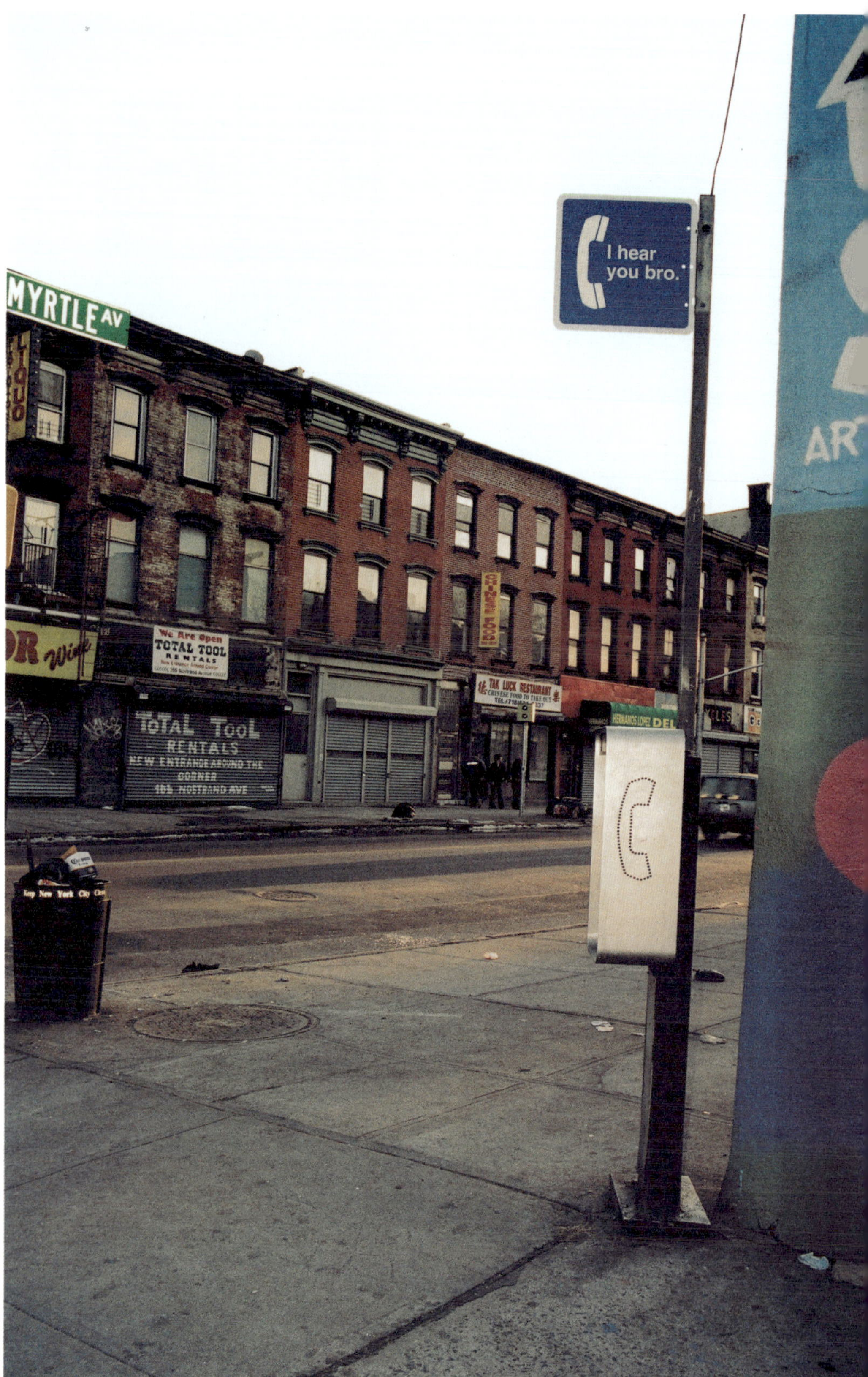

I hear
you bro.
MYRTLE AV
LIQUO
OR Wine
We Are Open
TOTAL TOOL
RENTALS
TOTAL TOOL
RENTALS
NEW ENTRANCE AROUND THE
CORNER
NOSTRAND AVE
CHINESE FOOD
TAK LUCK RESTAURANT
CHINESE FOOD TO TAKE OUT
HERMANOS LOPEZ DEL
Keep New York City Clean
ART

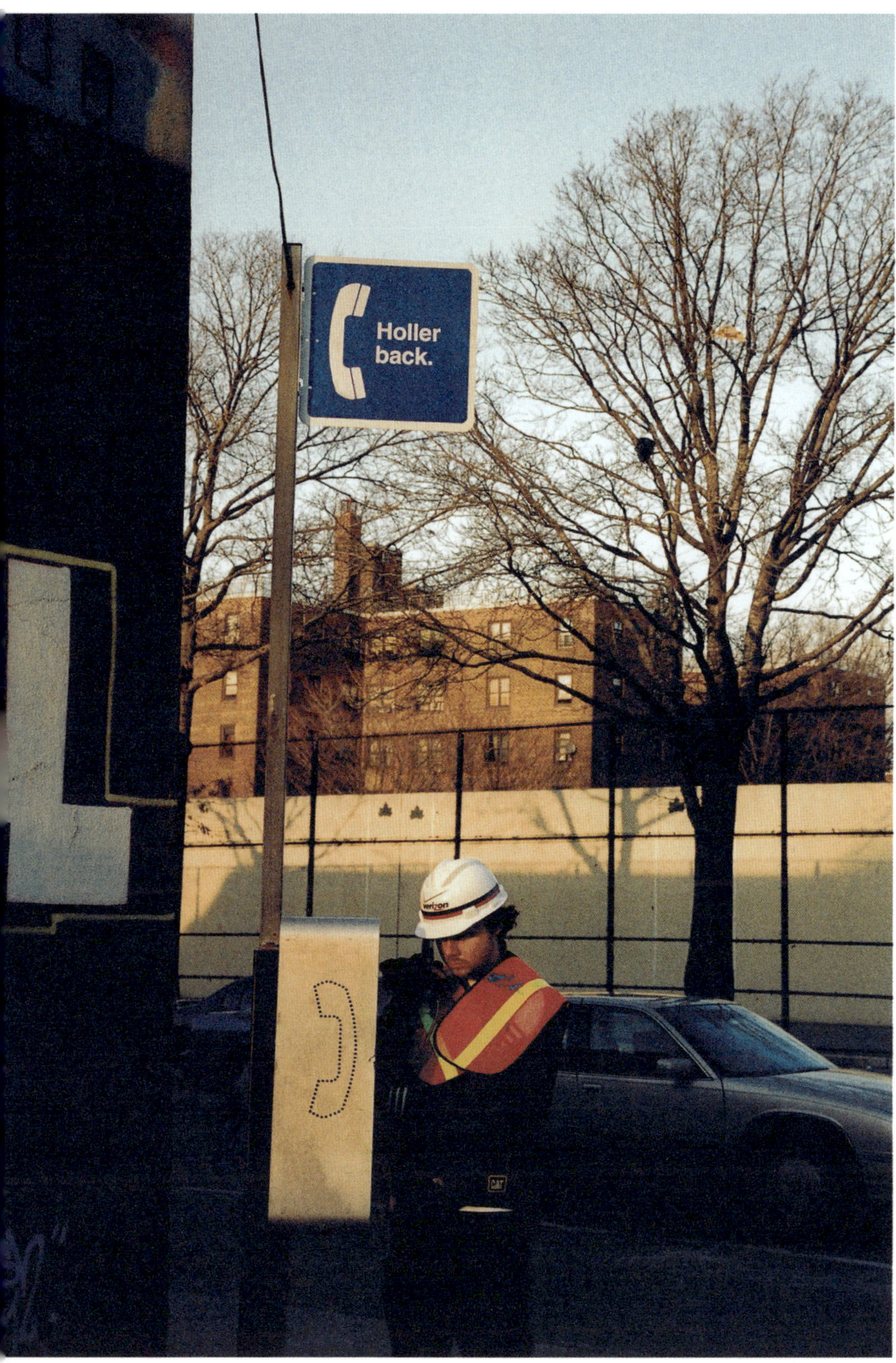

I Hear You Bro/Holler Back (front and back), Darius and Downey, 2003. Brooklyn, NY.
Duration: 4 years and counting. Photo by Tod Seelie.

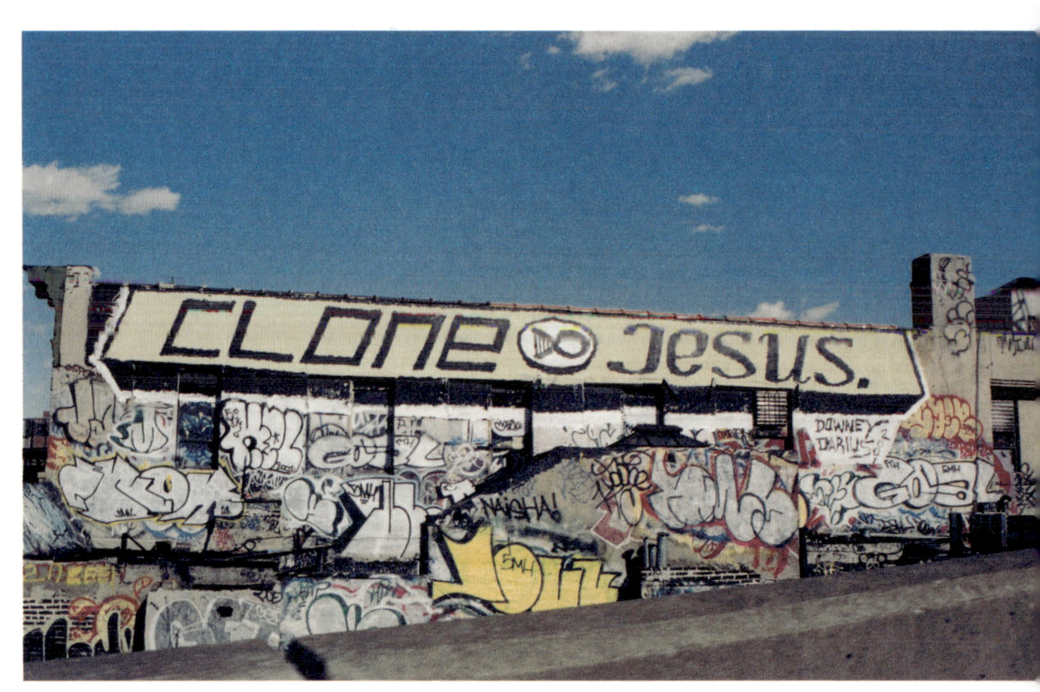

Clone Jesus, Darius and Downey, 2001. New York City, NY.
Duration: 3 years.

THE HARD WAY

2001 | With a verbal permission slip signed by Espo, Leon and Brad do their damnedest to go over a famed Espo/Amaze NYC boom at the base of the Manhattan Bridge. Having recently been riddled in disses by Swatch (Omar), it was fair game, but with Espo's blessing plus a few hints that got lost in translation, the boys were looking at a golden ticket situation. Everything was going gravy until company showed up with the sunrise.

In the March of 2001, with Brad, Leon, and Quenell all living together on Skillman Street in Brooklyn, the three felt, for the first time, a real sense of stability. Brad and Leon's urge to collaborate was stronger than ever, and although Leon was spending most nights at Polina's, he and Brad decided to spend their days coming up with pieces that they could work on together, in a similar fashion to the work Leon had been doing alongside Andre back in Cincinnati.

One afternoon while the boys were walking down Myrtle Avenue to pick up some lunch, talking about ideas they had overflowing from their sketchbooks, Brad remembered a phrase he had come up with that previous summer which might be a good fit for what they had been planning.[*] As they waited for their pizza to be reheated for the cold walk home, Brad mentioned his idea.

"So I've got something that might work, a piece that we could do together," he said. "What about writing CLONE JESUS?" Brad took a napkin and drew it out with a pen.

"Let me see that?" Leon motioned for the napkin and looked it over. "I like it, but well, what if we did this?"

Leon drew a Jesus fish with a DNA double helix above it and an arrow pointing between the two words.

"Ohhhhhh." Brad smiled. "I think we've got something here."

And as simple as that, the two picked up their slices and started the walk back home to sketch it out again, on something a little more durable than a Liberty Pizza napkin.

Once home, Brad told Leon where he was thinking the piece should go. Having recently, but not collaboratively, gone big on a building on the Brooklyn side of the Manhattan Bridge, on a location chosen and shared by Eric Adorn, Brad thought that if they were going to do

---

[*] Whenever he was down in Atlanta, Brad would go to the Judge's house to talk. During his summer 2000 trip, they had talked about religious archeology, which was a hobby of the Judge's. Brad joked that they should just use those artifacts to go ahead and clone Jesus. They agreed that the Shroud of Turin would probably work. Everyone could have a pet Jesus. The two laughed and joked about it for several minutes, and it stuck in Brad's head.

something even bigger as Darius and Downey, then going up on the Manhattan side as well would be the move to make.

A recent feud between Espo and Swatch had left a landmark Espo/Amaze mural riddled and ruined with tags. The mural was atop a building in Chinatown, one that was front and center when coming into the city from Brooklyn. If they could get that spot, they would have significant shine on each side of the bridge.

But Leon was hesitant. Although the mural was dissed and the spot ready to be repainted, he had too much respect for Espo to assume that it would be alright to go over it, even when the rules allowed it. Under some pressure from Brad, he eventually sent Espo an email, testing the waters and asking permission.

A few days later, Leon came up to Brad and shared the good news. He had gotten a response email from Espo, giving them permission to go over that prime piece of graffiti real estate. As it turned out, they would be doing him a favor. The NYPD Vandal Squad had freshly busted Espo and the court was planning on handing out heavy destruction-of-property fines for each individual piece of art that was still up by the end of the trial. Espo was so keen on the idea, he even shared a hint on how to get up on that roof.

It felt like they were being handed a key to the city. The imposing space atop that building in Chinatown was getting passed down to Brad and Leon from their graffiti elders. Here was an opportunity to go big, in a spot that would be seen by every person who crossed the Manhattan Bridge, as well as a chance to help out someone they respected. They were finally catching a break, and a big one at that. With the location and concept set, and the piece they would use to kick the door open, it was time to get started.

The email from Steve Powers (Espo) to Leon:

> Date: Wed, 7 Mar 2001 22:13:23 EST
> Subject: Re: I have a question.
you have my blessing and thanks, blow that shit up proper, though. there was a french lady that lives underneath the roof, say hello, and she should be cool.
steve

Brad, Leon, and Quenell gathered up gallons of paint and other supplies that they had "rescued" from storage in the basement of Pratt's physical plant and started packing up for the trip. Brad, only having been back for a matter of weeks at this point, still had the new luggage his parents had gotten him for his return to New York. Mentioning to Quenell that it might be big enough to fit one or two things, Brad watched as the expensive baggage was packed with the sixty-five pounds of paint that had to be lugged to the location. That bag's immediate future was an ugly one. It was full to the point that it had to be pinched with four hands to pull the zipper shut, and before long those zipper teeth were snaggled at best. That night was the last time Brad would see that suitcase in one piece.

They had been planning this mission for weeks, devoting themselves to getting everything as perfect as it could be, and suddenly they were running late. Leon's anxiety level shot through the roof. Starting late is a pretty big problem when your personal safety is based almost entirely on the timetable of a dark night. With the shot clock already running, they started to get a move on over to the subway.

Brad's luggage might have had wheels, but once swollen with stolen paint, it had to be pulled through snow, ice, and a seemingly unending barrage of wet newspaper and C-Town grocery coupon pullouts, all of which gummed up the wheels and chipped away heavily at their spirits. No part of getting from Brooklyn to anywhere in winter is easy, but add an enormous overloaded case, backpacks of painting gear, and a bunch of extendable rollers besides, and things get complicated when having to deal with the subway system.

Dragging the whole mess down three sets of stairs and through the service entrance next to the turnstile to the subway platform, the three finally made it inside the Metro system. All this hassle was only made more difficult by having to look as casual as they could, keeping it cool and shrugging off whatever behavior might hint at the fact that they were about to go and break a handful of laws on a stranger's roof.

After waiting forty minutes for the train to arrive, they pulled their equipment on board for the paltry seven-minute ride to their destination. Hauling the wheeled luggage up the stairs and directly past the front door of the police station that makes the Canal St. subway stop its home, the three stepped up to street level. As they pulled the equipment into the crisp, cold air, they were momentarily deafened by the blaring horn of a midnight bus going the wrong way down a one-way street. Welcome to Chinatown, NYC.

Almost giddy to be within blocks of the spot and no longer an East River away, Brad, Leon, and Quenell felt refreshed with purpose. The subway was done and things, for better or worse, were getting more concrete. One thing was for certain: they were at the spot with about four hours less slack than they needed. Time was officially the enemy.

They made it behind the building quickly enough and soon were shivering in the alley, staring up through eleven flights of fire escape. Already late, they didn't have time to really look things over and take in the environment, but some specifics were slowly sinking in.

This being a residential building, most people would be present and accounted for at 1am, each in varying stages of winding down. The three would have to be as silent as possible going up the fire escape. That would have been fine, if it were just a mad dash to the top. The trouble began when they took into account the enormous case filled to the brim with what might as well have been bricks.

All concerns were duly noted and dismissed with a series of shrugs and nods. And with that, they started the ascent. Leon got a boost from Quenell and was up on the escape in seconds. Once on higher ground he solved the problem of how to get the heavy paint up before anyone even got a chance to hypothesize. Leon just took one of the rollers, flipped it like he was fishing for DuPont, hooked the paint, then used the hand-over-hand method to lift it on up. About twenty seconds had passed and the first issue of getting the heavy paint buckets onto the fire escape was settled.

"That nigga just lifted some shit that I've been dragging for two hours, like he's some kinda Superman," Quenell whispered to Brad. "I carried that bullshit since Skillman. He's been resting his arms for this." He continued complaining under his breath as he pulled himself up on the fire escape ladder.

With everyone on the fire escape, the next step was to get to the roof as fast and as quietly as possible. An above-ground subway line that ripped through the adjacent bridge every five minutes or so, just thirty feet from the fire escape, gave them an all but deafening sound blanket. However, since it switched back and forth from industrial thunder to whisper silent, the train wasn't nearly enough cover to allow for easy breathing.

Brad handled the rollers and extensions while Quenell and Leon lumbered the big suitcase full of paint buckets up the stairs. To hustle the bag along, just inches away from people's windows, took some serious coordination. Lifting the cumbersome suitcase, turning it so it didn't slam into the window, all the while holding the front flap tight, not trusting the zipper to stay closed, then grunting up the next flight – round two through eleven, each floor took a solid minute to climb.

Brad stuck with them for the first couple of floors, but when Quenell and Leon turned around on the fourth floor, he was gone, bolting up the stairs.

"That nigga finna git himself killed," muttered Quenell.

"Let's worry about us," Leon shot back.

Leon was cursing and complaining for the whole ascent, but his was all inner monologue. He had a strong belief in professionalism in all things; if he was going to be a cook, he would think through and through that he was a chef. If he were a mall cop, he would learn the Miranda Rights backwards and forwards. Whatever he was, he would take it seriously; he would be far more than the job demanded. If they were going to commit a crime, they had better act like real criminals, and the way he saw it, real criminals don't talk unless they absolutely have to.

On the seventh floor, there was an industrial air conditioning unit with its blades tilted to just the right angle to allow Quenell to see through and into the apartment. There he glimpsed a bootleg poker table surrounded by middle-aged Asian men gambling. He paused to watch one of them throw some chips on the table, totally unaware of this young black man staring in at them, their poker hands, the table, their faces, taking a mental photograph of the scene. A world that was never going to be accessible to Quenell was, for a few seconds, completely his own.

Meanwhile, Brad was already up on the roof, just standing there in awe, staring past the bridge. He hadn't gotten shook and split on the whole mission; he had just done what he thought was logical at the time. Seeing that he couldn't help them carry the load any faster, he figured his presence could only hurt the momentum. So he took off, flying up the stairs. He had gotten to the roof as fast and as quietly as possible, and was feeling pretty proud of himself for doing so.

Reaching the top, he stepped over the ledge onto the roof, turned around, and in one crystallized moment, the whole city opened up. It was his first real glimpse at the view that hits you behind your eyes: Manhattan in the crisp, clear air of winter. For someone who wasn't born, raised, and jaded in NYC, it was staggering. Much more than just another Midtown "luxury panoramic view," with all the banality that implies, this was Downtown, where the city still has eccentricities worth looking at, seen from the top of one of the tallest buildings in the neighborhood. It was the first time Brad had really taken in the view, and it was hypnotic.◗

But Brad's romantic moment came to a swift end as soon as Leon and Quenell reached the roof. They walked past him, set the heavy suitcase down by the wall, walked back and started reading him the riot act in as much of a hushed tone as they could maintain. The three debated

---

◗ If you were one of the people that bothered to notice how amazing the Twin Towers looked before they got blown up, you'll always know what all the fuss was about. You can fake it if you want to, but you're only fooling yourself.

flawed modus operandi and semantics for all of thirty seconds, and then decided to table it for the time being, until they could scream at each other full tilt in the comfort of their own home.

Walking over to the wall they had been dreaming about for weeks, Brad and Leon slowly gave it a once-over while they laid out their materials. The roof wasn't the easiest terrain to move across quietly, with zigzagging iron girders waffle-printing the entire floor plan, just waiting to take a divot out of someone's leg. That someone was naturally Brad. About two seconds after the temporary truce, Brad turned around and smacked his shin against one of these booby traps lying in plain sight. Brad bit his lip, but believing in "no hairline fracture, no foul," he limped through the pain.

Opening the five-gallon bucket, which was filled to the brim with dull green paint, one bucket of black and one of gray/white, the boys had a great deal of color before them and were eager to get started. Painting started off well enough: Brad and Leon assembled the twelve-foot extension poles and began slowly rolling over the Espo/Amaze joint.

This affected Leon a little deeper than Brad or Quenell. As a former teenage graff writer and newly converted street artist, he found it surreal to be going over two of his heroes. But with each pass he made with the gigantic roller, he reminded himself that he wasn't erasing their work but adding another layer to the history of the wall. This was an empowering moment for Darius and Downey.

By the time they finished with the green paint, the paint pans had been long abandoned. Instead Leon and Brad had started pouring the paint directly on the ground beside them and using four-foot patches of the roof as roller dipping points. The majority of the green paint was on the wall, but you wouldn't know it to look at them. Their gloves were soaked through with paint and starting to freeze to their hands, so they pulled them off rather than lose the skin the gloves were adhering to. Brad and Leon had paint raining down on them so consistently that by the end of the night they were more annoyed than terrified to have to wipe latex paint out from under their eyelids again and again.

Quenell walked around looking for good angles, nice framing, and whatever additional light he could find and take advantage of. But in between shots, he had to deal with a fair amount of down time. The cold weather was only amplified by the windy rooftop in the middle of Chinatown, and any time when he wasn't fully focused on his camera, all he had to think about was his freezing extremities. Also, this mission wasn't going to be a quick thing. This was the largest boom that Leon and Brad had done together up to this point and it was going to take hours, if it was possible to finish it at all before sunup.

Quenell did have one piece of good luck: he found a folding chair just waiting for him in one of the corners of the roof. It was the closest any of them would come to comfort for the rest of the night, and he settled into it and took twenty-minute catnaps that put him perilously close to death. Brad and Leon might have been working themselves warm all night, but with a sturdy chair and more free time than he knew what to do with, Quenell could have just dozed off into a full-blown case of hypothermia.

Leon and Brad worked as fast as they could, but before they knew it the sky was near-purple through the heavy clouds and it was clear they were getting down to the wire. When the green was done with, they poured out the black paint and Brad went to the left to put up CLONE and Leon went right to paint JESUS. They had to step it up if they wanted to finish before the morning traffic came tearing across the Manhattan Bridge.

As the sky turned a shade somewhere between deep blue-black and reddish-purple, a cop car came flying across the bridge with a "wip-woop," that little puppy bark they do when they flick the siren switch for a quarter second. All three were kissing the roof tar before the "woop" ended – though it's a safe bet that NYC's Finest were just clearing some cabbie out of their lane so they could keep their speed above seventy-five miles per hour while entering the city. (Firing up the siren while still on the bridge isn't the best way to sneak up on three trespassers if you want to catch them in the act.)

With the police still speeding down the bridge, the boys slowly got to their feet, each feeling a little embarrassed for diving to the ground as if they were under fire, but no one said a word. There was no time to joke around; it was clear to the three of them that within as little as a half an hour, it would be bright blue morning and traffic would start flying across the bridge. They were out of time, not to mention out of paint. By the time they were finishing the lettering, they were scraping the black paint bucket dry.

Brad and Leon rushed to put on some final touches, while Quenell rested his back against the metal door to the building's stairwell, taking one last break before capturing the final result of a hard night's labor. As they were wrapping up the piece, he left his little oasis to catch the last of the work on tape. He was about ten feet away from the wall when the door he had been leaning on was kicked open with a thunderous crash, putting the thing nearly off its hinges. Flying all the way open, the door smashed into the wall and stayed there, having no spring to pull it shut. Everyone in the building would have heard the heavy steel hit the concrete wall. That sound was deliberate and sent a shockwave across the roof.

Two white men ran out of the dark stairwell and onto the roof towards Leon and Brad. Everyone froze. The two men stared at the three by the wall, sizing them up. If a pin had dropped on the top of that building, it would have blown their eardrums.

The boys were clearly busted. Leon was caught off guard with the rest, but being Leon he wasn't at all surprised that they were getting run up on.■ The two men came towards them. They were all but by-the-book undercovers, one husky enough to have a bulletproof vest under his jersey, the other taller and skinnier, but also a little too top-heavy

■ Leon is a surprisingly daring and prolific artist for a "defeatist" at heart. He prefers the term "realist," but you tell me what you would call someone whose inner voice says "It's about time you fellas showed up" when caught in the act by the police.

not to be protected. Both came through the door with real authority and the standard "This city gave me a gun and put me in charge" personality.

Leon dropped his paintbrush and awaited further orders. Brad, however, decided that if he was caught, he was caught. He wouldn't do their job for them; if the police wanted him to stop what he was doing they had better go ahead and make him. Quenell just stood there, silent, waiting to see what would happen next.

It was dead quiet. The traffic and trains slowly faded into the ambient hum of the background and disappeared. The sky was light blue now, and in the silence of that moment, it began to snow.

As the boys waited for the police to launch the terrible day they had waiting for them, with handcuffs, bail, and court dates, the two men waltzed right up to the CLONE JESUS boom and started respectfully tagging beneath it. Leon had trouble breathing for a moment, having completely left his body when he realized that he wasn't looking at police officers at all, merely fellow graffiti writers.

"Sheeeit," Quenell smirked and chuckled, as he exhaled a breath that carried the weight of prison on it. "Boy, I thought we were busted." He smiled at Brad.

"Yo, what's y'all's names?" Brad asked the two men throwing tags up on the wall.

"Yo man, I'm Kel. What's up man, your name's Clone? That's cool. This is Rebel. Brooklyn, right here. Which one a y'all's Jesus? You?" Kel asked as he pointed at Leon.

"No… not quite, I'm Darius. That's Brad. We're just writing Clone Jesus," Leon explained.

"What you mean, you're just writing Clone and Jesus?" asked Kel.

"Yeah, but I mean it's like, to clone God. Like you know, clone Jesus," Leon responded.

"What are y'all God heads? This some like, get into the Bible, shit?" asked Rebel, now curious about the boy's intentions.

"Well no…" Leon started.

Brad cut him off. "How did you guys get up here? It looks like you guys been gettin' up all over this roof." He sensed that religion might be a dangerous road to debate on the rooftop.

Kel and Rebel were so bored with talking at this point that Kel just carried on tagging while Rebel explained things to the boys.

"What are you talking about? The front door to the building doesn't lock. It never has. It's open twenty-four hours a day. We wanted to stop by and write a little, so we walked up the stairs," explained Rebel. "Hold up, how did you get up here?"

As Leon was explaining the intricacies of their trip, Rebel slowly turned to the wall and began tagging it up. That was as good a cue as any for Brad and Leon to begin packing up their gear, and they decided it was best to get while the getting was good. They were as lucky as they could imagine that these two weren't the police, and decided against pressing their luck by chilling.

Still skeptical of two guys who decided to begin tagging once the sun was up, and with more stubbornness than intelligence, they took the fire escape back down, carrying significantly lighter gear, but now crossing each window as alarm clocks fired off, waking the tenants up for work. They made the entirety of the descent in full, bright daylight.

By the time the sun was fully hanging above, the piece was as done as it ever would be and people rolling across the bridge were already smirking, honking their horns at the bumper sticker that was expertly painted thirty feet across and ten feet tall. There it was, larger than life and twice as surprising. Darius and Downey had hit the ground running.

THE TETANUS FLOWER

1998–2003 | Leon finds his first love and, with that, his first heartbreak. Turning frantic denial of rejection into fateful inspiration, he creates a rough masterpiece in his hopes for reconciliation, only to find a higher meaning in his work. With his new way of thinking, and a motivating kick in the ass from Quenell, Leon suddenly finds himself heading to London.

By the spring of 2002, Leon had been with Polina for about two and a half years. He was working in a metal shop steadily and spent his free time with his best friends. The days, for the most part, were passing without incident. Leon's life was going well enough and so like most things hitting their stride, it was due for a strong hiccup. With graduation coming fast, there were major changes on the horizon, no matter how hard he would fight the tide. But bigger, unseen clouds were gathering.

Spring in Clinton Hill, Brooklyn, is a tense season. Pratt Institute's graduating class, oblivious to the weather report, is suddenly thrust out into the real world and everything goes through a severe disconnect. The people you see day-to-day move, get on with their lives, disappear completely. Even the people you are closest to are compelled to do the same. It's a point of departure, a transition only slightly less traumatic than birth itself. What's hard to grasp while attending is that college is a temporary manmade habitat. No matter the strength of the friendships you make and how real every moment is, in the grand scheme of things, the time you are there is slight. As accustomed as you may become, your stay will end on the day you find yourself most adjusted.[*]

Leon had met Polina during freshman year, the way everyone meets in college – a shared class, a friend in common, a smile across a court-yard. For one reason or another, it wasn't until a year and a half had passed that they spent any real time together. But when they did, the conversations came easy, which is saying something for Leon. From the very first talks that they had, just getting to know this girl with the pretty smile, Leon found himself hooked.

Leon became more and more infatuated with everything he learned about Polina. She was Russian born and raised, yet spoke better English

[*] It would be a safe wager that the percentage of soldiers who reenlisted for a second or third tour of Vietnam matches well with those who get their graduate and doctorate degrees. Once you adapt to a situation, once you acquire a taste for it, it's hard to pull yourself out and leave it forever.

than Leon and at least half the state of New York. Her parents, both scientists, had no problem getting American citizenship after the fall of Soviet communism in '89, certainly an easier road than others with less desirable IQs and vocations. Coming to America in her teens, Polina's childhood took place in the Jewish housing projects, and she knew what it was to have a harder life. This was strong currency in Bed-Stuy; Pratt was brimming over with privileged kids pretending with all their might to come from the 'hood, but in reality terrified to leave their dorm's lounge. When Polina first got to Pratt, she wasn't shocked by the surrounding poverty and crime; she went out of her house, unafraid, and made her neighborhood her own.

More jaded than fragile, yet still somehow maintaining a child's sensitivity, Polina was making Leon fall hard. All the pieces of her past just colored-in her personality, answered questions her acerbic humor posed, and pulled Leon in so close he didn't know what he was feeling. When he saw her art, the emotion she could tap into, Leon was done falling. He loved this girl.

In the two and a half years that followed, Leon learned what it is to be in love. Never having felt this way before, he realized that this was the kind of feeling people throw themselves in the way of a bullet to save. This was the feeling that he would trade it all for. It was certainly new.

Being twenty years old, he felt all of that, intensely and real as anything, and still couldn't be the best boyfriend that young love could buy. The two had their problems, their arguments, like all couples do, but Leon wasn't emotionally mature enough to know how to properly show what he was feeling. Friends had opinions, but Leon wasn't going to be told how to fix things. Polina certainly wasn't mature enough to carry the burden alone, either. How could she be? How could either of them be expected to be competent adults in this arena? At twenty, you're basically the same maniac you were when you first hit puberty, with little to no idea why you're doing anything, but committed like lockjaw to your idealism.

Eventually, after the relationship had begun to deteriorate through Leon's mixture of workingman's absence and home-life complacency, not to mention Polina's inability to express her unhappiness, she decided she had had enough. She started talking things over with her girlfriends. When she had run out of different ways to say the same thing to them, she realized it was over. It wasn't his fault or her fault; it was just the end of the relationship. Even Leon, while getting as comfortable as he'd ever been, and working day and night on his senior show, felt it coming.

One night, fittingly a rainy one, Leon picked Polina up from a long evening of talking over at the house of one of her girlfriends and walked her home. She broke the news to him in the rain and as they climbed the steps into her apartment he felt like he was outside of himself, watching his wet body being dragged through the front door and sitting down on the couch near her bed. The shock, sinking depression and sudden hollowness of his body pushed down on Leon with a new gravity. He slept on the couch that night.

At work the next day, Leon was miserable. His job at the time was in a metal shop fabricating the variously sized LOVE sculptures created by Robert Indiana. He was one of the many hands that cranked them out endlessly at high speed to pollute the landscape, and every sculpture he put his hand to mocked him. As much as he tried to work through his pain, Leon was unfocused, tense, and filled with an anguish he'd never known before. Adding an element of fear to his day was the fact that lack of focus while working with welding gear can end you up in the emergency room, or worse.

Finally, after catching himself turning a valve and zoning out without lighting it, filling the room with gas, he knew it was getting too dangerous to stay any longer. He asked his unforgiving boss for the rest of the day off, knowing full and well that people had been fired for less. He cited "woman problems" and for the first time he saw his boss make an exception to the rule. He was sent home.

As soon as he walked out of the dark metal shop and into the bright light of day, the answer came to him. He was going to win her back with a classic romantic gesture. As the idea formed in his head, Leon raced his bike to the subway. He was so excited that he smacked hard into a parked car and was thrown to the street. Getting back on the bike, he pedaled a little slower, a little unevenly from the pain, but was still busting at the scams.

Getting back to Pratt campus, he rushed to the metal shop and decided he would weld a gift to Polina, a symbol of his love, a symbol of how much she meant to him. The shop boss was walking out and was in no mood to do anyone a favor, but one look at Leon spoke volumes. He was on the verge of a breakdown. It was better just to let him in and limit the time available rather than push this man over the edge and have him snap.

Giving him one hour to do what he needed and then get out, the boss left. Leon went to work, blasting out petal after petal with the plasma cutter, and welding them to his ramshackle iron flower stem. When it was done, it was still very rough, but it was a six-foot-tall flower with a little horse at the base. On the horse Leon had painted "Pomni Ya Vsegda Ryadom" which is "Remember I'm always next to you" in Russian. As gestures go, it was a hell of a start.

He grabbed the hammer drill that he and Brad had only recently acquired, a tool that was recommended by their longtime friend Al for drilling into any material imaginable and installing their work wherever they chose. They had experimented with it before, drilling into the back lot behind their apartment on Skillman Street, but had never employed it to install a piece. Feeling willful and determined, Leon decided that now was the time to try it out for real. "If I get busted I get busted. If it's gonna work, it's gonna work right now."

Leon dragged the six-foot steel flower fifteen blocks to Polina's apartment building and saw that next door there were four old women sitting on the stoop, gossiping, pointing at people and whispering – just enjoying the day the way the elderly will. He was going to have an audience, no two ways about it. Keeping his head down, he walked up, and professional as possible, started drilling.

After getting the first hole finished, he blew hard into it to clear the dust. A pile of powdered concrete shot right into his eyes. He paused for a second and let the moment wash over him. It was the middle of the afternoon, he was illegally installing a sculpture that was taller than he was on his ex-girlfriend's front stoop, in front of an audience who perhaps knew the landlord of her building, and now had momentarily blinded himself with gritty concrete dust. But he simply wiped his eyes clear and got right back to it. When driven nearly insane from heartbreak, some temporary pain and potential jail time are no deterrent.

After it was bolted down and he could see that it wasn't going to be removed without a fight, he took off towards Pratt. He was going to have to wait a few hours until Polina got off work and came home to see her gift. It was going to take a few more minutes after that for her to realize that she had made a huge mistake and quickly call Leon to take him back. It would be sometime later that evening until they were back together and everything would be right again in the world… the most perfect of all perfect worlds.

A few hours passed and Leon got no call. Pacing in his apartment he decided she must have walked right by it, or maybe it had been removed before she got home and he was waiting for nothing. He called her.

"Polina."

"Hey Leon," Polina replied after a pause.

"So… How was your day?" asked Leon.

"Ok, I guess…" she said.

"So, did you see it?" Leon asked impatiently.

"…See what?" she replied, cautious.

"Go out front and check it out. I made you something." Leon's heart was pounding.

"Ok, wait one second, I'll go look," she replied.

She walked outside with her cell phone. The technology picked up her every step down the stairs and Leon held his breath, not allowing himself to make a sound.

"Oh, Leon," she said.

"So…what do you think?" he asked.

"It's beautiful." Polina sighed. "How did you do this?" she asked.

"Can I come by to explain it?" he asked.

"I'll be here," Polina said, as she hung up.

Pressing "end" on his cell phone, Leon ran straight to his bike. It had worked. Everything had hung on him doing it right, doing it fast, all to save the sinking relationship. He had done it. Problem solved. Now he just had to get over there and start the long road to recovery. Now everything could go back to the way it was.

Polina was waiting on the steps when he got there. He jumped off his bike and ran up the steps to her, heart in his throat. He stopped short; the look on her face said it all. It was too late. What was done was done and there was no undoing it. Slowly, awkwardly, they hugged. They talked for a while, looking at the piece from the steps.

Everything just became slow motion for him. His day had been spent at breakneck speed, getting everything together for this moment, and now here, it was for nothing. And that nothing was taking forever.

"I love it," she said, more for him than her.

"I love you." Leon countered, then paused. "What do you want me to do?"

"I don't want you to do anything," she replied. "I'm leaving in a few weeks, I'm going to Thailand for a while. Then maybe I'll move out of the city for a bit."

Leon couldn't breathe for a second. In one swift move, she would be leaving all of this pain behind her, the breakup, the flower; everything would be left for him alone. He envied her, and hated her, and began to pity himself. He felt himself getting angry over how helpless he felt and then immediately depressed over getting angry. "What's in Thailand?" he asked.

"Thai people? I don't know," she replied. "It's just different. Don't you ever want a change of pace, Leon?"

They continued to talk into the night, and again, Leon slept on the couch.

In the coming days, word of the metal flower got around the street art community, and a friend of Leon's named Noah went to check out how it was installed. Bending in close to inspect the short work the hammer drill had made of the sidewalk, he clumsily caught the back of his head on one of the petals and gashed it open. Heading directly to the hospital for stitches and a tetanus shot, Noah called Leon and told him what happened. Leon found himself distraught at how it seemed like the flower had proved better at hurting than helping.◗

Word of the flower also reached Polina's landlord. When it came time for her security deposit to be returned, the landlord informed her that if she wanted any of it she had better pluck that flower first. Next thing Leon knew, the landlord was calling, ordering him to handle it. Bitterly, Leon removed it the next day and Polina promised to put it in storage with the rest of her things.

With Polina finally in Thailand, and bodegas, bars, friend's houses, and parks all reminding him of better times that would never return, Leon turned heavily to his work at the metal shop. He resigned himself to the apparent inevitability of sinking into a long depression.

A week after that most recent devastating blow, Leon was walking by her empty apartment and saw the flower resting on a pile of scrap metal on the landlord's patio. It was just the knife in the heart that Leon needed to reclaim a little dignity. He went back to Pratt's metal shop and devoted himself to making a flower that was ten times as intricate and well crafted. If Polina wanted to throw away the flower that was made for her and her alone, Leon would break his back making one that was more beautiful in every way and give it to the whole of Brooklyn. Still chuckling over Noah's scar tissue and tetanus shot from the first flower, the street art community dubbed the new sculpture *The Tetanus Flower*.

◗ Leon was also terrified at the thought of his work hurting anybody else. He wouldn't have been able to live with himself if the flower had hurt a child. He never left a sharp edge on a piece of art after that.

Unable to look at another LOVE sculpture, and feeling that he owed himself a change of scenery as well, Leon got another job as a carpenter making windows at a factory in Brooklyn. Still hurt, but surviving, he was soon finding a new stride in his slumped depression. It took the better part of Brad and Quenell's senior year to convince Leon even to think about coming with them to England. The two had applied and been accepted early to master's programs there. Leon, stubborn as ever, was choosing to be left behind. Quenell and Brad both took it upon themselves to try their best to convince Leon to at least apply for his graduate degree abroad.

Finally Leon, under protest that it was "stupid," conceded that he would apply to a school. Upon receiving his rejection letter, he was satisfied with his effort and settled down to mope in the depths of his depression for the rest of his life.

And that's when Quenell gave him "the talk" – which is how they lovingly refer to Quenell showing up at Leon's work during his lunch break, taking him aside, and reading him the riot act.

"If you think it's stupid to apply to England, and you're fine doing it, don't be half stupid. Be all the way stupid. Apply to five schools or you shouldn't have applied to any at all!" Quenell got angry. "Your best friends are going to leave you here to be depressed, all by yourself. We're moving on to bigger and better things. What, are you going to sit here in your cheap ass apartment and make windows for the rest of your life? You're gonna let some girl ruin the rest of your life? Come with us to England."

Quenell raged for another twenty minutes while Leon just sat there passively. Once Quenell had done screaming and cursing, Leon looked up at him and sighed. "Fine, I'll be all the way stupid."

It was just the tough talk Leon needed.[*] He applied to a few more

---

[*] There was another thing that helped, in a strange way: getting his thumb and forefinger shredded in a machinery accident at the carpentry job. The damage was to his right hand, his drawing hand. Never so close to losing his abilities before, it woke him up to just how much he had taken for granted. It was the first sign of life Leon had shown in months, and things began to look up from there.

schools, just making the deadlines. By the end of the following spring, Leon was accepted to the prestigious Central St. Martin's, and he was on his way to London, the biggest change of scenery yet.

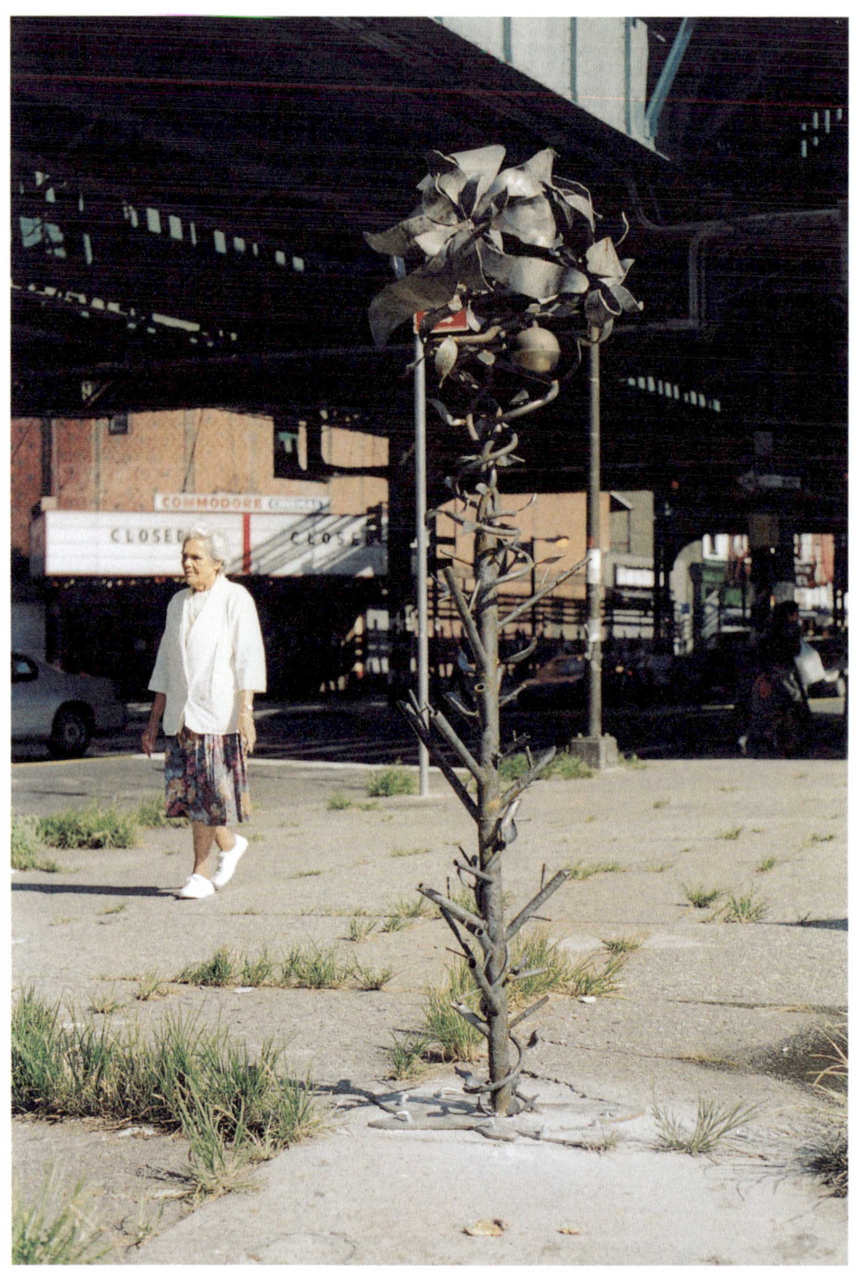

Fleur d'Acier, Darius Jones (Leon Reid IV), 2002. Brooklyn, NY.
Duration: 5 years and counting.

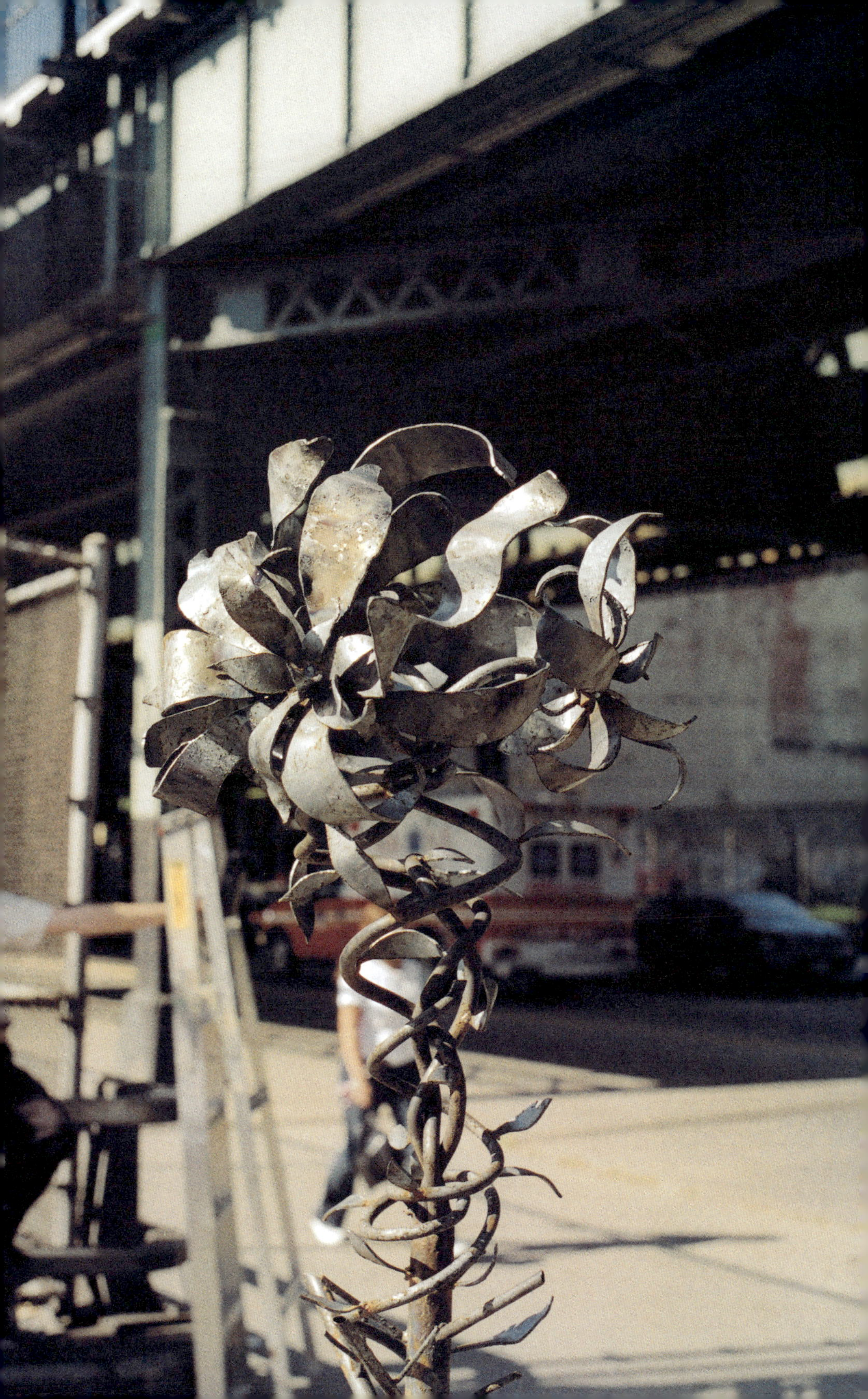

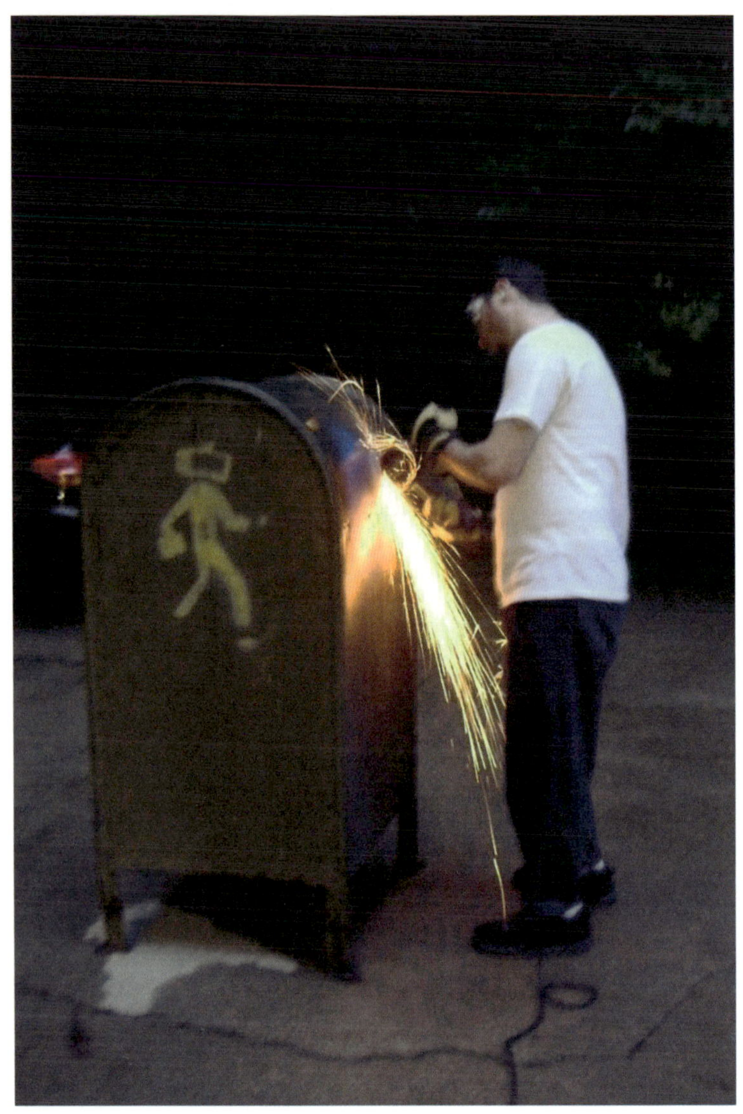

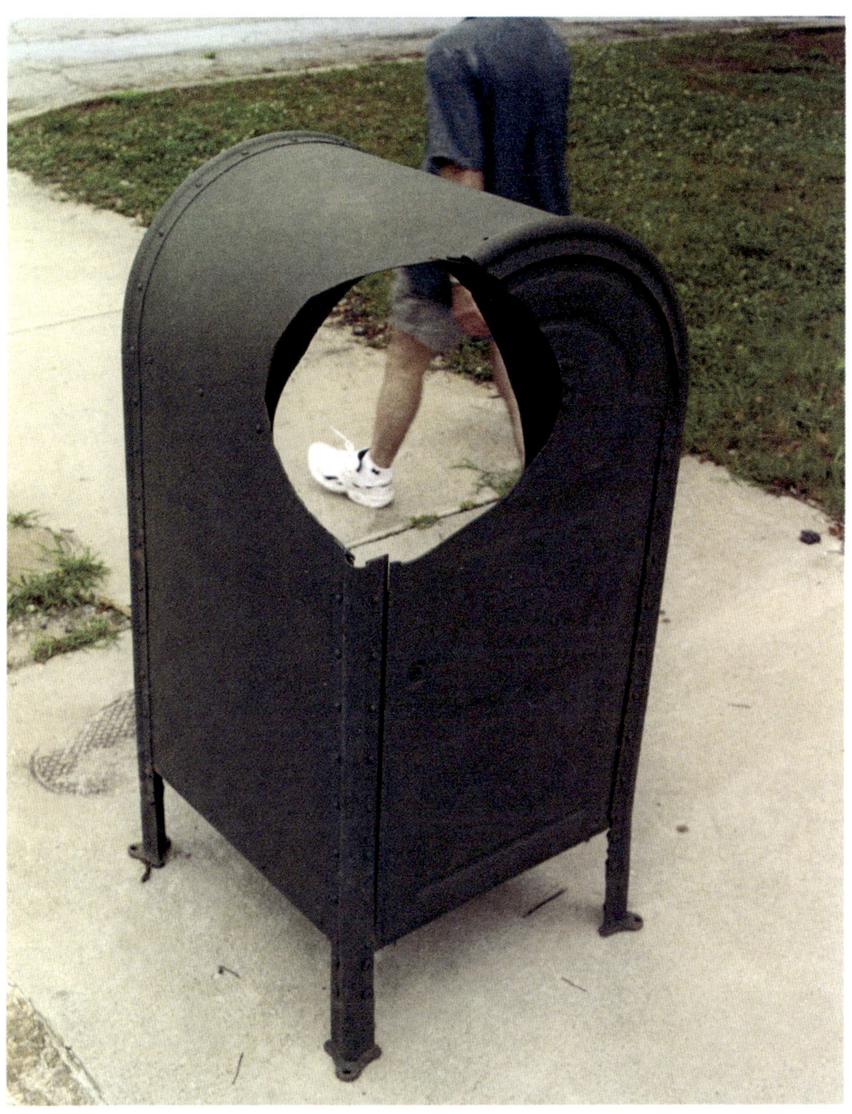

The Orifice, Brad Downey, 2005. Atlanta, GA. Duration: 6 months.

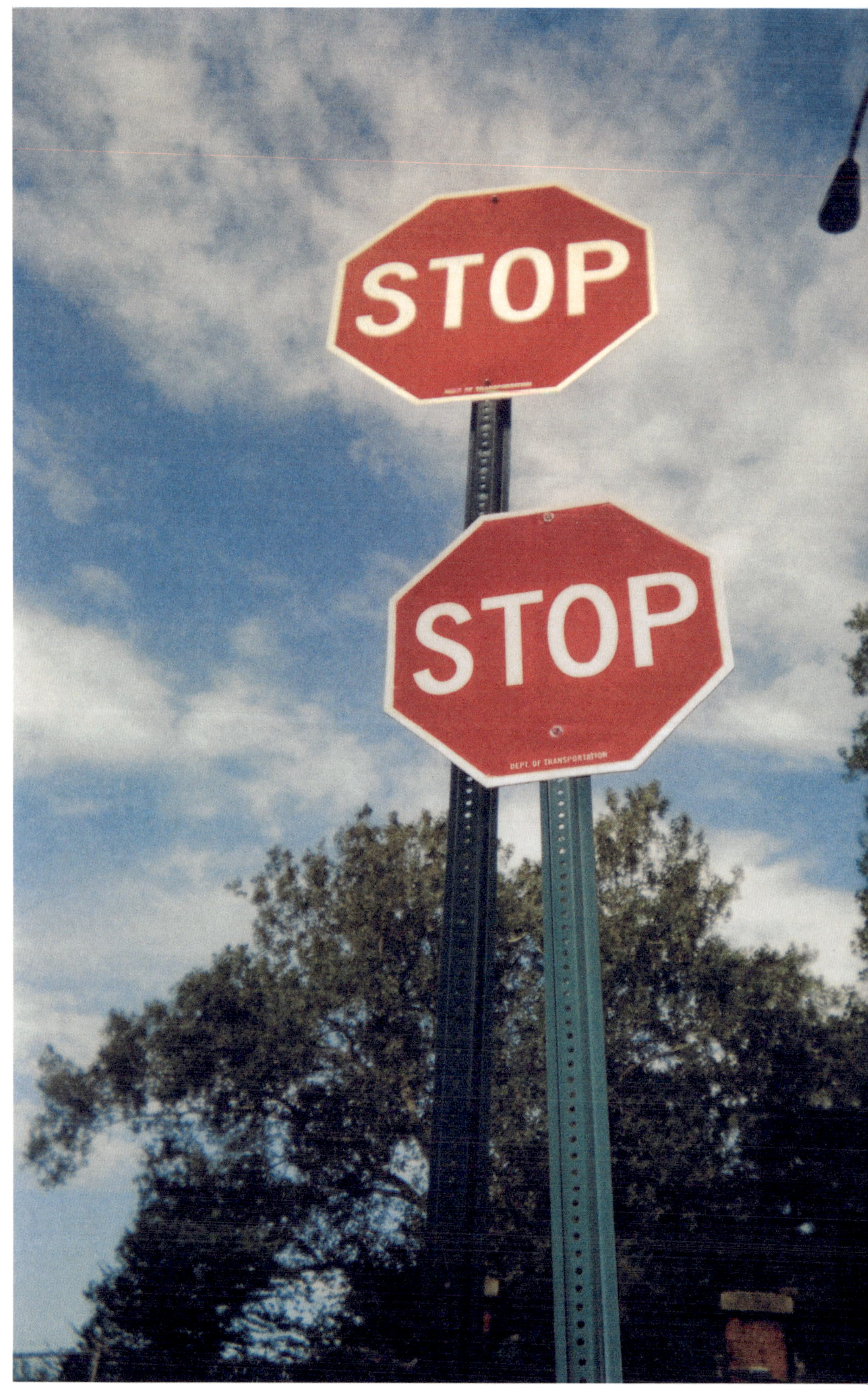

STOP
STOP
DEPT. OF TRANSPORTATION

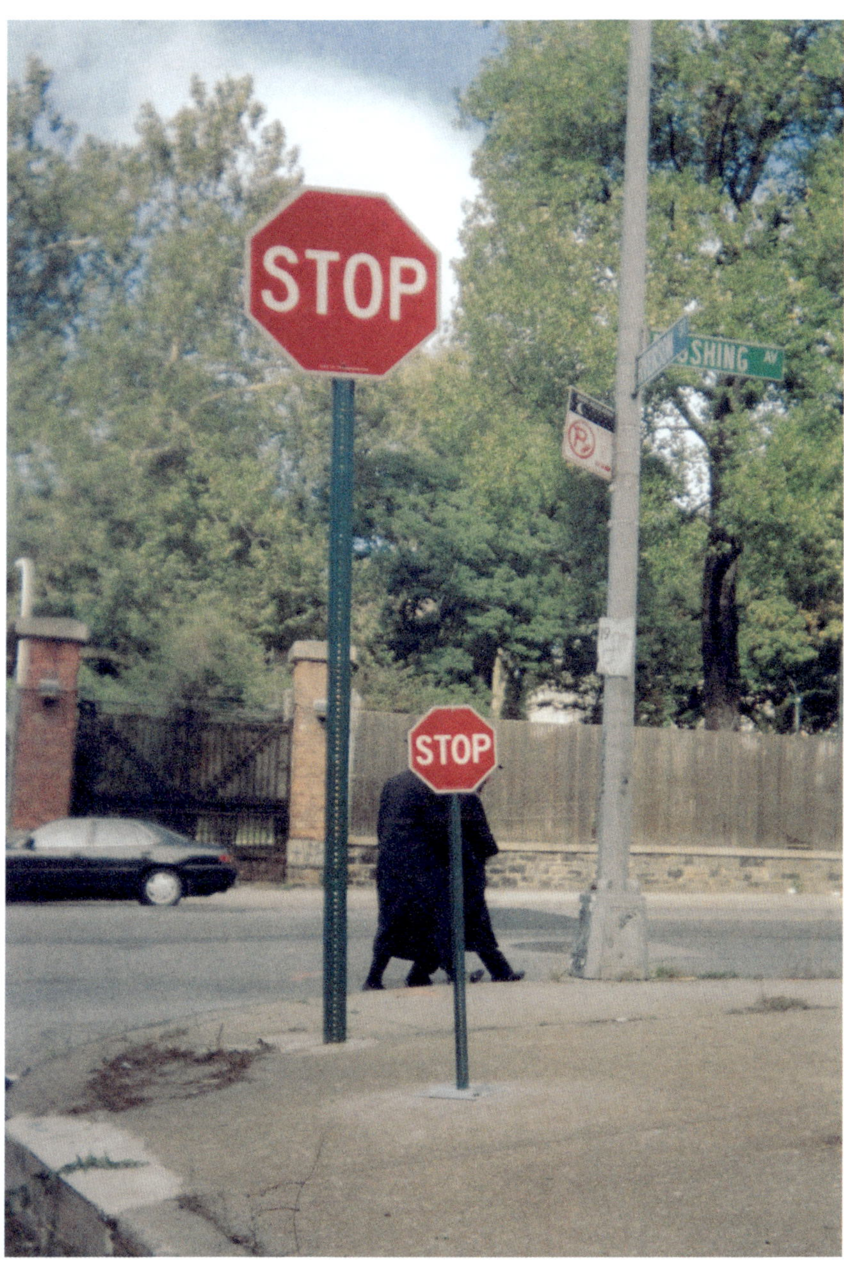

Baby Stop Sign, Darius and Downey, 2002. Brooklyn, NY.
Duration: 2 days.

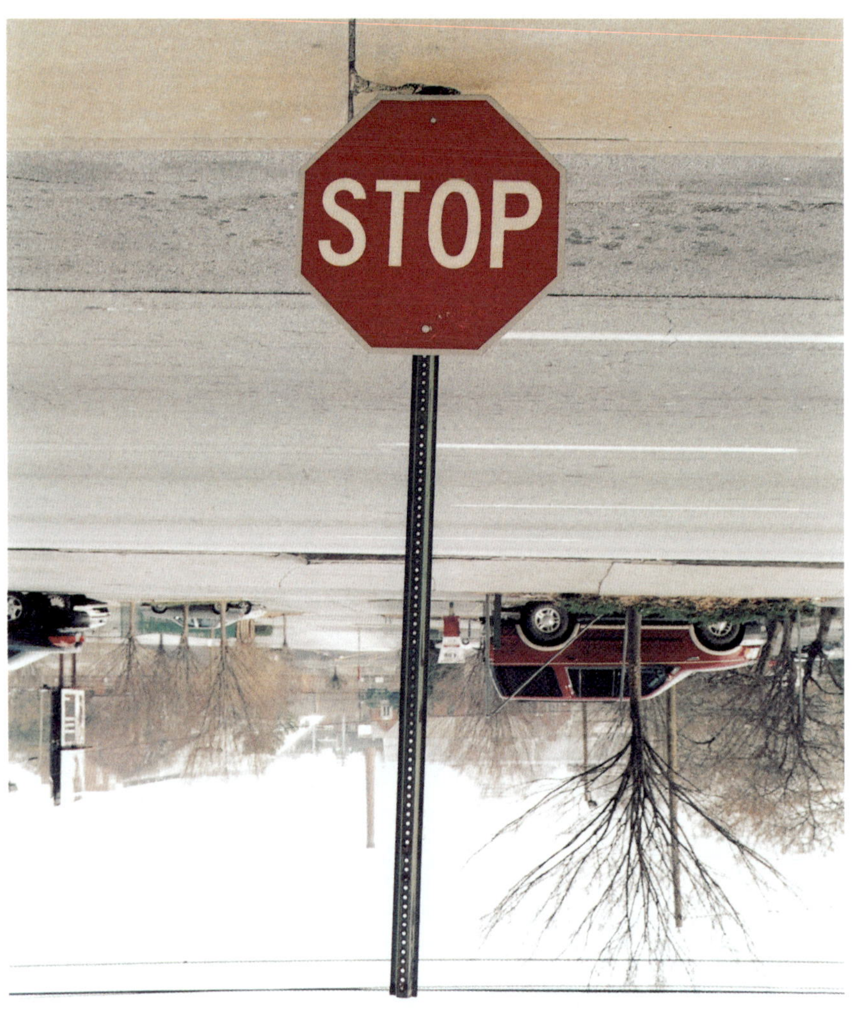

UpSignDown, Brad Downey, 2004. Atlanta, GA. Duration: 2 days.

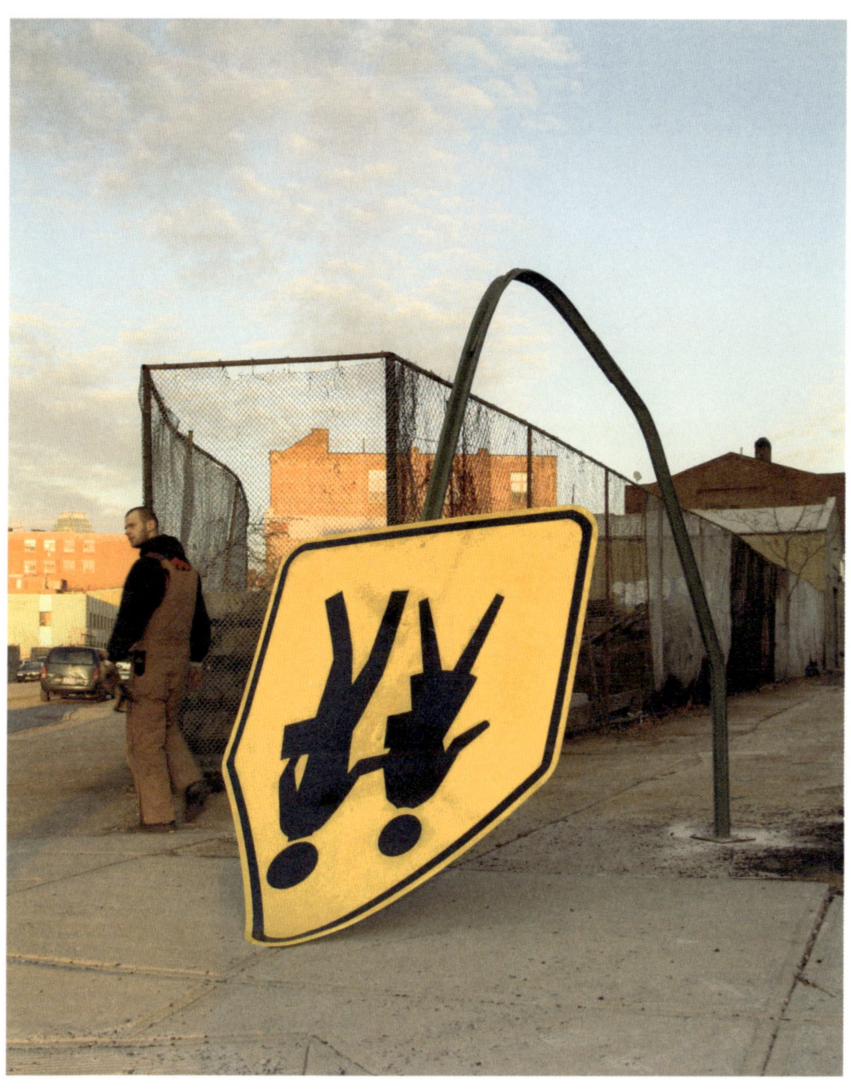

Over-Sized Sign or *The Burden of Children*, Brad Downey, 2006. New York City, NY.
Duration: 5 weeks. Photo by Tod Seelie.

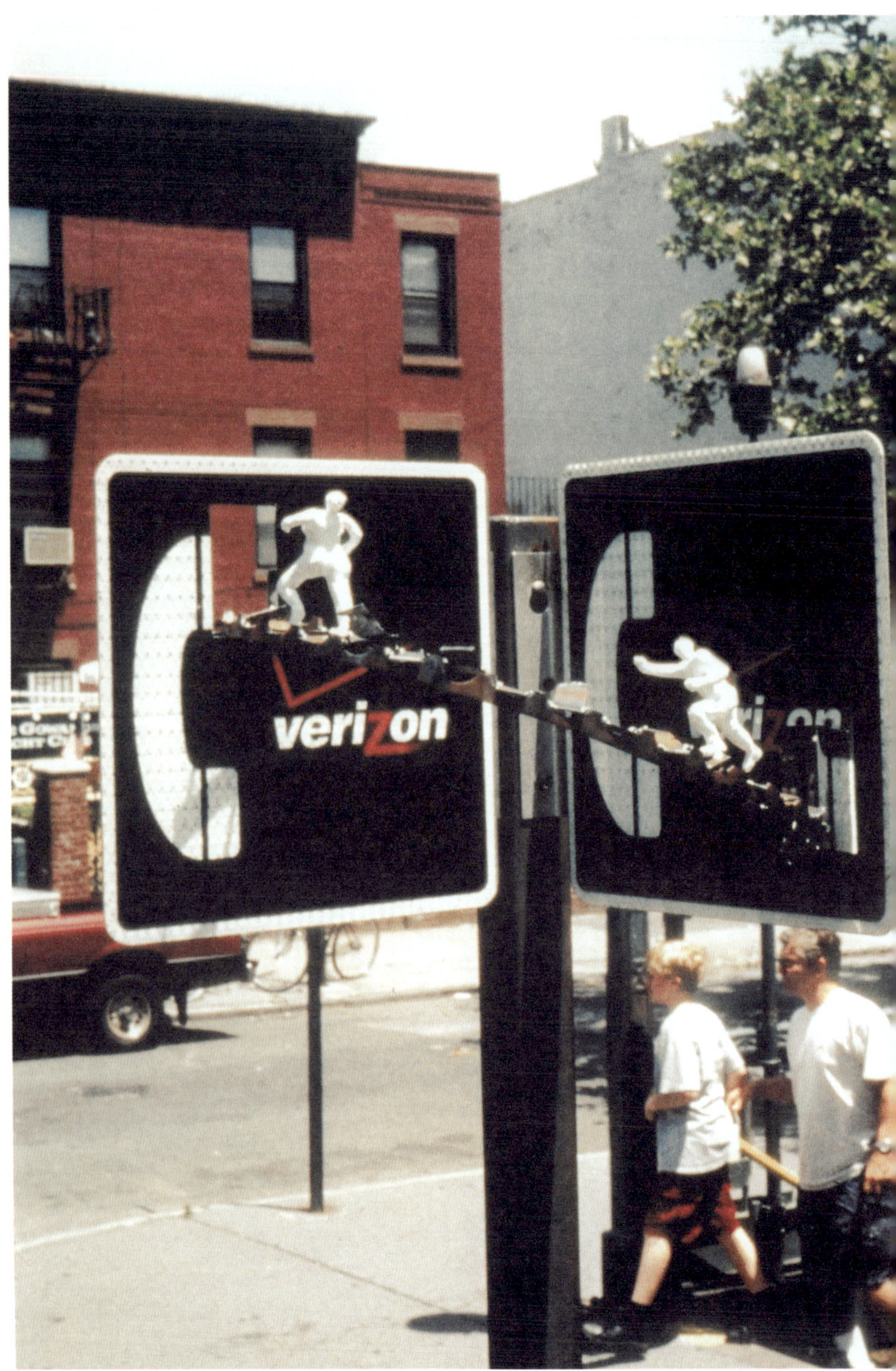
verizon
verizon

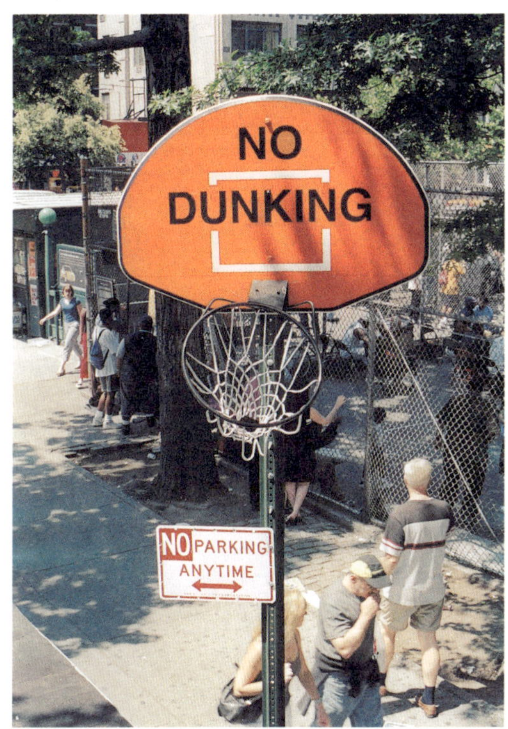

OPPOSITE *Phone Tag*, 2002, Darius Jones (Leon Reid IV). Brooklyn, NY. Duration: 4 months.

THIS PAGE *No Dunking*, 2002. Darius Jones (Leon Reid IV). New York City, NY. Duration: 3 months.

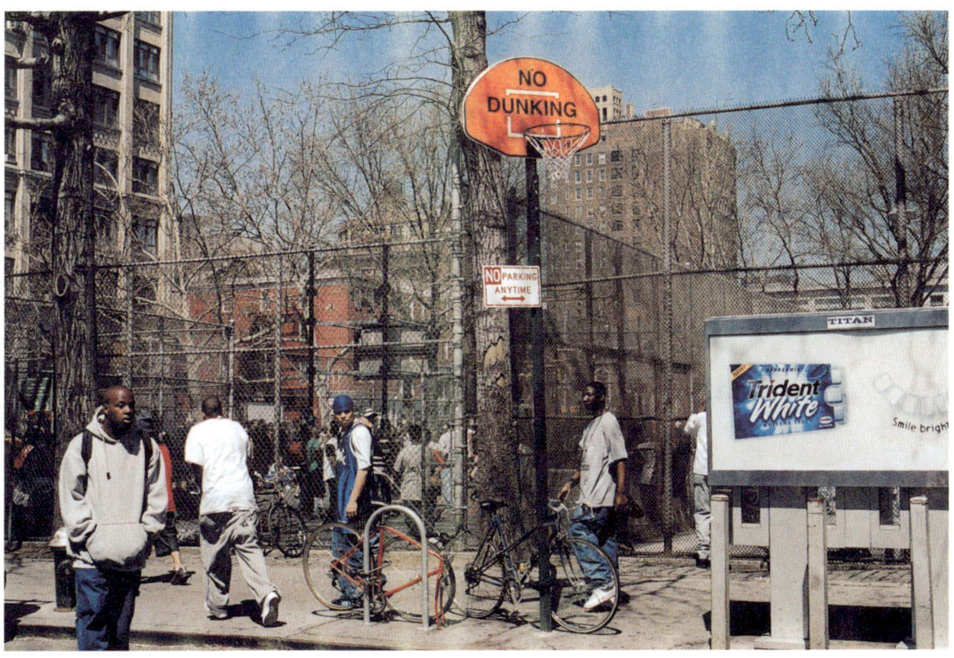

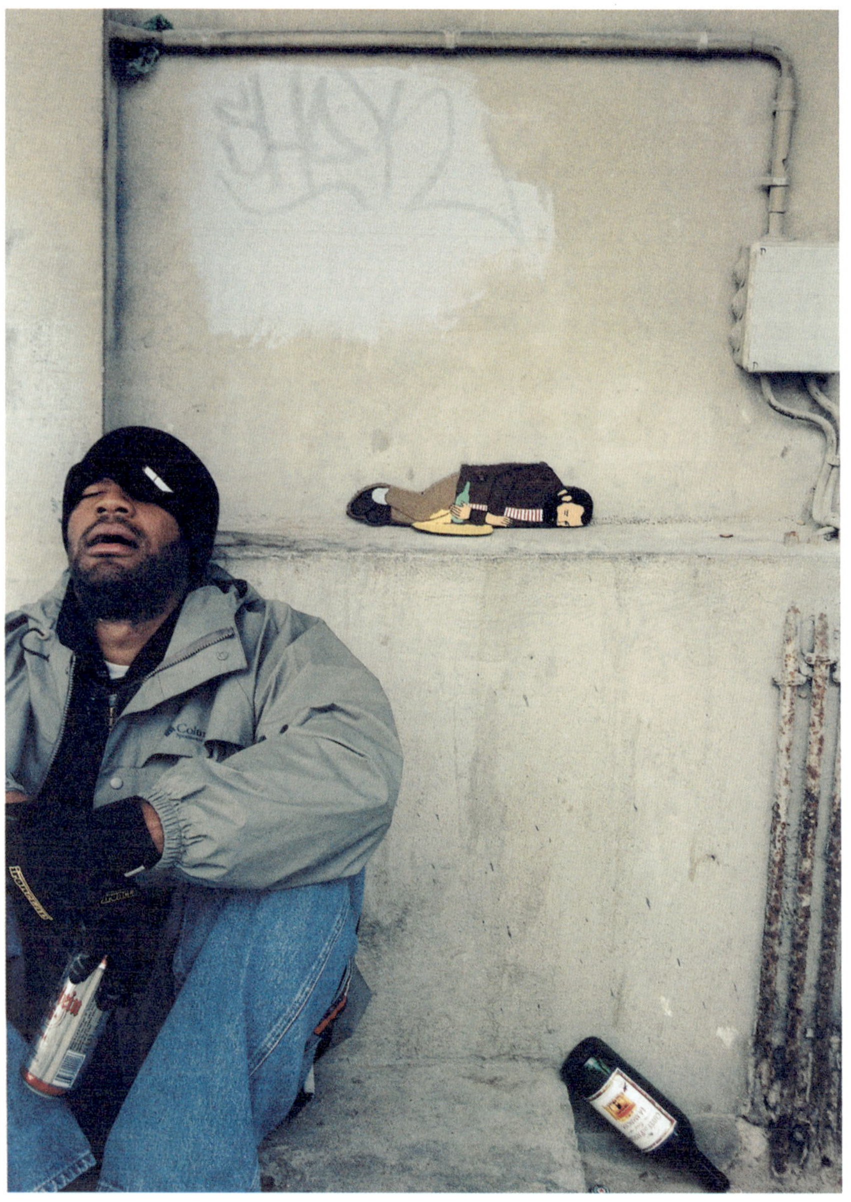

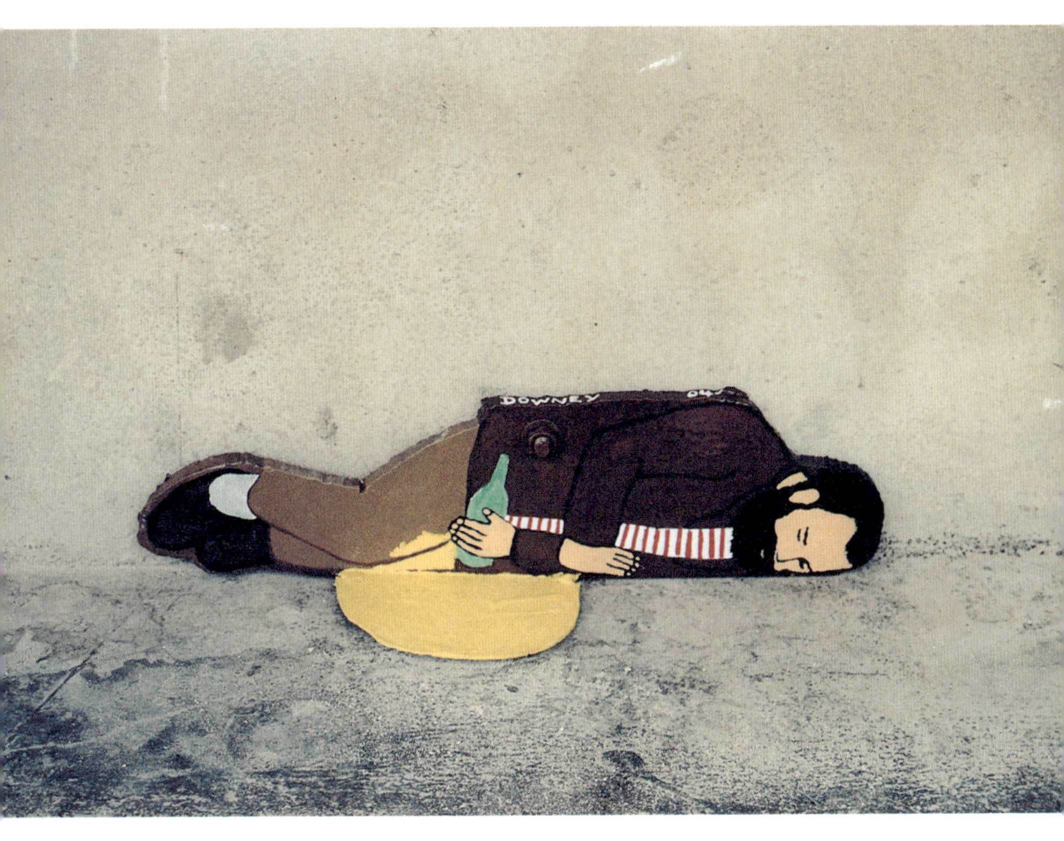

Le PoivRot, Brad Downey, 2004. Paris. Duration: 1 day.

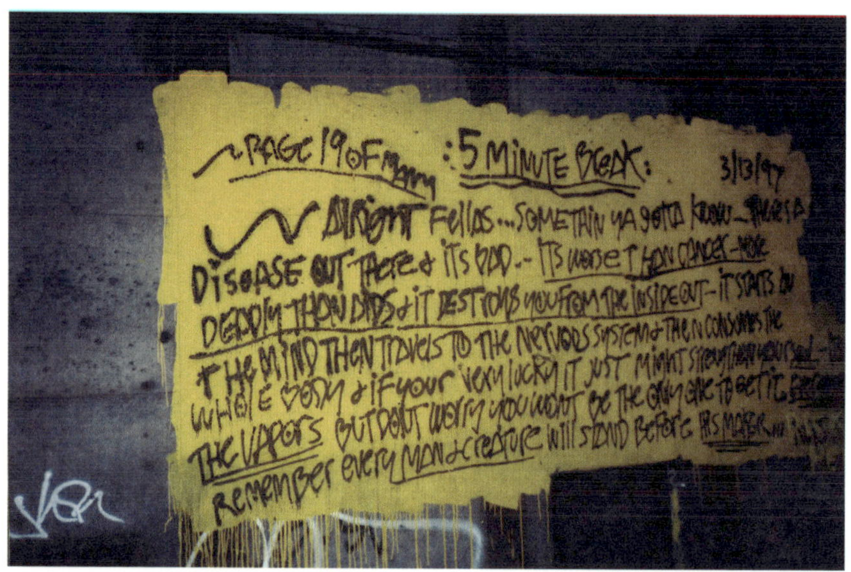

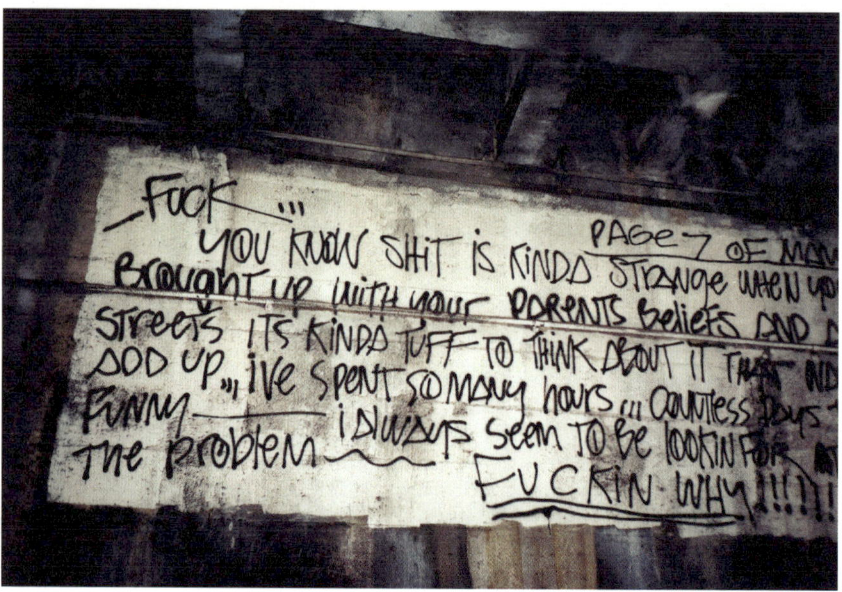

Tunnel diary entries by Revs, early 1990s, New York City, NY.
Photos by Stephen Schuster.

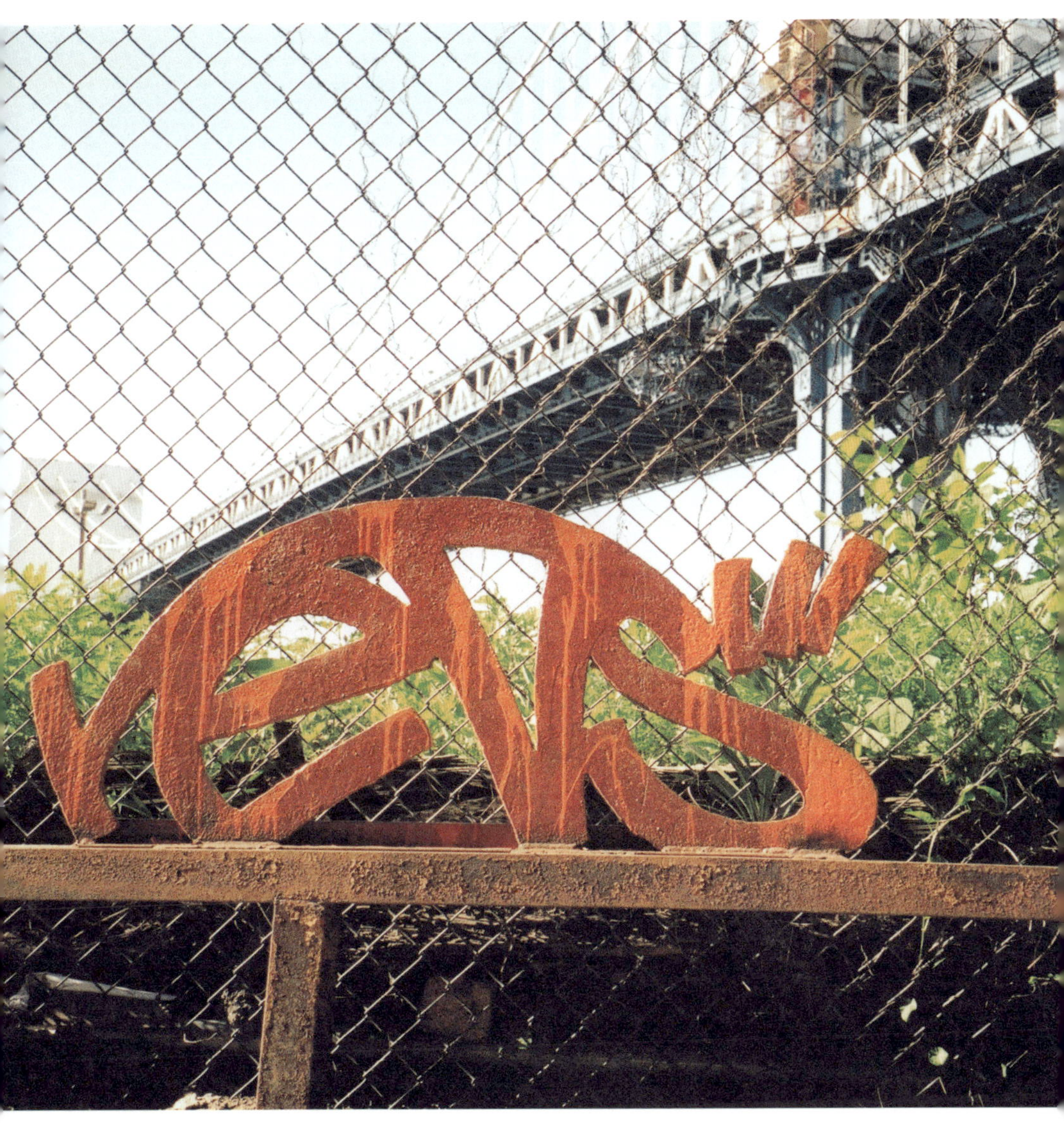

Revs, Brooklyn, NY. Photographed in 2001.

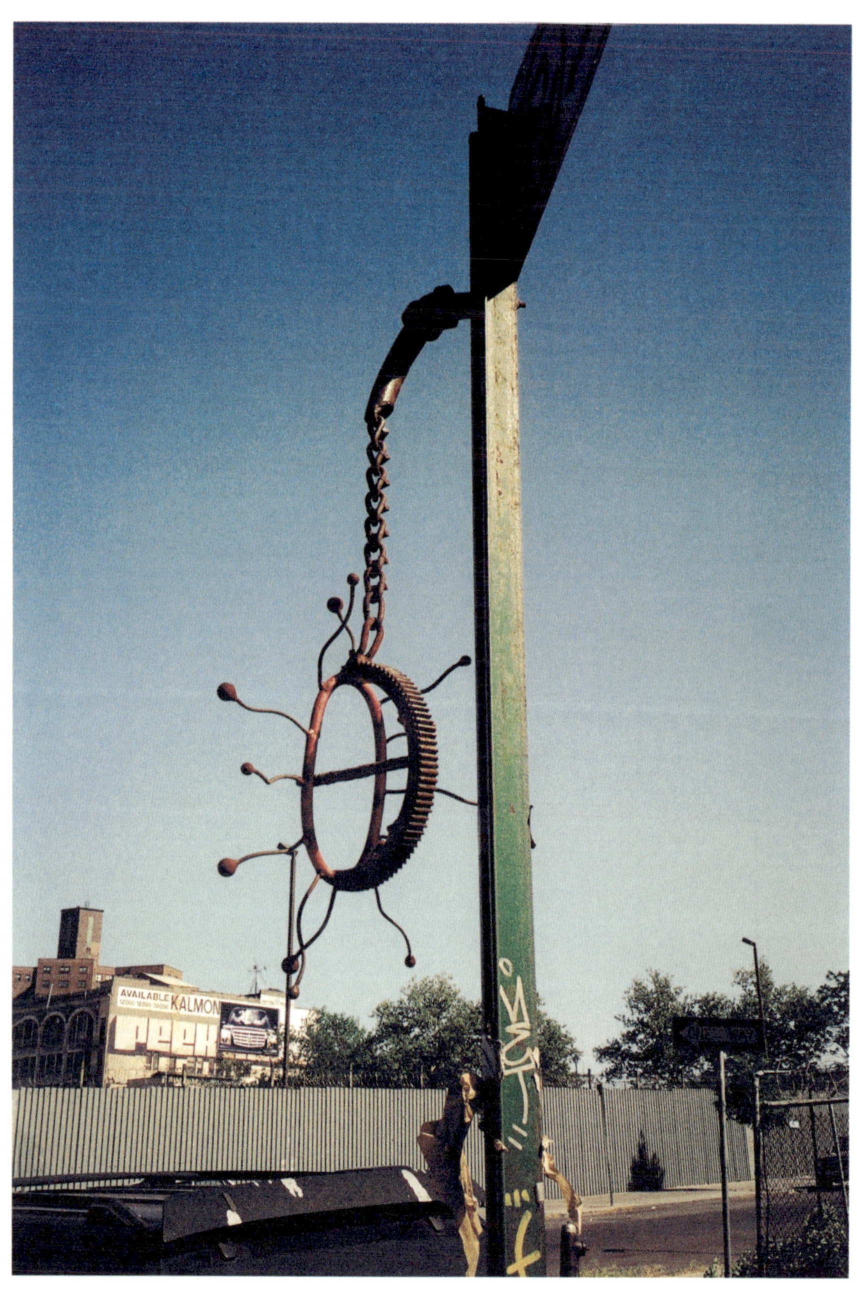

Jantar Mantar, JJ Veronis, 1996. Brooklyn, NY. Duration: unknown.

THE SKILLMAN YEARS

2000–2003 | Leon, Brad, and Quenell move into an apartment together, establishing a base of artistic operations in Bed-Stuy and learning advanced tricks of their trade from JJ Veronis and Shepard Fairey. Brad also meets the devastatingly pretty Alto, soon to change her name to Swoon, and in her finds someone to talk and spend his days with. As the building begins to fall apart around them, they seek refuge elsewhere one by one, until Brad is left alone with his thoughts and has the biggest epiphany of his artistic career.

Part 1

Skillman Street in Brooklyn, home to Brad, Leon, and Quenell from the first weeks of 2001, was just a few blocks away from Pratt Institute. Quenell and Leon had done their homework and found the apartment while Brad was still down south completing his half-year stint of forced family bonding. Hasidic[1]-owned, like the majority of the neighborhood, the building had been recently remodeled and looked to be on the up and up, which was saying something for the area.[2]

The winter was already a cold one, which can make one sign a lease even faster than the mere prospect of homelessness. They didn't talk to other tenants in the building, or give it a real once-over, checking the water pressure in the shower and the like, to see if things were up to personal snuff. The price was right, the location was good, and the floors were wood, which was the local equivalent of shin-to-ceiling windows and marble inlay. All things considered, they had found a little piece of high living in the middle of the ghetto, and things were looking fantastic.

Brad and Quenell were well pleased with themselves. Leon too was happy with his new home/storage locker, although he rarely stayed the night there, preferring to sleep at Polina's in this honeymoon phase of the love of his young life. Seeing Brad and Quenell, so broke from paying

---

[1] *American Heritage Dictionary*
Hasid or Hassid also Chassid
A member of a Jewish mystic movement founded in the eighteenth century in eastern Europe by Baal Shem Tov that reacted against Talmudic learning and maintained that God's presence was in all of one's surroundings and that one should serve God in one's every deed and word.

[2] The entirety of the Bed-Stuy zip code is a wasteland presented in long rows of dilapidated, ramshackle houses owned by proper slumlords whose neglect has left them just steps above shanties. The whole area seems to hold true to the 1970s and early '80s depression that almost consumed New York. When tourists visit the city's sanitized Lower East Side, or deep-bleached, pressure-cleaned Times Square, they take for granted the fact that not everywhere had that salability which makes a massive overhaul worthwhile to City Hall. There is no tourism in Bed-Stuy to maximize; there is no trade to boost or blossom. The star maps that do exist show the birthplace of Jay-Z and Biggie Smalls. And for lack of a celebrity benefit or a séance, they rarely visit.

first, last, and security, have to sleep head-to-toe in the same bed for the first week straight certainly did nothing to change his mind on this.

Soon enough, the apartment was furnished, and the boys could relax in their new home. The weather just kept getting colder and colder, so to aid in heating the apartment, Quenell started making a daily routine of turning the oven up to 500 degrees and leaving its door open, blasting heat at the rest of the apartment. On bad days, he would opt to live dangerously, turning the four top irons on to maximize the available facilities. All in all, things were working out surprisingly well. That is, until the gas leak.

The three had been living there about a month with every intention of paying rent, when one day the oven had trouble lighting. Leon, the calmer and relatively more cautious of the three, being absentee, Brad and Quenell didn't hesitate to fiddle around with the gas tubes and handles for a few minutes. But then, upon smelling gas and knowing that the rent they paid also covered upkeep, they called Jacob the landlord. With unforeseen urgency, Jacob had a gasman banging on their front door inside of an hour. Entering the apartment, he walked directly to the oven, slid it out of its crevice, twisted a few knobs, and announced that it could no longer be used in the conventional sense.

"You can put a toaster oven on it. Maybe a microwave," he said to Brad.

"What the hell you talking about?" asked Quenell.

"It is just part of the countertop for now. You have extra counter space," he replied as he sniffed at the air. "It's very dangerous. Talk to Jacob, he'll fix everything."

Then, without another word, the gasman walked out of the apartment, into the basement, and shut off their gas altogether.

"Wait, so now we don't have heat because of this bullshit?" Brad yelled down the stairs.

The gasman, like Jacob, was a Hasidic Jew. Hasidic communities are modern-day isolationists. Huge fans of *Time Life* DIY books, if there is something to be done – construction, gas, plumbing, healthcare – they have their own people take care of it.

"Too dangerous!" he replied as he lumbered up the stairs and out the front door.

Quenell and Brad sat in the living room, leaving messages on Jacob's phone as the apartment got colder and colder. They then called Leon and told him the news, and Leon, after not much thinking about it, decided not to stray from his usual plan of spending the night at Polina's. He would deal with the issue of heating his home away from home the following day.

"Well… So we'll get space heaters?" Brad asked Quenell, as he put on a sweater.

"Well I ain't payin' rent if I have to live under a buncha heat lamps." Quenell had three sweaters on at this point, over two heavy t-shirts.

Brad agreed. "I just want him to fix shit, but if not paying him the money will get it done, then fine."

"I'm gonna put on another pair of jeans, and then let's go to Kmart."

The following day, Brad eventually got through to Jacob and told him that until the heat was fixed, they wouldn't be paying rent. A minor argument followed, and they agreed to disagree on whose problem it was. On the 15th of February, Jacob knocked on the door.

"Do you have the rent?" he asked.

"Are you going to fix the heat?" asked Brad.

"I'll have someone come tomorrow," Jacob responded.

"Well when he finishes, we'll give him the check. We're not paying until you fix it."

"He'll be here tomorrow," Jacob said as he walked away and down the stairs. "Have the check ready for him."

Brad made sure to have the check ready, but no one came that afternoon, or the day after that, or for the rest of the month. On the 13th of March, Jacob was driving his black SUV down the street, saw Quenell, honked violently on the horn and pulled over.

"Hey there! Jones!" he screamed out the window.

"Yeah, what you want Jacob?" Quenell shouted as he walked over.

"You got the rent on you?" Jacob asked.

"What? No I don't have the damn rent on me. Fix the gas and you can have the rent. Don't you pull up to me in the middle of the str…"

"No check? Ok!" Jacob cut him off. "I have to go, I'll send someone over to fix things, you have the check ready!" he yelled out the window and pulled off down the road.

Two more months of no heat passed with zero contact from Jacob. Spring was starting to show in Brooklyn, bringing with it hints of warm weather and a complete lack of interest in paying rent. Brad, Leon, and Quenell started feeling like that gas situation was the best thing that could have happened to them, and began worrying that much less about pulling in rent money, and much more about making art and loving life.

Back in April the previous year, while wandering through the halls of Pratt Institute's Engineering Building, Brad had walked into a large room in the basement. This room was completely empty, save one short, very pretty girl printing designs in the far corner. Noticing that this was the same sticker work that he had seen around the neighborhood, Brad walked over to say hello.

Never one to be at a loss for words, Brad mentioned that he had seen her stuff around and was into it, and the two spoke for a little while. She really wanted to learn about wheat-pasting, and Brad, who had just been taught the ins and outs himself a few nights earlier while on a mission with his friend Eric Adorn and Shepard Fairey, said he would be happy to show her a few tricks. Brad explained the documentary he was working on, asking her if she'd like to be involved.

With that one afternoon of aimless exploring, Brad had met a girl that he couldn't stop talking to, a girl who called herself Alto – a girl who would soon go by the name Swoon.

When Brad had to go down to Atlanta, everything was put on hold for six months. But as he was walking down Myrtle for a sandwich on the first warm day of the new year, Brad bumped into her, literally, while turning a blind corner.

As she carried on hurrying past him, Brad called out, falsely threatening, "Whoa, whoa, whoa! Hold the fuck up!"

Alto spun around. "Brad? Brad!" She ran full speed, jumping to hug him and knocking him a few steps back.

"How you been, girl? What are you dressed like that for?" he asked.

"Very well, thank you. And I'm dressed inconspicuously," she replied, giving a little twirl to show off her miniskirt and tights, which made her look about as jaw-dropping as he had ever seen her. "Would you look at me and think I'm out there being a vandal?" she asked.

"I can't take my eyes off you. I wouldn't give a damn what you do to my storefront." And with that, they were linked up again.

Brad started taking Alto around with him more and more, at first just hanging out at the house parties that started heating up with the weather, then on long bike rides to parts of Brooklyn she hadn't even heard of yet. She had been putting work up near the Brooklyn Navy Yard and other spots along the Brooklyn waterfront, but Brad was the one who showed her DUMBO (Down Under the Manhattan Bridge Overpass), which became one of their favorite destinations to bike over and spend the day. They would walk around for hours, looking at the dozens of Revs ⬛ sculptures that were installed in the ten-block radius. As they explored dilapidated and fenced-off parts of Brooklyn, they became lost in long, winding talks about art and who they were into, who they thought was bunk, who was getting hype for no reason, and who was gonna be huge if they ever got discovered.

One night, as the two were sitting on a concrete slab that stretched out into the East River, Alto seemed preoccupied, and Brad asked what was on her mind.

"Well, I think I'm going to change the name I go by," she said.

"Good," Brad replied a little too quickly. "Alto kinda sucks." He chuckled. "What are you thinking of changing it to? You gonna use

---

⬛ Revs pioneered roller-paint tags and wheat-pasting graffiti in New York along with Cost in the early 1990s. He went on to make his tags in 3-D metal, welding them around New York's five boroughs. But he is most known for his obsessive diary entries, which he wrote in New York's subway tunnels. His goal was to have at least one entry in every tunnel in New York.

your real name?" Brad was a strong believer that an artist should take responsibility for what they create and that the work should speak for itself.

"No… I have a friend back home who had a dream about me. She said she had a dream that I was a famous artist that went by the name Swoon." She smiled shyly, but her eyes got excited. "I think I'm going to call myself that."

"Ok…" Brad bobbed his head. "That's that name you want to use?"

"…Yes," she replied.

"Well then Swoon it is, girl." Brad smiled. "Own that shit. Better than Alto, huh, shorty?" Whatever he might believe himself, it was hard to be anything other than supportive of the girl.

Unfortunately, as soon as the summer really started to kick off, Swoon left for Florida to spend some time with her family. She had had a crazy year, living and working in Amsterdam for a good part of it, and she wanted to get back to basics for a while. And as for all people lucky enough to have one, things don't get more basic than visiting the immediate family still living in their old hometown.

That summer was the summer Brad had dreamed of the year before. House parties day in and day out, a city packed with friends that he would smack into again and again like they were the only ones on the street, and the freedom to start doing work on a daily basis. Money was tight, but he knew the hustle. Food was either pick-pocketed from the school cafeteria or picked up by friends with credit cards that were still billed to their parents' houses. Drinks were bought by semi-pretty girls with stipends for accessories, and bar tabs in general were drink-and-dashed. He was night-living off the land, a land full of kids still hanging out on their parents' checking accounts.

But eventually fall arrived, and the temperature began to drop. Swoon was back in town and started putting up work seemingly as soon as she stepped off the plane. While picking up supplies at Pearl Paint in Chinatown, Brad and Leon walked to the back alley behind it where the spray paint was kept. There before them was Swoon's latest work, and it was vastly different from what she had been doing just months prior. The wheat-pastes, now cut out, were intricately crafted portraits conveying life and character through skillful combinations of positive and negative space.

"There's your girl," said Leon. "Looks like she's stepping it up."

"Yeah... wow. What is this?" Brad asked aloud. "A reverse stencil? Oh wow, yeah this looks great. She's gonna blow up if she keeps this up, no one's doing shit like this right now."

"You think anyone doing wheat-pasting is gonna blow up, period?" Leon asked. "I think it's too limited. Not enough possibilities with that stuff."

"No man, she's gonna get huge," Brad replied.

"Doubt it, but she should stick with it, see where it goes," said Leon as he moved on to pick up an aerosol can.

The following week, Brad got a call from Swoon, and very soon she and Brad were back on their bikes and riding around again. Brad told her how much he was into her new stuff and eager for her to show him her process and what else she had been working on during her stay in Florida, so they rode back to her house to look it all over.

Once there, she unrolled three big sheets of heavy paper in which she was cutting portraits of her grandfather and little brothers, two of the nicest little hellraisers in central Florida. She showed Brad her reverse-stenciling technique. It was a strong evolution in her work. Brad was impressed and a little intimidated that she had found her natural style in her medium, her craft. After that, he knew that everything else would fall into place for her.

As the summer's roof parties started tapering off, it began to dawn on Brad that he should start facing the fact that the weather was going to get a lot worse before it got any better. The ignored phone calls from Jacob chasing the rent had been getting less frequent, just when his voice would have been starting to sound pretty good. It was soon going to be time to break those space heaters back out.

As Brad and Quenell were sitting around one day, flanked by open-faced toasters set to full blast, there was a knock on the door, with Jacob behind it.

"Ok boys, do you have something for me?" he demanded. "If not, it has been a year… move out."

"Hold up, we're not moving anywhere. Have you looked around Jacob? You are breaking so many codes in this building it's illegal for you to have anyone on this property," Brad responded.

"You see this here, Jacob?" Brad pointed to the front door, which only had a deadbolt. "If there's a fire, the door's going to be too hot to use a key to get out. This is a death trap. But it's our death trap, so fix this stuff and we'll start paying you again. I don't want to move."

"Then pay the rent," Jacob insisted.

"Fix the heat today and I'll pay you the rent for this month when you're done." Brad was dead broke without hope of a real payday in sight, but with a brand new winter ahead of him, it was worth the gamble. "We've got all the back rent ready to pay you," he bluffed. "You fix the heat and the rest, we'll give you a year's rent right now."

"Just pay the rent today, or get out!" Jacob yelled.

Suddenly, from behind Brad, Quenell was no longer able to keep himself out of the argument. He had been holding his tongue and letting Brad handle it, now he had to speak his mind.

"Now hold on! Lower your motherfuckin' voice." Quenell boomed from behind Brad. "You want to kick us out, you go get a court order saying we've got to go. You've got so many fines waiting for you if you let an inspector up in here, you ain't gonna do shit. So just fix the heat, and we'll give you the rent. Until then…" and Quenell slammed the door in Jacob's face.

Brad and Quenell could hear Jacob cursing through the hallway as he stormed out of the building. The two sat down in the living room and watched through the front windows as he drove down the street.

"Shit. I was going to call him today to try to negotiate a truce," said Brad.

"Like you've got a year's rent in your back pocket to give Jacob," Quenell shot back. "We're lucky as hell that he doesn't fix anything. Shit, we're living for free, baby. Get through the winter and we got eight months of free housing."

"So… space heaters?" asked Brad.

"Space heaters," Quenell agreed.

And with that, the two started looking around for power strips to load up with as many space heaters as they could find.

Part 2

Brad had the apartment to himself that winter, with Quenell spending most of his nights at his (newly acquired) girlfriend's house and Leon still doing the same. With his home mostly vacant, it became the perfect place to prep for missions or have visiting friends stay for months at a clip.

January was cold, but it took until February to really drop below freezing. When it finally did, with the Brooklyn streets covered in filthy snow and ice, Brad and Swoon decided to go wheat-pasting around town. They set out a few hours before sunup, that being her preferred time to schedule a mission, planning to go where the morning took them, starting with the areas around the Brooklyn Navy Yard. To prepare for the harsh conditions, Brad mixed salt into the glue to keep it from freezing over before the poster was in place.

The salt was a trick that Brad had picked up from Shepard Fairey. As it happened, one of the many things Brad and Swoon had in common was an inability to position their posters as level and precise as those Obey poster clusters. Shepard was talented at keeping things aligned to near OCD perfection, while Brad and Swoon were stuck having to think their way around such aspirations. Brad cut his work out, wanting to put it as high as he could without worrying about orientation. When Swoon had still been making her rectangle and square collages, she had slapped them down after a quick eyeball of the aesthetic balance of the terrain and never looked back. With her cutout work, she too was now free of the constraints of ninety-degree worry.

Both Swoon and Brad believed that art should communicate and interact with the environment around it, whatever that environment may be – a graffiti-covered wall anywhere in the world or a vacant lot along New York's East River. When the work was made to communicate with its surroundings, the entire location would become part of the art piece. Neither of them had the money to make the massive Christo-sized art they dreamed of, but in this way, they believed their work could become exponentially larger than if viewed in isolation.

After about four hours of putting up a handful of Brad's posters and a few dozen of Swoon's, it was 8am and the two went back to Skillman Street to relax with some tea and make a little breakfast. Brad was as excited to sit and eat as Swoon was to drop the enormous bag, still holding twenty-eight leftover posters, off her tired shoulders and onto the floor. As she did that, standing noticeably taller than she had all morning, Brad put the teakettle on one half of the two-burner hot plate, and started unplugging space heaters.

"That's going to take at least ten minutes to boil," he said. "But when it does, take it off and throw the frying pan on with some eggs, maybe? There should be some in the fridge."

"Why don't I just turn on the other burner?" she asked. "And what are you doing with all the space heaters?"

"That other burner never gets all the way hot. It's broken. And I'm going to take a shower, so I'm putting these in the bathroom with me so I don't die in the cold water."

"Are you serious?" Swoon was half giggling, half terrified.

"Hell yeah, I'm serious. You think this is a game?" Brad shouted, and then doubled over with laughter. "I'll be back in a little bit, go ahead and get comfortable, kick the shoes off… whatever."

When Brad walked back out about eleven minutes later, fresh and clean and layered back up with new gear, he didn't even recognize his kitchen. Swoon had taken him up on his offer and put up every one of the posters she had left over from that morning's mission. She covered the walls, every cabinet, and every drawer. She even cut around the edges of the kitchen units, making each drawer and cabinet open up like an enormous diorama, a lifesize 3-D popup book of her art. It was nothing short of amazing.

"You like it?" Swoon asked, batting her excited little eyelids like a cartoon beauty queen.

"Um, wow. Yeah, girl. It's incredible," Brad replied, still wrapping his mind around what he was looking at.

"I'm soooooo relieved," she shot back, waving her hands around. "I thought it would be nice, like, it might look really cool and would, you know, be cool with you, but then I remembered, like halfway through, that you live with Leon and Quenell and I was like, oh my God, I totally just wallpapered Brad's entire kitchen without really asking and I thought that I was going to get you in trouble with the boys and oh… I'm so glad it's ok. Phew!" And with that she took a big breath, sighed, and fell back into her chair. "Oh, and the tea's ready."

"…Cool. I could use some hot tea," Brad said as he sat down.

"Um, it's already kind of cold," Swoon replied, and gave the shyest smile Brad had seen in his whole life.

They decided to go for a walk over to John's Diner for some hot tea and a proper breakfast instead of struggling to cook on the hotplate. There Swoon started telling Brad about her fascination with Gordon Matta-Clark, an artist working a decade or two earlier who had been slicing apart architecture on a scale then unheard of. He did multiple variations of cutting entire houses in pieces, as if a laser had made a clean slice through staircases and the rest, as well as gone spelunking through roofs and floors, cutting geometric shapes from the top down in buildings scheduled for demolition in the Bronx. In vision he was an inspiration, in scale he was a deity.

Part 3

As the weeks went by and the ice finally started to melt, cracking under its own weight, life became bearable again in the apartment Brad was sharing with his best friends' possessions. He would still see Leon and Quenell nearly every day, but he was the only one who slept in that apartment day in and day out, rain or shine, warmed by the summer's heat or cold enough to see his breath in the bathroom. That late April, as the sun finally came out, curing the Tri-State area of its collective seasonal depression and making the place more livable by the day, Quenell and Leon started spending more time at home.

One afternoon in early May, while the three were eating lunch, Leon got a call from Albert Zuger inviting them to JJ Veronis's studio in Long Island City. JJ had just lost the space, and was ripping out ten years' worth of groundbreaking work. He needed help, and if Leon and Brad were willing, they were welcome to stay and hang out for a while. Neither hesitated, they just asked what was first on the list of things to do. Brad and Leon had long been die-hard fans of JJ's, even before they knew his name and simply called him "sculpture guy." Any chance to meet him was worth running towards. Brad was especially excited, having long wanted to interview him for his film.

JJ picked them up in his truck and drove the boys to the studio. Taking the scenic route, he showed Brad and Leon every piece he had installed between point A and point B. The two were gassed and full of questions. JJ was flattered, seeing them still wholly respectful of him and his work. He had seen the Darius and Downey work and knew that these two were on their way.

Walking into the studio, both Leon and Brad were amazed at the sheer amount of work before them. JJ had kept busy over those ten years, filling the space the size of a shopping mall with sculptures made from everything you can imagine. As they walked in, the floor itself split open to reveal kinetic mosaic sculptures. There were huge jet engines hanging from the ceiling in suspended flight, navigating between giant safes that seemed to threaten a thunderous fall. Brad couldn't stop staring at one piece, a full car frozen just after impact, busting through a roll-down fence and into the studio.

Later in the day, Brad and JJ were having a few beers while removing a giant metal safe that was suspended from the ceiling. Very soon it was dangling by a single bolt.

"Whoa, how is this not totally dangerous?" Brad asked. "This safe has got to weigh at least 300 pounds."

"More like 400," JJ replied, not sweating it in the least. "And each anchor bolt can hold up to 500. Maybe a little more." JJ smiled as Brad's mind got blown right there on the spot.

The rest of Brad's evening was spent asking JJ every question he could think of, while he and Leon put their backs into removing amazing work of art after amazing work of art. As the two were leaving, JJ grabbed a box off one of his workbenches and handed it to Brad.

"Go ahead and put these things to use," he said.

Brad looked in the box and it was overflowing with the same anchor bolts that were strong enough to suspend that safe from the ceiling.

Later that same week while collecting more scrap metal to work on, Brad and Leon found metal bars that looked as if they were used as pieces of a shelving unit.

"Oh look, these look exactly like..." started Leon

"...Mini street poles" finished Brad.

The two quickly collected all the poles and carried them back to Leon's studio for safekeeping. They weren't sure what they wanted to do with them yet but, feeling inspired by their afternoon with JJ, they were sure they wanted all of them.

With the closing of the shortest spring on record, summer was soon in full effect and Brad headed down to Atlanta to see his folks for a month. With Brad gone, Quenell started staying in the apartment again full time, not trusting the neighbors not to steal them naked or Jacob not to change the locks. Just days after Quenell got comfortable having the place all to himself came the breakup that shattered Leon's heart, firmly reinstalling him in Skillman Street as well.

Completely distraught, Leon buried himself in his day job and his art, repeatedly looking over his older work for inspiration, trying to think of anything other than his failed relationship. One day he was struck with an idea to use one of those small metal bars as a mini street pole, as he and Brad had thought, with a shrunken-down version of a Verbs sign that he had installed in the past. Positioning it alongside the original, he called it his *Baby Verbs*.

When Brad returned to a full house for the first time, he too was primed to do some fresh work. He was also returning to the mountain of editing and shaping that "Public Discourse" was going to need. He and Quenell would be spending the better part of the next nine months attached at the hip, working near sixteen hours a day just to finish their documentary by May.

One late morning around 11am, Brad and Quenell were still sleeping when there was a thundering boom that shocked them both from their sleep. About eight seconds went by, and there was another crashing boom that shook the building. Brad came running out of his room towards the living room that housed Quenell's bed.

"What the hell was that?" Brad screamed, sliding into the room in his socks and boxers.

Quenell was already pulling his belt tight with one hand and his head through his shirt's neck hole with the other. "We about to find out, right the fuck now," he said as he pulled his workman's boots on without socks.

As Brad and Quenell came running out of the front of the apartment building, there was another crash. This time glass could be heard shattering and a motor was starting up. They started towards the noise, but only had to walk another ten feet.

The neighbors were running screaming from the house immediately next door to them, which was also owned by Jacob, as men smashed through the windows with sledgehammers and table saws. The saws had been ripped loose of their tables and were being used without any safety gear at all, cutting through window frames, the front door, and the columns that supported the front porch.

Brad, Leon, and Quenell had been very aware that they were living next to a crack den for months, but had no idea it would come to this. Most days, when returning from work or the studio, the boys would have to clear the crackheads selling drugs from their stoop. They assumed the final straw was when the house had its electricity shut off from never paying bills, but the crackheads solved that problem by powering the entire house with two fifty-foot extension cords that were plugged into a lamp pole that had its low panel ripped off with a crowbar.

One of the demolition men was guarding the front door with a sledgehammer, threatening the squatters. He slowly walked them backwards out into the front yard, screaming that if they went back inside the men doing the demo would not stop tearing the building apart just because they were in danger. One of the tenants ignored him and quickly dashed past, grabbing as many of his things as he could carry before he ran back out again.

Other terrified neighbors were gathering outside now. These demolition men weren't professionals, they were just local guys who usually spent their time drunk at the bodega down the street. Now here they were, cutting through loadbearing walls and smashing pipes with sledgehammers, more than ready to crack the skull of anyone who got close.

Suddenly, the two evicted men got heated with the man guarding the entrance and started walking towards him. When one of them picked up a piece of wood, the demolitionist swung the sledgehammer to keep them at bay and came inches from killing one of them.

"Whoa!" screamed Quenell. "Don't any y'all motherfuckers have a cell phone?" he screamed at the neighbors. "Call the fucking police!"

"Mind your fucking business, nigga! You want to stop us, why don't you walk over here and stop us?" one of the men with the table saw screamed from the second floor. All the demolition men stopped their work and stared. No fool, Quenell shut his mouth.

These men were so unprofessional that they were working their way from the ground floor up, smashing out every wall they could on that floor, then climbing the stairs. They smashed at the floors from above and below, standing on a couch and cutting through the ceiling of the first floor with a table saw, then going upstairs and smashing at the wooden floors with sledgehammers. Brad thought of Gordon Matta-Clark as he and Quenell watched in awe for three hours. Not one police car stopped to investigate.

Eventually the men, covered head-to-toe in plaster dust and soaked to the bone from ripping apart all the plumbing, pushed a huge section of the front of the house back on itself and the entire structure started to collapse inwards. When the outer walls on the left and right started being pulled in by the weight of the collapse, they began to affect the buildings that were attached on either side.

The house on the far side, two doors down from the boys' apartment, got the better end of the deal. The partition wall on that side broke free of the collapsing building, giving it a second outer wall's worth of insulation. Brad, Leon, and Quenell's building, however, had worse luck. As the next-door building collapsed, it ripped the outer wall clean off of their house too. Across the lot from the boys, watching the whole time, were about a dozen Hasidim leaning against their cars, bearing heavy smiles and looking at their watches, as the building collapsed into rubble at their feet without them having to lift a finger.

All of the pipes that were once sandwiched inside the wall of the boys' building were now on the outside. The sharp ends of the nails and pins holding up their posters were visible from the street. But it was still summer, so from inside the apartment it was impossible to notice the difference. Brad and Quenell thanked their luck that the demolition men didn't take their building down with the crack den, and went back inside, safe and sound.

That evening, Leon came home from work, stopped on the sidewalk and flipped open his cell phone.

"Yellow?" said Brad.

"Hey, um, Brad?" Leon said, "What in the fuck happened to the house next door?"

"Oh, man, it was crazy. Where are you?" Brad asked.

"I'm outside. Our place is fine right? I mean, you're inside the apartment?" Leon asked "Quenell there?"

"Yeah man," Brad replied. "We're inside having a beer, trying to relax. Come on in."

Leon walked up the stairs, came into the apartment, and saw Quenell and Brad sitting in their chairs drinking their day away, with piles of beer cans at their feet.

"So?" Leon asked.

"Jacob hired some guys to finally evict those crackheads."

"That's what an eviction looks like around here?" Leon dropped himself down, sitting on Quenell's bed.

"Jacob probably just rolled up in a van to those fellas on the corner and screamed, hey niggas! Want to tear some shit down? Then gave them a couple hundred dollars each and some tools, and let them fucking tear the neighborhood apart." Quenell laughed.

"Jacob was there?" Leon asked.

"Naw, Jacob wasn't anywhere around. That shit was ignorant as hell today," said Quenell. "All them niggas nearly got themselves killed. Shit was gonna be bloody as a motherfucker."

"So we gonna start looking for a new apartment?" Leon asked. "I mean we can't stay here anymore…"

"Why the hell not?" Quenell asked.

"Cause we're next man!" Leon yelled. "We haven't paid rent in over a year! What's to keep him from doing the same shit to us?

"I'm not moving a fucking inch. This shit is free and I'm staying till he does rip this bitch down," Quenell shot back.

"I don't have the money to just up and move. I'm staying," Brad chimed in. "Listen, Jacob hasn't said a thing to us in a long time, and I think the upstairs and downstairs neighbors all pay rent. The downstairs ones have a kid, dude. He's not going to tear shit down."

"I'm looking for a place tomorrow. If y'all want to stay here, cool with me, but I've got to go." Leon had made up his mind, and the following day made plans to move into a room in his friend Noah's apartment that had recently been vacated by Swoon.

Brad and Quenell, far too busy with the film to hold down a day job, continued living on the cheap all through the fall. When it did start getting cold out, it got freezing inside the apartment. Brad started seeing Quenell pack his backpack with a few days' worth of clothing at a time before heading over to his girlfriend's house, and knew what was coming. He would soon be all by himself in the cold again. It was already cold enough that the house was uncomfortable to hang out in, much less sleep inside of. And it was still only November.

Part 4

The winter of 2002–3 was the one that gave New York its record-breaking blizzard. It snowed without mercy for days on end, freezing out the city and causing mass transportation to slide to a complete halt.

Brad, still living in the apartment when the blizzard peaked in February, took refuge in his room, taking every space heater in the house there with him and turning them on full blast. He would wake severely dehydrated each morning, but alive. Too busy working on the film to socialize, and with no one offering any favors, Brad was forced to play the hand he was dealt.

When the pipes froze, and the apartment no longer had running water, Brad wondered whether it might be time to leave, but then quickly realized if he were to shower in that degree of cold, he would get sick anyways, so what was the benefit of running water? He began buying drinking water by the gallon at the bodega down the street.

One day, with Brad's cell phone long disconnected from not being able to pay the bills, Quenell stopped by, worried about his friend. When he walked into the apartment he feared he would be seeing Brad destitute or worse, only to find him sitting in the living room in a t-shirt. The apartment was no longer cold; in fact it was warm for the first time since they had signed the lease.

"What in the hell is all this about?" Quenell asked. "It feels like we got heat in this bitch. What did you do boy, start a fire?"

"I don't know, I woke up and it was warm in the whole apartment." Brad smiled. "I'm just enjoying while it lasts."

"Well shit, boy, I'm gonna get my ass comfy then. Take this carpet off." Quenell started laughing as he unzipped his Carhartt vest and pulled off his sweater, now in a t-shirt as well. "I was gonna tell you how usually you're the lucky motherfucker with a girlfriend and a nice place to stay. This time I lucked out nigga, I don't know how, and now… You're the only motherfucker I know, stays in this bullshit in the middle of the coldest winter I've ever seen in Brooklyn, and suddenly, this nigga's got a heated apartment."

"You want to see something really crazy?" Brad asked as he flipped on the television. "Check out what was going on with the kitchen this morning."

"What... in... the... hell?" Quenell studied the television screen as Brad flipped his video camera on to the play setting. "Where is that? Is that the kitchen?"

"Uh-huh. It was raining in the kitchen when I woke up," Brad said, still shook from the experience. "Warm rain, man. Jesus... Just terrifying."

And it was. Brad had woken up a few hours previous to Quenell stopping by, his room significantly warmer, with the sound of a shower running. Scraping the extra crusty, dehydrated flakes from his eyes, he had stumbled out of his bedroom and into the kitchen, and was immediately soaked.

The kitchen was a rainforest, not dripping drop by drop, but pouring rain from every crack, crevice, and fixture in the ceiling. The water was warm, and gallons of it were flowing over every bulb hanging in the room. Still in complete disbelief, Brad ran to the living room, tossed a fresh tape in his video camera, and started recording the spectacle.

Miraculously, the water didn't pool and collect; there wasn't even the hint of a flood. Every single drop that hit the floor rolled into the corner by the cabinet under the kitchen sink and disappeared. Brad set the camera down, worried about what assuredly was flooding the downstairs neighbors and ran over to the sink cabinet.

When he opened the cabinet doors, Brad had no idea what he was looking at. It was bright and the cold hurt his face. There was nothing behind the cabinet doors but a blanket of snow and ice and beyond that, the outside world whipping the elements through the hole. The wind from outside was laced with tiny hail rocks that stuck to his eyebrows and quickly melted. Brad closed the doors and opened them again.

It was too early in the morning; he had seen too many crazy things happen too quickly to process what he was looking at now. The water was being funneled outside via a hole in the kitchen leading directly to a blizzard.

As he crouched there, soaked, just staring into his cabinet, through the hole and down the street, the rain suddenly stopped. He stood up, the last of the water rushing past his bare feet. And that was when he noticed that even with the hole blowing icy air into the apartment as best it could, the apartment was warm. He slowly closed the cabinet, started stripping his wet clothes off, and threw them in the sink to drain.

Drying off, he pulled on a t-shirt and jeans, opened a beer, and sat down in his chair in the living room. He played the video he had just recorded to make sure everything he had experienced was real, rewound it, and sat there drinking until Quenell happened to stop by.

"That's what you missed…" said Brad, still not believing it himself.

Quenell got up and walked into the kitchen.

"It's not even wet in here!" Quenell shouted over to Brad. "How in the fuck did I just watch a rainstorm on video and this shit not even be wet?"

"Look under the sink!" Brad shouted back across the apartment, then got up and walked over to see Quenell's reaction.

Quenell opened the under-sink cabinet and jumped back. "That's the street!" he screamed.

"Told you." Brad laughed.

"That's the motherfucking street!" Quenell couldn't stop laughing and pointing. "That's crazy!"

"Want a beer?" Brad said, arm outstretched with a cheap warm beer, the refrigerator long broken.

"Shit. Yeah I do!" Quenell laughed, still in disbelief, wiping the tears from his eyes. "I can't get my head around this shit!"

The two walked back to the living room where it was warmest and kept drinking.

"I haven't had those space heaters turned off since September. This is incredible," said Brad.

"How long you think this is gonna last?" asked Quenell.

"I don't know. If it lasts to the end of the day, that's amazing. But who knows? It might last a while," replied Brad.

And with that, there was a loud knock on the door. "I'm here about the pipes! We got a leak! Open up!" a man screamed through the door.

Brad opened it up and a Hasidic repairman walked into the living room, where he started testing the ceiling with his knuckles. He was pushing them deep into the ceiling material, denting it.

"The leak was in the kitchen," said Brad. "Not in the living room."

"The pipes are busted. The pipes outside froze and broke and it's leaking all through the building. Very bad," the man said. "Here, look." And the man walked over to the wall in the living room that used to have a house on the other side of it. "See this?" he said as he pushed his finger right through the wall, like it was no thicker or stronger than pudding skin.

"Whoa! What the hell are you doing?" Brad screamed. "Stop it!"

The man slowly pulled his finger out of the wall. A beam of light followed his finger into the apartment and shot a tiny circle of daylight onto the floor. There was a peephole now, out into the vacant lot. From the other side of the room, it looked like someone had spilled a drop of light blue paint on the white wall.

"No! This is no good!" the man yelled, putting his meaty hand into the hole and peeling it out. Like silly putty, it started to flap and slap down onto the outer side. "Look! It is no good! It is all water damaged!" he pulled the flap of the wall in, suddenly opening it three feet across.

"Yo! Stop it!" Brad screamed, stepping towards him. "I fucking live here!"

"You got anything to patch this hole with, man?" Quenell boomed. "You better have something in your van, you want to keep ripping up the walls!"

"But look at this! It can't stay like this!" the man cried out. "It all has to be fixed!"

And with that, the man stormed out of the apartment, ignoring Brad and Quenell's demands that he come back and fix it.

Brad slumped onto the edge of Quenell's bed and just went silent, staring out of the new hole in the wall.

"It's 'bout to get cold as hell in here, you better toss on a little something more than that t-shirt, my man," Quenell said as he walked back into the living room, putting on his sweater, heavy vest, and other pieces of warm gear.

"…Yeah," Brad replied and didn't move.

"I'm gonna go to the bodega and grab a sandwich, you want to come with?" Quenell asked. "Or you want me to grab you something?"

"Nope." Brad replied. And with that Quenell walked outside, and down the street.

Brad could see Quenell through the hole, walking in the distance with his hands flat on top of his head, shook by the morning.

Brad looked out of the hole and around the hole. He compared the room before it and now with it. He reflected upon holes in general and he thought about the power of that missing piece. The wall was suddenly more present than it had ever been before. The whole room was no longer sealed and separate from the outside world. With this one act of removal, this act of subtraction and destruction, it was now connected to the outside world. Joined through subtraction. Fused through removal. Looking through that hole he felt so bad he almost wished that he were standing in the waiting room to heaven. As if he might float through that hole straight to the clouds above and all this pain would be over.

Brad was lost in thought as the wind kicked up suddenly and changed direction. It began to snow in the living room, lightly at first, and Brad watched and reflected on his situation as the snowflakes melted into his beard and he sat on a chair in the middle of the room and stared.

The following week, with a sheet of plastic stapled over the hole, Brad finally came up with an idea of what to do with the remaining mini street poles he and Leon had found. Both of them had long desired to escape from fixed street poles as the sole destination for their work, wanting to be free to install their sculptures anywhere they imagined. With the hammer drill, they now had the tool with which to do so. They could put work directly into the concrete sidewalk if they wanted. And with the lessons learned from JJ still fresh in their minds, the two had an open terrain before them.

Brad liked Leon's mini Verbs sign placed next to its full-size counterpart. It was done well, but he thought that their next piece could be more successful by being more accessible – something every passerby could grasp. His idea was to make a baby sign to put on a mini pole, which they would install at the base of a full-grown street sign, creating the idea of parent and child.

This would not only take advantage of their newfound ability to install their art wherever they chose. It also upped the role of the context in giving the work value and meaning. Brad was still very concerned about the theft of their street sculptures. The only way he could see to deter the street vulture Omar-types was to make work whose setting was so essential that it would have no meaning or value out of context. Removed from where they installed it, it would become a mere trinket.

At first, Brad planned to create a miniature No Parking sign, to suggest no double parking. But wanting it to be precisely to scale, he discovered that the small-print text at the bottom of a standard sign was impossible to replicate at the appropriate size. So he opted instead for a shrunken Stop sign. Unable to create stencils that would produce the necessary quality, Brad asked Eric Adorn to help him screenprint the text directly onto the piece of steel that he cut out at the metal shop.

Meanwhile, Leon was doing the meticulous job of drilling each individual hole into the mini pole with surgical precision, which he then attached to the base plate. Leon's fine attention to detail was essential, for the piece would only truly be complete if the fabrication looked perfect up close. The more closely it resembled the real stop sign, the less likely anybody would want to steal it.

Brad and Leon prepared themselves for the mission. Leaving early in the morning, they brought the *Baby Stop Sign* with base already attached, the hammer drill and fixings, their construction uniforms, and photographer Tod Seelie to document the installation. Tod was tight in the scene and definitely down for the cause. They headed directly over to the edge of the Brooklyn Navy Yard, and in broad daylight, in full costume, just feet away from the street and without a soul around, they smoothly installed the piece.

Biking back to the spot later that day, the two stopped and looked at the sign from a distance. The parent-child connection was unmistakable. This anthropomorphizing of their surroundings, this giving of human traits, this breathing of life into the inanimate was the opening of a new chapter in their work. Mundane objects no longer needed to be mere utilitarian slaves to function, duty bound to stand straight without thought or care. Brad was overloaded with the potential for these creations to empathize, to feel the work they did all day, to be cognizant of their position in the world.

With such new thoughts fresh in their minds, the documentary finished and already being offered international distribution, the summer was suddenly upon them. And with that, Brad, Leon, and Quenell all packed their bags and said their good-byes. They were headed off for Europe.

Although the boys had gotten away without paying rent for just under three years, in the final months before they abandoned the apartment altogether they started getting Con Edison utility bills for six thousand dollars and up, not including late payment charges. When they called the 1(800) number on the bottom of the bill and said that they hadn't had gas for three years, Con Ed had an official technician there the following day. Checking the basement, he found a little surprise; the gas had been rerouted via incredibly dangerous piping to the three buildings behind them. Jacob's plan was to stick Brad, Leon, and Quenell with the bill. By the time the authorities caught up with Jacob, the boys were already in Europe, free of the mess altogether.

BROOKLYN IN DIE HAUS

2003 | Brad and Leon are flown to Berlin to take part in "Backjumps – The Live Issue," an important street art gallery show. Dodging offers of prostitutes, the two dedicate themselves to putting up boom after boom on the streets of the German capital. With absolutely zero luck, they persevere through American stubbornness and fatalistic abandon, not to mention the grace and kind assistance of Juergen Grosse, Micha Bonk, Adrian Nabi, the CBS writing crew, and OKEGR.

In the early summer of 2003, Brad was invited to screen "Public Discourse" at a show in Berlin named "Backjumps – The Live Issue." The show would also be exhibiting Swoon, Banksy, Oclock, Shepard Fairey, Polina, Faile, Akay, and Adams, amongst others.

At Brad's encouragement, the curator agreed to put his and Leon's work into the show too. They were given a small but prominent wall in the second gallery show, a few additional weeks away. With the dimensions in hand, Brad and Leon went to work on a painting. Assuming that the curators would be expecting each artist to bring what was cutting edge and new in the city that they were from, Brad and Leon decided to do the opposite and brought their interpretation of German heritage and culture with them instead.

The gallery work would be a collaborative reworking and refining of an old piece of Leon's. They spent a solid month intricately painting Martin Luther wearing a construction uniform and tagging "Die Schönheit ist Der Prozess," "beauty is the process" – a play on the nailing of the 95 Theses to the Wittenberg church door. As in an old master's studio, they divided the painting's workload between them. Leon painted all of the background elements, such as buildings and trees, and Martin Luther's vest. Brad painted the foreground, all the animals and the gathered crowd, as well as Luther himself.

Completing the painting with a fine ornate frame that they covered in gilding, both were incredibly proud of their work. It was, they thought, a perfect use of the limited space available.

The illegal work they would bring to install on the streets of Berlin would be based on an old Downey piece, three transparent panels that stuck out from a tagged-up wall, creating the illusion that sections of the wall had been peeled off and made three-dimensional. Both Brad and Leon painted on either side, leaving some areas clear so the wall and the surroundings would always be seen through the panels and become part of the piece.

The following week, flying into Berlin at eight in the morning, Brad was unable to sleep and looked out the window. Noticing a piece of graffiti on a rooftop that was big enough to see from the sky, lit by the morning sun, he nudged Leon.

"Yo Leon, take a look at this," he said.

"Wow. How big do you figure that is, that we can see it up here?" Leon asked.

"Pretty damn big," Brad replied.

That piece was like a welcome to Berlin. Already it felt like this would be a good place to put up work. As Brad and Leon stepped off the plane, they were greeted at the terminal gate by a figure wearing giant hip hop sunglasses and gear straight out of a Bronx street manual from the late seventies. This was Adrian Nabi, curator of the show, creator of *Backjumps* magazine, and the man responsible for bringing the world's greatest street artists countless times to Berlin. Adrian and Brad bonded immediately. Excited to meet the two street artists, Adrian tried his best to make them comfortable and help them to relax after the long flight.

"Nice to meet you both! How was the flight?" said Adrian. "I have arranged everything. First, we will go to the Künstlerhaus Bethanian and see the show."

As they exited the arrival gate, Leon's mind was elsewhere, feeling the cold breeze of Berlin in August and cursing himself for packing clothes suitable for August in New York.

"So, would you like a prostitute?" Adrian asked, enthusiastically. "You both must be tense from the flight. I know a place nearby where they have excellent prostitutes."

"What?" Leon thought he must have misunderstood and asked again. "What did you just say?"

"Nothing, it is ok, we can go right to the space…" Adrian replied, embarrassed that he might have made the boys feel uncomfortable.

"I'm cool to go check out some prozzies," Brad joked, wanting to put him at ease. "But we're exhausted. Is there a place we can crash and rest for an hour or two? When I'm fresh and alert, then and only then do I want to start talking to prostitutes." Brad laughed. "It's a little early for some hooker action just yet."

"Ha! Ok! The apartment we have for you isn't ready yet, but I live nearby," Adrian offered. "You can rest there if you'd like."

Once rested, the boys were taken to the space and introduced to the owner of the gallery, Juergen Grosse, and his assistant and translator Micha Bonk. Juergen, a large, kind man who ran construction sites in Berlin and spoke only German, was a huge fan of street art and took photographs of everything that was put up with an efficiency that suggested total omniscience when it came to the city's streets.

Brad and Leon were then shown the wall that they would be putting work up on for the opening the following week. They glanced at each other in alarm. Instead of being six feet across as originally discussed, they found themselves faced with a giant wall twenty-five feet long. They were grossly underprepared for such a space, and began to stress with so much open ground before them.

Taking them up to the apartment, which was just upstairs from the gallery, Micha explained to Brad and Leon that the lock was broken and there were no keys for the time being. If they wanted to go in or out, all they had to do was jiggle the handle just right, stick a pen or screwdriver in the door at the correct angle and it would pop open every time.

It was a place all their own in a city that was new to them and it felt good to sit and have a place to set their things down. But Leon was unimpressed. This was far beneath his expectations after being flown in to the city for the show.

"Why the hell don't they have keys for us?" he asked.

"Whatever man," replied Brad. "Let's get downstairs and deal with that wall."

Walking back through the gallery, the two joined up with a skinny, polite young man who offered to show them around the city. He walked them down the street and introduced them to the local kebab joint (where they ate twice a day for the rest of their stay, being so broke at the time). After lunch, the boy let them know exactly where and from whom they could get supplies to do any work they had ahead of them in Berlin. Only much later would they learn that this respectful little graffiti writer who was kindly giving them the tour of the local cheap eateries and pubs wrote under OKEGR, one of the most notorious destructive forces in Europe.⟂

Deciding that they would definitely need additional materials to cover that wall, they followed his advice and went to see what exactly was available. Over in the larger gallery space, they were not only graciously giving artists materials and paint to do their work in the gallery, but also slyly providing materials well over and above what could be used in the space allotted. Without saying it, or explicitly encouraging it, the gallery had flown graffiti and street artists from across the world not just to come and do work inside the gallery, but to paint their city as well.

Once they had materials safely stashed in their apartment, Brad and Leon decided to walk around and check out the city. Maybe they could find some materials to do an installation with their giant space, maybe after learning the lie of the land they would be inspired to do something that would speak directly to Berliners. Picking an arbitrary direction and marshaling on, they began to decompress after their rough flight and to feel comfortable in the city.

Still walking through the streets that evening, they came across a construction site with no fence or protective elements. They had passed a few sites already, and at the most they were surrounded by an easy to open latch system, but this was completely exposed. Before Brad and Leon, mere feet away from the sidewalk, was a pile of German signs and street poles stacked waist high. The boys' prayers were answered. Without a second's thought or hesitation, they greedily grabbed as many of the signs

---

⟂ One artist who was at the opening decided he would push things as far as he possibly could and took an open gallon of green paint for a walk down the street. A few blocks away, he came upon a police station, pulled the strings on his hoodie tight to cover his face, and kicked open the front doors. Throwing the paint bucket into the middle of the lobby, covering a room full of cops in green paint, the boy then ran quickly back out into the night. Some think that the kid in question was young OKEGR, but no one knows for sure.

and poles as they could carry and started back towards the apartment.

They were four blocks away when they saw the lights and heard the sirens.

"Oh shit," Leon muttered.

"We fucked up," Brad confirmed.

The Berliner police parked fast behind them as the boys turned around and started setting down the signs.

"STOP! Bleib stehen!" commanded the officer.

As the two German officers started angrily interrogating Leon and Brad, another ran up to provide assistance. The three quickly realized that they would have to employ their limited English to deal with this pair. The conversation was stilted, and punctuated with shrugs and very conciliatory, nonthreatening gestures from the boys.

"What are you doing with the signs?" one officer stuttered out.

"We thought they were trash," explained Brad.

"What? You stole them from behind a partition," the same officer replied, getting into his role as inquisitor.

"No, they were just there in a pile, we thought they were trash." Brad pushed the ignorance card as hard as he could.

After some further gentle questioning, and a little smart thinking on Brad's part, the two were let go, but only after the police had got all their information, including their passport numbers and the name of the gallery they were showing at.

Leon and Brad were kicking themselves all the long walk home. They felt like total amateurs for getting caught, tagged, and released back into the wild after only being in the city a matter of hours. Totally depressed, they got back to the apartment and jimmied the door open. It now being around 1am, Brad flipped the light switch so they could see around. Nothing happened.

"Oh. No way," said Brad

"Are you serious, the bulbs are dead?" Leon said from behind Brad, still in the hallway. "Shit. Where the hell are we gonna get bulbs for this place at this time of night?"

"I don't think the bulbs are dead…" said Brad.

Pulling his cell phone out of his backpack, Brad flipped it open.

"Who you gonna call with that? You don't have service in Europe, dude," Leon reminded him.

"It's not a cell phone right now, it's a flashlight," Brad shot back.

That's when Leon noticed a single electric cord running under the front door and into one of the back rooms. He followed it to a small desk lamp powered from the gallery downstairs.

"Man, this place is totally a squat," said Brad

"Oh you think so? I'm tired of this shit," Leon replied. "I'm going to sleep."

Next morning, Leon checked the shower and found they had no hot water. He was furious. Heading out of the apartment, through the gallery and outside, he and Brad walked down the street for some coffee. Leon was neck-deep in a defeatist funk and laid down on a bench, already calling it quits for the day.

"This is bullshit. The space they gave us makes the painting look wack, the apartment they gave us is totally illegal, and we got busted like punks last night. Man, fuck this," he fumed.

"Whatever man, we're in Berlin," said Brad. "Let's go walk around."

They decided to dedicate the day to figuring out how to deal with the mismatch between the giant wall and the small but incredibly ornate painting they had made for the show. Walking in, they were pulled aside by Micha.

"So I'm glad you slept in," he said. "The police were here this morning looking for you."

"What?" asked Leon. "The cops were here? What did they want?"

"We got into a little trouble last night," Brad admitted. "But they let us go. What did they say?"

"They wanted to bring you down to the station and properly finish putting you into the system. Ask you more questions I guess," Micha replied. "It doesn't matter."

"Well, why doesn't it matter? It matters a lot to me," said Leon.

"That's my ass we're talking about."

"Yeah, no I know, but they won't come back looking for you, I told them that you left the country very early in the morning." He laughed. "So they gave up."

"Yeah, Micha. That's my man right here. Thinking on his feet…" Brad smiled. "Thanks for taking care of that, dude."

"Yes, no problem. I'm happy that you are having a good time here. Let me know if you need anything…" And as simple as that, Micha was off helping another artist.

The two went outside to get some air.

"Well that's it man, we're done," said Leon

"What do you mean we're done? We just got here. I'm not done." Brad replied.

"We've been here twenty-four hours, and the police already know our names and where we're staying. We do something now and we're fucked," said Leon. "I'm not going to jail in Berlin, man."

"Listen I don't give a fuck if I go to jail in Berlin. I'm just happy to be here," Brad shot back. "Dude you've got to relax, worry about one thing at a time. What do you want to do about the wall?"

After some discussion, the two eventually came up with a solution that would be big and attention-grabbing, directing everyone's eyes right to the painting. They made the requests to the gallery for supplies and with their newly acquired materials, started painting a gigantic golden arrow stretching eighteen feet along the wall, pointing at their painting.

As they worked they were joined by Swoon and Polina, who decided they preferred the vibe in the smaller, but still spacious, gallery. The two women worked on the floor on the street art they would be putting up in Berlin, while the boys stole glances at them and what they were creating.▐

▐ Swoon was working on the cutout *Beuys Don't Cry* based on the German artist Joseph Beuys's New York performance piece *I Like America and America Likes Me* (1974), for which he wrapped himself in felt and spent three days in a room with a coyote.

With the issue of the gallery wall out of the way, Brad and Leon pulled together and started feeling more positive. Wanting to make the most of being in Berlin, they decided to go out that night and test their luck again. The two got ink from the gallery supplies and went out writing witty quips on the walls of buildings and storefronts just to shake how shook they were. Phrases as silly as "Brooklyn in Die Haus" were scattered around the blocks surrounding the gallery and beyond into other parts of the city.

With this night a small but effortless success, they got their land legs back and began rethinking their luck. This time they started planning big. With one night's reckless abandon, they felt refueled and hopeful. They decided they would spend the entirety of the following week doing two enormous booms, three if they could manage it. With that in mind, they spent each day that followed from sunup till sundown arranging for the mammoth work before them. As Darius and Downey, they had only done five or six booms total, and to plan on doing two in a week was no small task.

Besides having to find the locations that would properly showcase their work, and ways to get up there in order to paint it, they would also need rollers, roller extensions, and a great deal more paint.

They turned to Adrian for the paint and when they told him of the plans, they were met with a smile from ear to ear. They were still working out the specifics but they wanted to go big, letting everyone know they were there, and Micha and Juergen were excited to see what they would come up with.

Brad and Leon had been thinking about who exactly would be the first to know they were in Berlin making street art. The city's other graffiti writers would clearly be the first to notice, but after them, coming a close second, would be the police – the only other fan base that turns graffiti artists into minor celebrities. Poking fun at their own luck thus far with the police, Brad had an idea to paint a detective's magnifying glass high above the street with themselves lifesize inside it. Underneath the painting they would write "Actual Size" in German and sign it Darius and Downey.

After calling upon Micha's help for a translation, Brad and Leon mentioned to him that they had brought the hammer drill to Berlin and planned on installing some work there. They asked Juergen, through Micha, if he would be able to find them a construction vest. The man chuckled and said that it would be no problem; the gear would be in the gallery when they got home from going out that night. Then Juergen asked if they would wait a moment, as he ran over to his briefcase. Walking back with a folder in his hand, he handed it to Brad and Leon.

The folder was full of developed photographs of each and every tag Brad and Leon put up the night before.

"They are yours right?" Micha translated for him.

"Yeah… wow," said Brad, amazed.

Brad and Leon later hypothesized that he must have taken the pictures when the ink was still wet for him to have them developed by morning.

Going out the following day to buy more supplies, Leon and Brad jumped on the subway, riding the mass transit system the same way they had been riding it for the past four days, without giving any thought to paying the fare. For the first time, they found some trouble. Almost immediately they were pulled off the train, taken aside, and ticketed.

"How are we gonna do what we need to do and still have time to figure out how to pay this ticket?" asked Leon.

"I'm not paying shit. We're already in the system and if we show up to pay it after Micha lied for us… no. Fuck that," replied Brad.

Leon agreed not to think about it for the time being, the two having more than enough on their plate already.

The first spot they picked was actually accessible from the squat apartment above the gallery. They were limited on materials and time, but they decided it would be best to test their luck close to home and gave it a shot.

Once up on the roof, they realized just how quiet the location was; every sticky slap of the paint-covered roller against the wall echoed through the courtyards below. Leon was steadily working on the magnifying glass while Brad watched, both spooked by the sound made at every pass.

As Brad stood there with Leon, about to start painting the stick figure self-portraits, they heard a car stop nearby and two doors slam shut. Freezing, they listened to the German men speak hurriedly and decided to play it safe. The boys had been having terrible luck and rather than risk it all and push through, they decided to take advantage of how close they were to home base, grabbed their supplies, and hurried back into the squat.

The following morning while at the gallery, Micha rushed over to them.

"Juergen showed me your new piece, it looks great, just great," he said.

"Um, no," replied Leon. "He must be mistaken."

"Really?" said Micha. "I'll go get him."

Walking back with Juergen, the boys were handed another folder.

"This." Micha said. "This is yours, right?"

They were handed a picture of the half-finished piece from the night before. Brad and Leon began to explain that it wasn't finished, but decided to leave things be, saying simply, "Check that out again tomorrow."

That evening Brad and Leon went back to the roof, eager to have a completed piece up in Berlin. Brad immediately went to work on the figures, but still not having an A-frame ladder to work from, he had to stand directly beneath the piece to reach it. He proceeded with great care, not having any room for error on the unforgivingly bright white wall, and knowing that any noise could stop the evening short and bring a great deal of unwanted attention. Then as he finished painting Leon's trademark Cincinnati Reds hat in stilted perfection, Brad stepped his entire right foot deep into the bucket of black paint, ruining his new sneakers.

"Shit," Brad whispered, quickly catching himself from cursing any further, knowing how easily his voice would carry down the street.

Admiring the boom, Leon asked Brad for the paper on which Micha had translated "Actual Size" for them.

"You've got it," said Brad.

"No… he handed it to you," Leon replied.

"Well, I don't have it." Brad.

"What do you mean you don't have it?" Leon.

"I mean I don't have it. I don't have it and you don't have it. So let's try and remember what he wrote."

"This is stupid. The man took the time to write it down and we lost it. This is just stupid now." Leon was getting upset.

"It's not stupid, it's just what it is, let's do it and get out of here," Brad shot back.

So Leon painted the German words as best he could remember them, they gathered their materials and headed back into the squat, safe and sound with one Berlin mission under their belt.

In the morning, walking downstairs into the gallery, Brad and Leon saw Polina and Swoon already hard at work, making as many new pieces to put up as they could. Seeing Polina was still difficult for Leon, but here was a chance to impress her, and he took it. Pulling them away from their work, the boys took off around the block to show what they had been up to the night before. Showing the piece felt good. It was one thing to feel like they had brought a little bit of their world of Brooklyn to Berlin without getting slapped with any jail time, but another altogether to show it to loved ones from back home – to revel in doing things that were larger than life, together.

Letting the girls get back to work, Brad and Leon went a few blocks away for some cheap breakfast. While walking back to see the piece again and take another picture or two they noticed some activity on the roof.

The owner of the building was up on a ladder, already buffing it out, painting over their work from the night before. The man fit exactly within the magnifying glass they had painted with rollers over the two previous nights, and as annoyed as they both were, Brad and Leon did take a moment to marvel at how precisely they had painted both the magnifying glass and their self-portraits. The figures truly were "Actual Size."

Walking back into the gallery, they were approached by Micha and Juergen.

"It's great!" Micha said.

"Was it spelled right?" Leon asked. "We lost that paper you gave us."

"No!" he said. "But it looks great!"

"Did we even get close?" asked Brad, feeling a little guilty.

"You only forgot one letter, but it is very clear what it says." He smiled. "It is very funny seeing it up there! Very cool!"

The boys felt revitalized. Inspired by their success in putting up a boom without going directly to prison, even if taunted by its short life-span, Brad and Leon decided then and there to get back on the horse and do another.

Planning a piece showing a Molotov cocktail flying through the air, they perfected the idea with a little help from Micha, who suggested they paint the slogan "But It's Art!" in German underneath. He said it with the inflection of a young boy explaining to his mother. Brad and Leon loved it and what it said about the way street art was just beginning to find public understanding and acceptance.

They decided to do the piece at a spot that Brad had noticed the first time he and Leon got off at the Kottbusser Tor train station near the gallery. Through the giant window in the station lobby, there was a wall that was perfect. Running low on time, they asked the crazily prolific and talented writing crew CBS for a little reconnaissance information. The boys from CBS knew how to get on top of most of the rooftops in Berlin and were happy to help, showing them a back alley and fire escape that would get them onto an adjacent roof, which led to an iron-caged ladder bolted to the exterior of the building in question.

Once they had their materials together, the boys hustled and got there as fast as they could that evening. The part of town they were working in was closer to the center of the city, and so was significantly busier and louder and not concerned at all with the sound of a paint roller slapping on a wall. The operation ran as smoothly as they could have hoped, and they finished up quickly and got back to the squat. That night they slept peacefully for the first time since their plane landed in Berlin.

The next day marked the end of the stay for the other artists in the show and Brad and Leon said their goodbyes. Having worked day and night up to this point, they decided to stay another day in order to relax and enjoy the city. They said goodbye to Swoon and Polina, and began hanging out with the curator.

The three met for a few drinks at a nearby bar and with the pressure of the show and the booms behind them, they were all significantly more relaxed.

"So, NOW, we get some prostitutes?" Adrian suggested enthusiastically. "You want a girl to suck your dick? I know a girl who gives the best head in the city."

Leon just looked at Brad, who, after volunteering to discuss it before, should have known this was coming.

"Do you know any good parties coming up before we leave?" Brad dodged the question. "Some place we could go and dance and pick some girls up?"

"Oh! You want to pick up some regular girls?" He smiled, looking at Brad as if he had said he believed in magic. "Sure, I'll call around."

Seeming to know everyone in Berlin, Adrian quickly made plans for Brad and Leon's final night in Germany. Showing up at the party and seeing the line that wrapped around the entire block, the boys felt that they might be waiting a great long while for their fun. Adrian, however, walked them to the front of the line, said his name, and the three walked in.

The next eight hours consisted of Adrian putting a massive amount of drugs in his system and, ever the generous host, offering a bounty of dope to Brad and Leon as well. Leon declined, having no interest in feeling even close to how Adrian looked, but Brad, already drunk and not wanting to be rude, went ahead and smoked everything he was offered, thinking it was nothing more than weed. Soon, with everyone at varying degrees of blind drunk and drugged, the three left the club and went to a house party that was still jumping at 5am.

Leaving the party just after 7am, the boys were mentally already on their morning plane, due to take off at 11am, when Leon, the most sober of the three by far, remembered that they still had the clear panel to install.

"Get it together man," Leon said to Brad as he stumbled down the subway platform with Adrian. "We have one more piece to do."

"No man, we're done. It's time to go," answered Brad. "Shit man, look at me." Brad was leaning against a wall in the subway and pissing horizontally, soaking everything within an eight-foot arc. "I'm wrecked, and we have to be at the airport in four hours…."

Walking up to Brad, Leon whispered. "We have to do it Brad, we told Adrian we would do it."

Brad took some convincing from both Adrian and Leon. He didn't want to push their luck any further, knowing how messed up he was on drugs and only having a handful of hours left before they had to be at the airport. But finally he relented, asking, "You really want to do it, Adrian?"

"Yeah, it will be excellent for the film!" Adrian said excitedly.

Without looking, his face still against the wall, Brad mumbled, "Fuck it then, let's just do it."

With Brad doing his best to stand upright, Leon took the lead as the three made their way to a deserted Kreuzburg alleyway heavily saturated with street art. On the way, they stopped at Adrian's apartment to pick up the sign, ladder, and drill. Leon grabbed the ladder, Brad took the bag and sign, and Adrian excitedly picked up his camera.

Brad learned later that the weed in the pipe he was handed was in fact not weed, but a drug known by a mixture of letters and numbers instead.

In the alleyway, a veteran drunk leaned his bodyweight against a far doorway, pissing all over his shoes as he slept upright. Leon chose a spot on the wall above a convoluted series of aerosol letters as Brad dumped the tool bag down in a fresh puddle of urine.

"Yo man pay attention to where you put my bag!" Leon snapped at Brad, who was already opening the bag, not noticing the piss that was soaking through the bottom.

Positioning himself to get the shot he was looking for, Adrian made no effort to keep matters discreet this late in the game.

As Leon started the hammer drill, the drunk suddenly came to, and looking at the men in construction uniforms working so close to him, shamefully tucked his business away and ran hunched over towards the exit of the alley. The first and second holes that Leon drilled to install the sign went smoothly, as did fixing the anchor bolts. But on the third hole, the drill bit snapped and was left sticking out of the wall like a steel splinter. The three froze in horror.

"Shit," Leon muttered looking at the broken end still in the drill. "Well, if this drill bit stays in, then it should be safe enough to stay tight," Leon said as he dismounted the ladder.

Brad, worried that any unnecessary time spent mulling around with their business out was foolish and likely to land the two in jail, took the ladder and folded it while Adrian paced back and forth capturing the sign from different angles.

"Yeah, it looks great. This is going to come out great for the film," Adrian said as he smiled at the boys putting away their gear.

With the sun now fully hanging over Berlin, the three escaped back to Adrian's apartment to wait for a car service to the airport.

"You two will always be welcome back in Berlin," Adrian assured them once their car arrived. Pulling out for Tegel Airport, the boys breathed a little easier, thanking their luck that Berlin was a city so incredibly welcoming to international street artists. As far as introductions to Europe go, Brad and Leon were very lucky indeed.

Aber es ist doch Kunst, Darius and Downey, 2003. Berlin.
Duration: 4 years and counting.

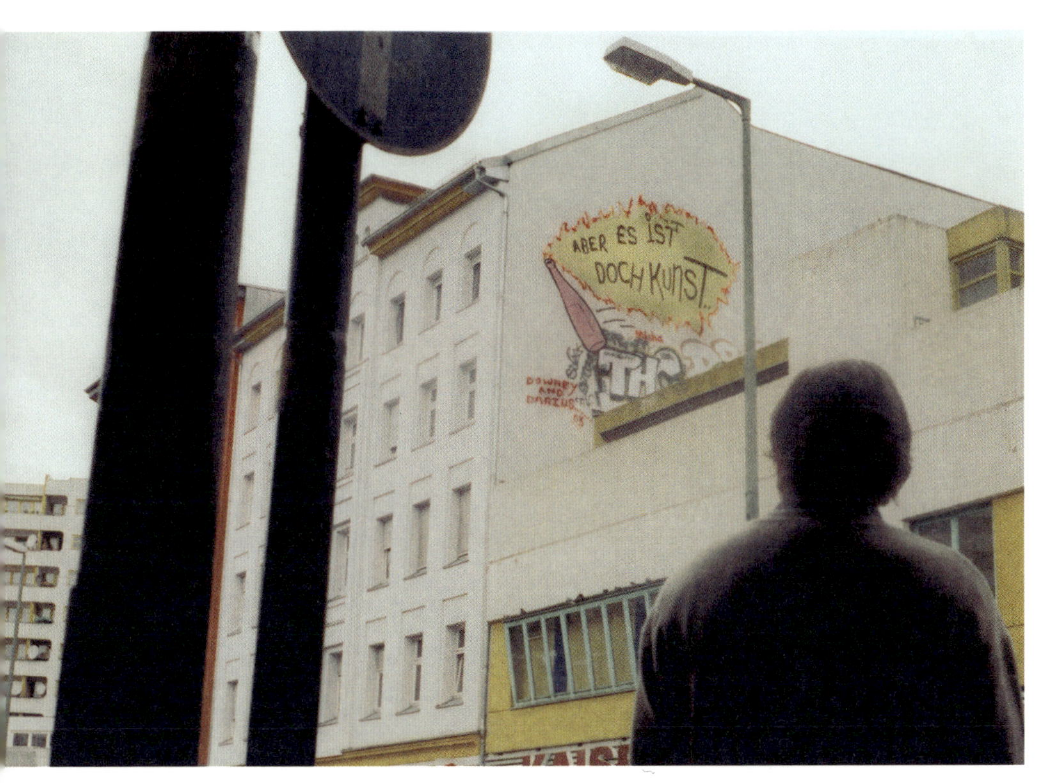
ABER ES IST
DOCH KUNST.
DOWNEY
AND
DARIUS 05

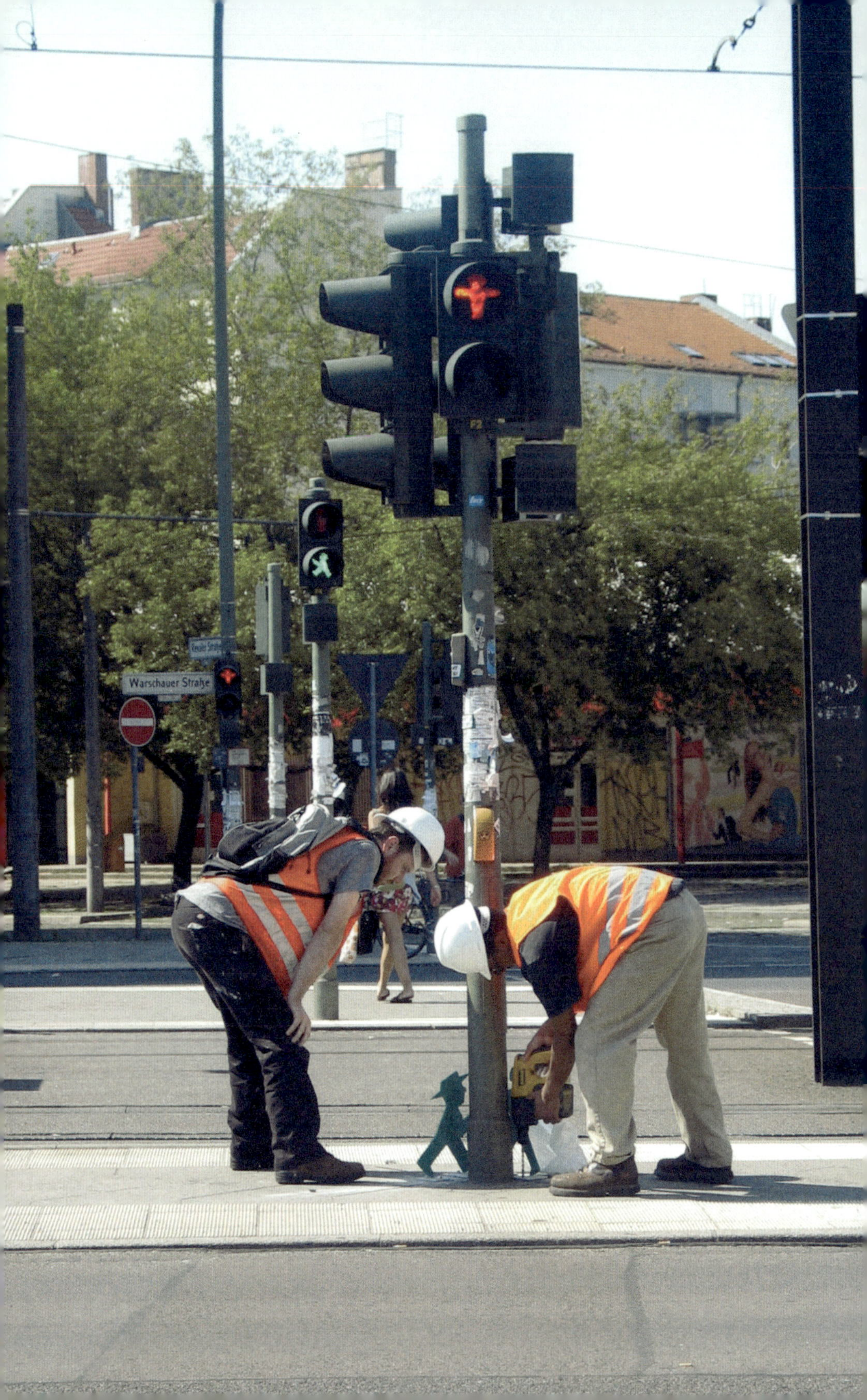
Warschauer Straße

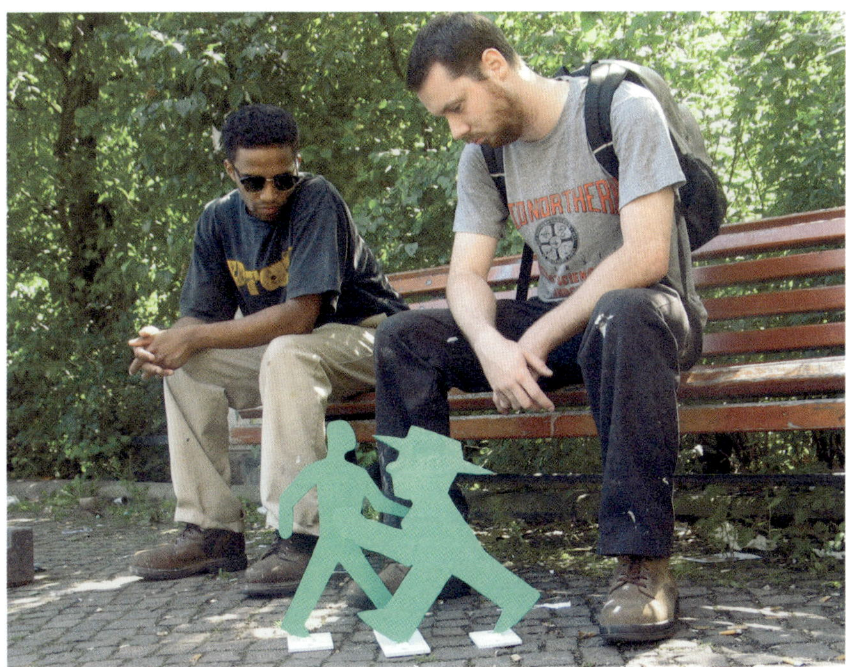

Ampelmännchen, Darius and Downey, 2005. Berlin.
Duration: East Berlin figure 2 hours, West Berlin figure
2 years and counting. Photos by Julia Tingulstad.

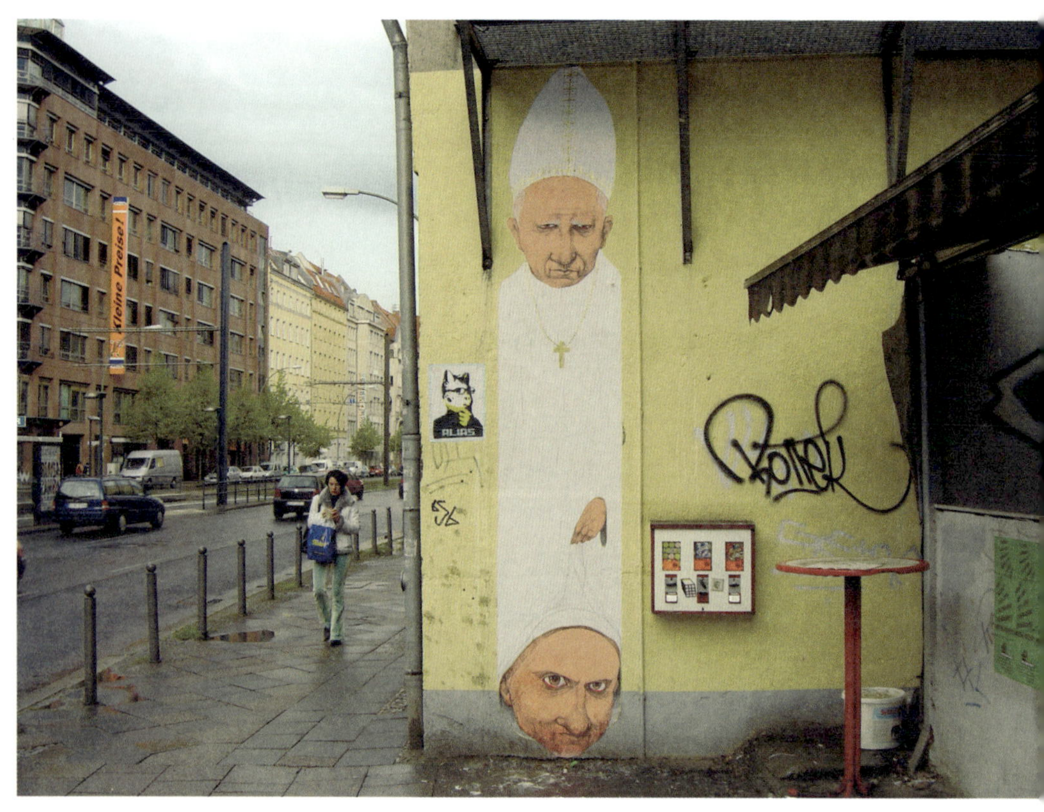

Revealing Benedict, Polina Soloveichik,
2005. Berlin.

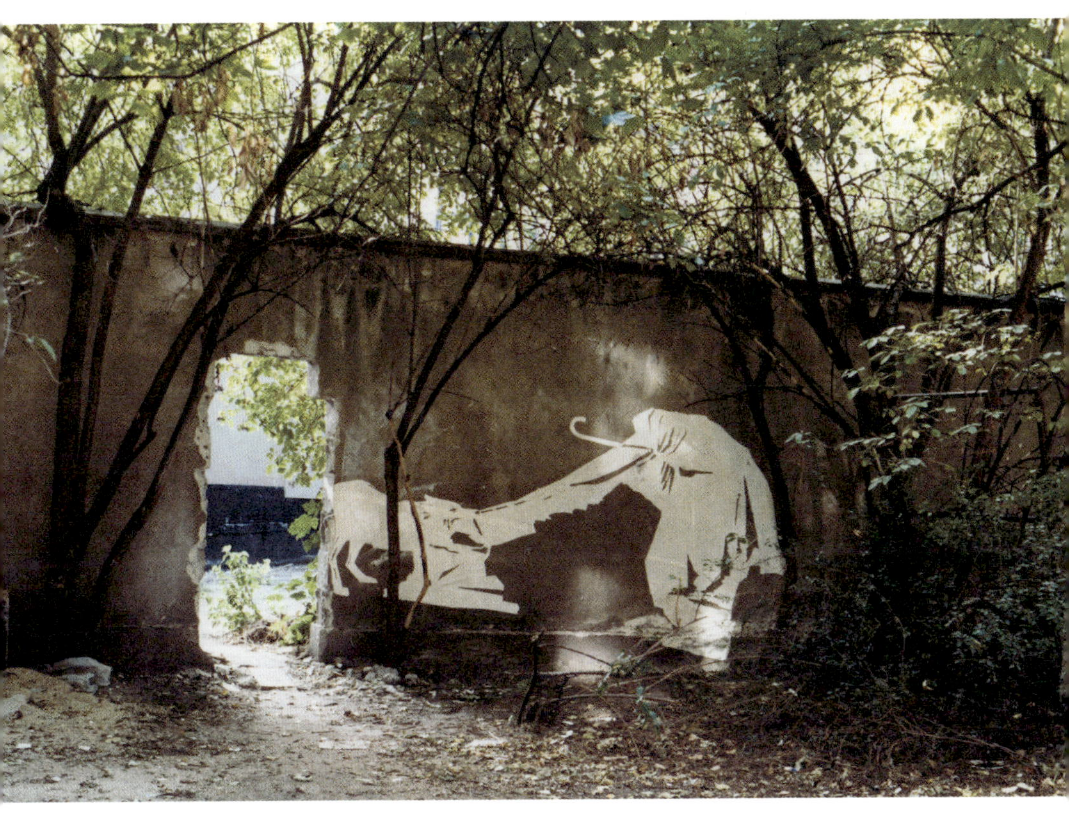

Beuys Don't Cry, Swoon, 2003. Berlin.
Photo by Juergen Grosse.

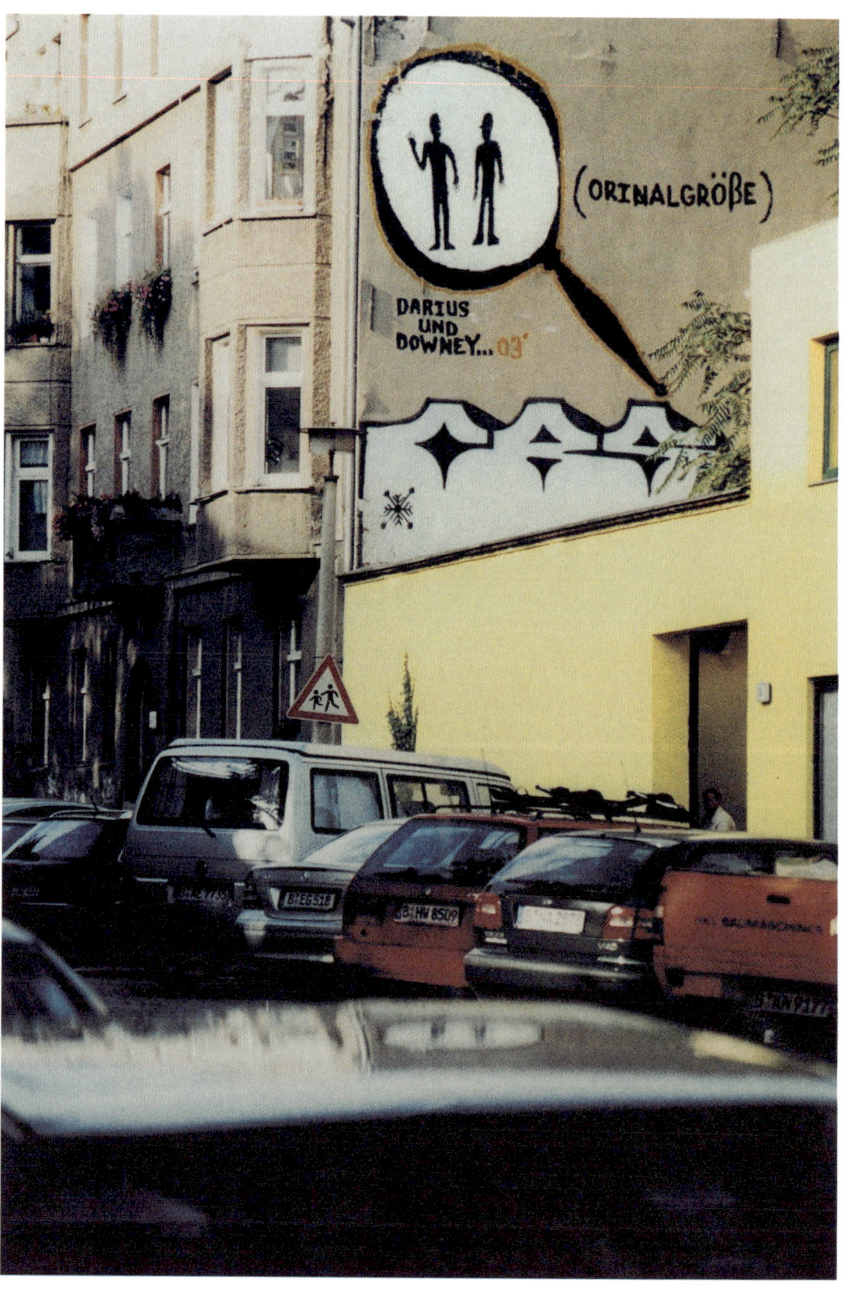

(ORINALGRÖßE)
DARIUS
UND
DOWNEY... 03'

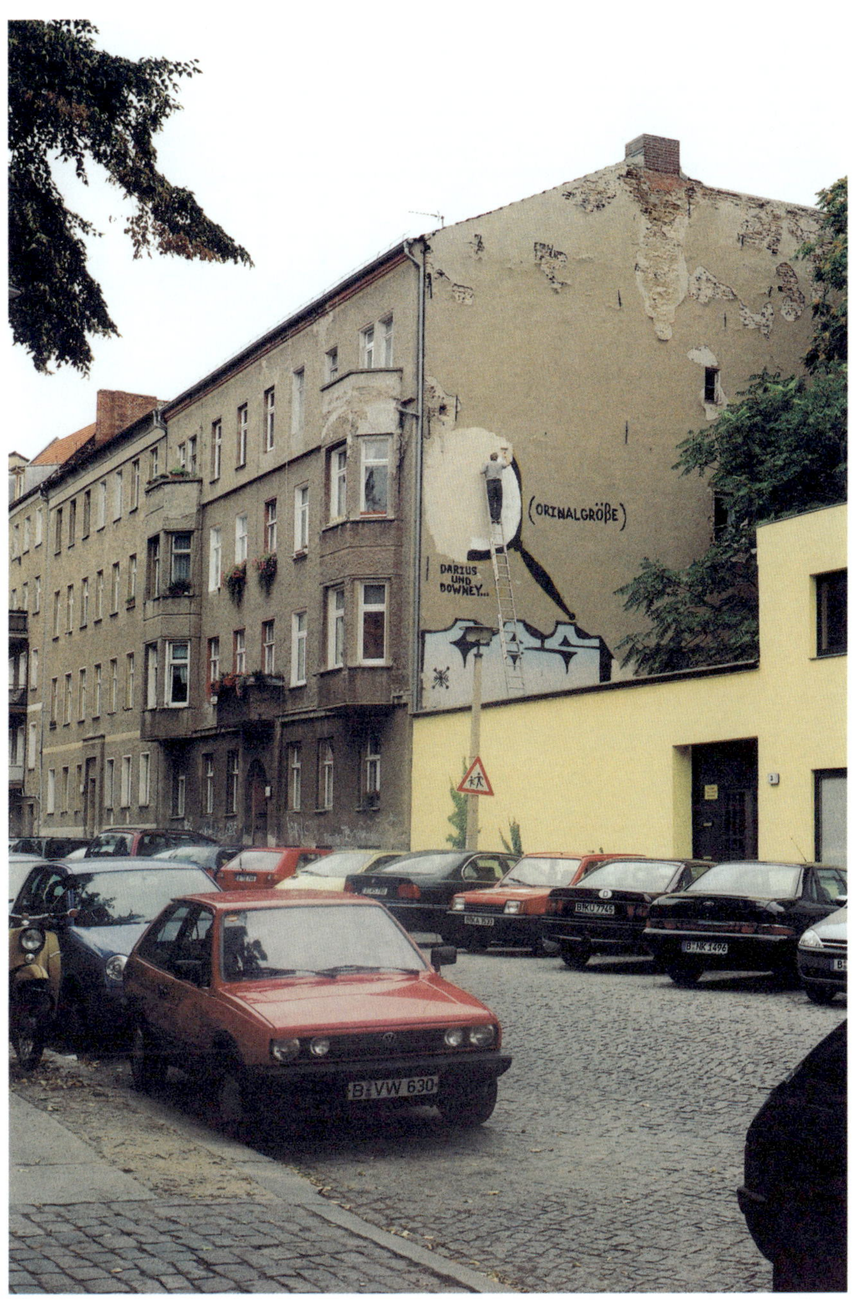

Originalgröße, Darius and Downey, 2003. Berlin. Duration: 3 days.

BELISHA BEACON – DARIUS

2004 | Leon and Brad land in London and are faced with adjusting themselves, as well as their work, to the new cultural climate. Leon, not having an easy time of it, soon begins to resent the new bold flavor of English bureaucracy. Unable to work with the ease he had grown accustomed to in Brooklyn, Leon makes a brash decision in the placement of one of his more beautiful pieces. He and Brad learn all too soon that street art has a very limited lifespan in the borough of Westminster.

By the late spring of 2004, Brad and Leon were living in London, getting master's degrees at the Slade School of Art and Central St. Martin's respectively.[*] Although they arrived together, their luck of the draw in the housing lottery differed greatly. The student housing for the Slade was in the heart of the city, while Central St. Martin's, despite the name, was far on the outskirts of town. In New York terms, Brad's apartment was in the equivalent of Union Square, convenient in almost all regards and within walking distance to the art scene, as well as fairly upscale. Leon was living in Tooting, the equivalent of Jamaica, Queens, miles away from any kind of civilization whatsoever, much less the art world. For the most part, this section of the city was reserved for low-income projects and offered cheap housing for the college to dump international students. Leon had drawn the shortest of short straws, and was visibly bitter and vocally salty.

But there were positives. Back in the center of London, near Brad's studio, the city had sectioned off a street corner with a flimsy temporary fence and was slowly filling it with damaged street furniture and equipment as well as what would be replacing it. To Leon and Brad it was a gigantic Christmas stocking and every few weeks when it was refilled was another yuletide payday.

Walking by this storage area one day, Brad saw two Belisha beacons (black and white striped lamp poles with a glowing yellow ball on top) pushed to the side, ripe for the plucking. With a quick phone call to Leon, the two were soon suited up in their construction gear and dragging away the city property. They agreed to house the beacons in Brad's studio for the time being, and set about inspecting their new toys.

One beacon was shorter and its pole slightly bent as if a car had clipped it, while the second was paint-damaged but straight. Leon looked them over, then looked over at Brad, who was drinking a beer he had found in the studio refrigerator he shared with other artists, the contents of which he had recently decided were communal.

[*] Quenell was also in England getting his degree, but he was at school in Manchester. He loved it there, but was rarely able to make it to London to visit.

"Can I have both?" Leon asked, and then without waiting for an answer said, "I've got this idea to have them talking to each other."

"Uh, no." Brad laughed, half upset. "I found them, I mean… I'll give you one… but that's it."

"Well… All right, all right. I just figured it couldn't hurt to ask," Leon conceded reluctantly.

"It's nice enough that I called you at all and decided to share one. You're talking about taking both?" asked Brad, a little indignant.

"Well, I didn't hear you talking about having an idea for them… I mean… whatever, man. Ok, ok." Leon backed down. "I'll take the bent one."

With the discussion closed and the beacons safely stashed in his studio, Brad finished his beer and they both headed out for the night.

Over the next few weeks, both were preoccupied with their plans for the summer. Brad's longtime college girlfriend, Susanne Hertell, was waiting for him back in New York and he would be leaving soon, while Leon was heading out to Spain with Quenell midsummer to run with the bulls in Pamplona. When Brad took off to the States, he gave his student ID card to Leon, and with it access to his more convenient studio space for the summer.

Leon found himself in London without a partner in crime, as it were, and had to make do on his lonesome. Always a complete workaholic (like Brad, for that matter), he found himself unable to think of anything other than the Belisha beacon. But before he could do anything, his first challenge was getting the hundred-pound pole to the metal shop he had access to, near his studio, several miles away. Not having a car available through either owner- or friend-ship, transportation of their work was always an issue. To move such a heavy object by himself… Leon felt like he was risking his neck, legally and physically. And he was.

It took him two hours to haul the awkward lamp pole to his St. Martin's studio in a handtruck through an unforgiving and densely populated city sidewalk. Upon arrival, he was met with a smile from the sole security guard left to man the lobby during the few summer hours the building was open. The metal shop, Leon was informed, had closed just the day previous. There was one school official on campus with the keys to the shop in case of an emergency, whatever that might be, but even the official wasn't permitted to operate any of the equipment.

Confident that this counted as an emergency, Leon tracked down the school official and, defying every prideful bone in his body, begged for access. The woman, against her better judgment, did the best she could do. Leon was granted access to the room, but just to the tools he needed to cut the pole into three slightly less cumbersome, significantly less heavy segments. It would have to do. For more complicated sculptural surgery the official told him of a less well-equipped but functional metal shop at Central St. Martin's sister school, Byam Shaw, six or seven subway stops away. With the pole chopped into three still weighty shorter sections, the trip wouldn't be fun, but it could be achieved solo. He was finally getting closer to being able to start thinking about what he would be welding.

After six trips back and forth on the Underground, everything was at last where it was supposed to be: Leon's hands were on welding equipment, however archaic, and were ready to go to work. His original idea, just an impulse really, was to accentuate the bend. Over the days spent just transporting the pole somewhere he could work, he had had a lot of time to think it over and he'd been doing a lot of sketches.

Leon at the time was dating a young French girl named Sophie, and so he was in a romantic frame of mind. His best work always came from love and loss, though when the idea for the piece finally came into his head, he didn't assign it to Sophie or anyone else, just to the emotion itself. Love would take control of the beacon. He would accentuate the bend, making it lean towards another light pole as if to give it a kiss.

Once the pieces were back on the operating table, the first thing Leon did was weld back together the two upper segments. Then he made shallow horizontal cuts along the length of it, chopping it bit by bit, six-foot-hero-luncheon style, nineteen cuts in all. At each cut, he bent the pole slightly, just a few degrees, and then welded it back together. Like every other aspect of this work, it wasn't the best way to go about executing the idea, but it was the only option available to him at the time. So he continued the monotonous, tedious task of cutting and welding, cutting and welding, until the job was finished.

With the Lover Beacon now in two pieces, back on the Underground he went, mutated city property in hand. He left both pieces in the hallway of his studio building, the proper storage room, like everything else, being closed at the time. That done, he took a well-deserved two-day break, and spent a little quality time with Sophie.

On the second day of Leon's R & R, he got a letter in his postbox at the dorm. It was a written reprimand for leaving the beacon in the back corner of the corridor, detailing the ways that it was creating not only a fire hazard, but blocking the better part of the hallway. For the letter to have arrived so quickly, it must have been written moments after he had set the beacon down, and put in express delivery. Leon wasn't catching a break. His London experience was in full effect.

The following morning, Leon showed up at the studio building ready to do what he had to do. Well rested, he was prepared for the hard work of hauling the heavy street lamp up four flights to his personal studio space, and out of the reach of further reprimand by absent/ invisible school officials. However, when he walked to the back of the hallway, he discovered that the base had disappeared.

Revisiting the security guard who was of little help before, he found him to be even less help now.

"Uh, hello sir?" Leon approached. "I left some of my art back there in the storage area, and now I can't find it. Have you seen anyone walking around with a striped post and stand?"

"Sorry mate, 'aven't seen a thing," the guard replied. "To be honest, I 'aven't been lookin'."

It wasn't a surprise. The only thing the Security Guard would have noticed was if the base itself had tried to walk into the school building…

without a current school ID. Otherwise, the guards pretty much turned a blind eye to every moment in their day. Someone could have easily walked out with it and taken it home.

Having spent time at Pratt Institute in Brooklyn, sharing studio space with privileged and unprivileged thieves and deadbeats alike, Leon didn't give it another second's thought: he immediately set about rummaging through every student's personal studio he could find. He had been around the block once or twice, and well knew that art students are more often than not selfish destructive egomaniacs who believe themselves invincible. Inside of ten minutes he was happily hauling the recovered base up to his own studio, as the paint he had kicked all over the thief's floor began to dry.

Having it all in one place, safe and sound, Leon went looking for his friend the school official; he had one more favor to ask. This round of begging (and the situation demanded begging) was considerably more difficult, she having been the one who took such issue with the "fire hazard." Blending apology with a renewed vigor for begging like a master saucier, Leon eventually turned the frigid Londoner into a soft touch. He was in.

A quick weld later, the two pieces were reunited and structurally sound; now all it needed was a paint job. Black and white stripes weren't the most complicated thing to paint, but for the sake of involvement, Leon called Sophie and had her help out. Once that was done, the piece was ready to go. And so was Leon: it was time to head to Spain.

While in Spain, Leon, and Quenell met with another friend of theirs from Brooklyn, Ed Zipco.[*] After bonding heavily through the adrenaline charge of the Bull Run in Pamplona and the citywide Basque riot of

---

[*] Ed had recently come into some money by bankrupting a short film with his signing fee, and with the collapse of said film, had plenty of time on his hands to travel. Hearing about the Bull Run, and missing his friends Brad, Leon, and Quenell, Ed quickly sold all his worldly possessions and bought a plane ticket. Following a stop in Japan for a few weeks of whiskey and peyote, he made his way to Spain via Paris. After several days spent living in a public park, he eventually found his long-lost friends, and soon they were all happily in harm's way.

the San Fermín fiesta, Leon, Quenell, and Ed said goodbye to Spain and headed back to England.

Back in London, Leon and Ed were counting the days until Brad's return from New York – which was difficult, since Brad is notoriously uninterested in dates and times when it comes to matters of air travel. He and Leon were scheduled to give a lecture at a street art symposium at the Urbis exhibition center in Manchester, and Brad was heading home early so they would have some time to practice. When he finally touched down and made his way to Leon's dorm, the two of them got serious, and before they knew it, they were on a train to Manchester.

The exhibit at Urbis featured street artists from around the world, including Swoon and Espo from New York, Os Gemeos from Brazil, others from Japan, and many from Europe. The show also featured documentaries on street art such as "Wild Style" and Brad and Quenell's film "Public Discourse." Before they knew it, it was time for the lecture, they were in front of a room of their very successful peers, and they had their game faces on. They came on stage to the sounds of Handsome Boy Modeling School's "Gorgeous" set to repeat, introduced themselves, killed the lights, and started showing pictures of their work and explaining what it is exactly that they do.

Suddenly, near the end of the presentation, museum security busted in the lecture hall, rushed the stage, and took Brad and Leon into custody, with screams of arresting them for vandalism done on and around the museum and Manchester as a whole. The entire audience scattered, most of them graffiti writers and street artists themselves who did not want to be picked out of the crowd and hauled off beside Brad and Leon.

What the crowd didn't know was that Leon and Brad had organized the stunt with the heads of Urbis days in advance. With the cooperation of two massive security guards in black leather jackets who were more than happy to violently hem up some skinny kids, everything came off very genuine. After hiding a while in the rear stairwell, the two took off running through the streets of Manchester and back to Quenell's dorm room fourteen blocks away, far from any questions about their arrest. The lecture was a roaring success.

After saying goodbye to Swoon the globetrotter,[*] Brad and Leon got back to business. At Urbis, Quenell had met a journalist who was interested in Brad and Leon's work, and had linked them up. The boys decided it might be interesting for him to come along for the installation of the Belisha beacon.

After meeting up at his office, Brad, Leon, Ed Zipco, and the journalist all walked the ten blocks to Leon's studio. Once inside, the two artists laid out their equipment and showed off the gear that they employed to install their illegal artwork: hammer drill, wrenches, construction worker costumes, and hard hats. It was an impressive display.

Leon was excited to install the piece, excited about the attention from the journalist, excited to get going. He started putting on the vest. Brad stopped him.

"Hey man, don't suit up now. We still have to walk out of here," he said. "Wait until we're closer."

Mixed with the excitement, Leon was anxious. Anxious enough to ignore rules that he himself set in stone years earlier, such as the one that said vests are only to be put on a block away from the installation, and taken off once a block away from the completed work. Day-glo vests make a pretty efficient profile description, but if you follow the rules, you put on the vest, do the job, drop the vest in a bag, and disappear.

But Leon had a near-terminal case of tunnel vision and he wanted to get going. As soon as they stepped foot outside the school, he threw the vest on, leaving Brad with little choice but to follow suit. The journalist and Ed stayed about twenty feet behind them as they handtrucked the curved beacon to its installation site.

---

[*] Days later, back in London, Brad, Leon, and Ed spent some quality time with Swoon, who rode the train back with them for a quick stopover at the BBC. Swoon was scheduled to guest star on a children's program to teach kids the "ins and outs" of wheat-pasting posters, and somehow was able to sneak Brad and Ed inside with her. The two walked around with wide eyes, like a pair of delinquent children let loose inside a government facility.

Through careful planning and investigation, Leon had found an existing Belisha beacon that was precisely the right height to interact with his sculpture. If he had placed his beacon next to any other, the kiss would have risen too high or fallen too short of the mark. Unfortunately its perfect match lived in Westminster. Referring to this neighborhood as upscale doesn't quite explain exactly how posh it is. The Palace of Westminster is the seat of the British government. As far as security goes, it is as high profile a neighborhood as it gets.

As Brad and Leon walked ahead of Ed and the journalist, slightly out of earshot, they began to argue.

"Why are you putting it here? It's not gonna last here. This is stupid," said Brad.

"Listen I don't want to debate with you where it's going. It's going where we're headed. That's all you need to worry about," Leon replied coldly.

"I don't want to see you just throw this piece away," Brad said. "I really like it."

"I'm not talking about this now. That's the end of it," Leon shot back.

"This is stupid. I'm not gonna tell you how this is stupid later tonight. It's stupid now." Brad gave up. "Fuck it, whatever."

There had been tension between the two since Brad got back from New York, but they hadn't had an opportunity to really get into it. Neither of them had had a chance to catch their breath since Brad touched down three weeks ago. The long and short of it was that Leon wasn't having a good time in London. When Brad left, he felt ditched

---

Admittedly, Leon was having a bad time even in his daydreams at that point. After the year of absolute life-wrecking depression that followed his breakup with Polina, he had gone with his best friends to another country to help get his mind off of the sadness and into new people, places, and things. The dismal rainy weather did not make London the greatest choice. Even so, Leon felt very strongly that on top of his personal issues with London, illegally installed street art did not stand a chance in the city. Every piece that was removed or stolen only further fueled his theory that England was not the place to be a street artist. He has since modified that theory, acknowledging that he was having a rough time in his life during his stay.

by his only real friend in the city, and it stung. The only comfort Leon could take was in his work, and the last few months had done nothing if not highlight the problems he was having working there. Meantime Brad was seemingly having success after success. Now that Brad was back, Leon was damned if he was interested in hearing his advice.

Once they reached the spot, Ed and the journalist positioned themselves on the opposite side of the street and tried to blend in with the tourists while Leon and Brad set down the beacon. The two spent a few seconds adjusting the placement; Leon wanted the beacons' light balls only centimeters apart, creating a spark of energy between them, the suspense of a kiss about to be delivered. Ed very slyly videotaped the entire installation, while the journalist discreetly snapped photos with his tiny digicam.

About five minutes into the twelve-minute installation, while Brad held the pole straight and Leon used the hammer drill, three men walked directly up to them. Everything stopped. Slowly, Leon stood up, and he and Brad turned to the men, both calm as anything. The three men began apologizing profusely for interrupting and unfolded a map. Then very politely they asked directions to the nearest Underground station. Not bothering to put on any kind of accent, Brad and Leon looked over the map and gave quick clear directions. Smirking to each other as the tourists walked off satisfied, they got back to work.

Once finished, they gathered their materials and set off back towards Leon's studio. As soon as they were a few blocks away, they stripped off the costumes and walked into the school looking just as they had a half hour previous. Ed lingered around the installation taking photographs of people interacting with the new beacon. Girls giggled, businessmen hung off it, a couple stood next to it and smiled. It was well received in the immediacy of people's reactions.

The journalist caught up with Leon and Brad sitting in front of the school and after getting lost for fifteen minutes, Ed joined them. The three friends said goodbye to the journalist, and went off to have a celebratory jacket potato, the cheapest hearty meal in town. After talking and eating away the adrenaline jitters, Leon split off to take another look at the beacon while Brad took Ed to see his studio.

A full three blocks away, Leon could hear a heavy "klang! klang! klang!" and his heart started to sink. Trying to get there as fast and as discreet as could be, Leon knew what he would find. Two minutes later he proved himself right. He got there just in time to see the beacon get uprooted with the moan of stretched metal tearing. Construction workers made short work of Leon's inanimate lothario, with sledge-hammers and spikes that ripped the metal around the bolts. Seeing it happen was more than Leon could handle. He quickened his step and walked a few blocks away, finally coming to rest on a park bench.

Feeling like his soul had just gotten ripped away from him, Leon thought about the events of the day, the last few weeks, the last few years. They had all rushed by him so quickly. He couldn't focus, he didn't know where he was. All his memories were so fluid, he couldn't grab onto a single one. He would think of something and just as quickly as he thought he had something concrete, it would mix with another memory from another time, all spilling into each other. He felt like he was coming apart.

It wasn't just the piece getting ripped down by this city, it wasn't just Brad waltzing in and out of his life on a whim,[*] it was everything, all together. It was right then he decided he needed to get back to Brooklyn. He needed to get himself together. He needed some American concrete under his feet. That would be a start. Just deciding that, he could feel his heart slow down. It was a step in the right direction.

Taking a deep breath, Leon dialed Brad's number.

---

[*] Growing up a military brat, Brad was constantly moving, and sees it as completely normal. Every now and again he gets out of Dodge quick, but usually to fulfill some commitment elsewhere. He won't leave anyone high and dry, but if he is uncommitted, he has no qualms leaving. He gets accustomed to new places quickly, and as an outgoing gentleman, he makes fast friends.

That's not to give the impression that Brad was innocent in the squabble that followed his departure. He was completely unable to see the damage him leaving was doing to Leon, who was, at that point, fairly codependent. The rift that was created in the Darius and Downey partnership is something that is being worked on to this day.

"Yeah, Leon. What's up?" Brad picked up his cell phone.

"They got it man, I could hear them taking it down with a sledge-hammer from a few blocks away. They took it," Leon explained.

"Shit… I'm sorry, man. You wanna meet up?" said Brad.

"Nah. I'll see you at the apartment," Leon replied as he hung up.

Leon just sat there for a second, and then got up. He went for a long walk and actually slowly started feeling better, knowing that this would be the last time London could hurt him like this.

When he got back to the apartment, having already accepted the loss of the piece, Ed showed him the photographs he took and handed him the video that captured the whole installation from start to finish. The photographs had Londoners, the real desired audience of the work, loving Leon's piece, leaning on it, hanging off it, staring wide-eyed and smiling at it. Leon's art did all of that in the time it was up, no matter how short that ended up being. The piece *The Kiss* remains Leon's favorite work of street art made by his own two hands to date.

BLINDING BIG BROTHER

2004 | Brad is made paranoid by the over-abundance of security cameras in London. After several lengthy discussions with Leon, he decides to strike back against Big Brother for the greater good of the public psyche. With close friend Jess driving the getaway car, Brad goes on his most stressful mission to date.

In London, Darius and Downey were surprised to discover they had another environmental element to take into account when picking locations to install their art. Not only did they have to adopt "English" construction worker costumes, they also now had to be constantly on the lookout for video cameras.

Both Brad and Leon had been struck dumb upon their initial arrival in London as they began to notice not one or two cameras in front of banks, police stations, pawnshops, and other high crime areas, but literally hundreds of them over the course of even a few city blocks. Big Brother was not only alive and well in the land of his birth, but it seemed they had upped his allowance and he had gone high tech.

Going to locations again and again simply to spot cameras that were spotting them quickly became as essential as their uniforms. It was a twisted game of *Where's Waldo*, looking for not only the large and obvious CCTV cameras, but also the more innocuous glint of glass that invariably meant they were being recorded by more discreet means, whether by bank, government agency, or wealthy private citizen.◤

Seemingly in tandem with Leon and Brad becoming more sophisticated in their disguises, with their official uniforms and mannerisms, Big Brother had been working smarter as well, installing his own version of functional street furniture. While the two artists had co-opted elements of the city environment that people had taken for granted and made them into positively oriented artwork, the city had

◤ Brad made the rampant use of video cameras in London the subject of a presentation during his master's program. The presentation took the form of a tour through Tavistock Square where it joins Woburn Place, an area adjacent to his studio. He assembled his tour group at one end and slowly led them down the street, inviting them to count every video camera they saw while walking the short distance. Not counting the street lamp at one intersection, which had three rings of cameras at different heights pointed in all directions and totaling eighteen cameras on the one pole, the higher counts were near thirty, topping off at thirty-one. Brad led them back to the beginning of the block and showed them the nine cameras they missed. This was by no means an official count, just a leisurely walk with an open set of eyes. Tragically, months later, this was the same London city block that terrorists bombed.

done something much more sinister and put up lamps, trash cans, and street poles that all doubled as video cameras.

These new technological leaps in surveillance weren't flawless yet; the black glass of the lens was still visible, for now, and the boys were fast becoming experts in the field. They would pick locations where there were blindspots in the all-seeing eye, though these were few and far between. Once they knew where the cameras were, and in what direction they were pointing, they would turn their heads, angle their bodies, and shield their faces from view whenever in uniform.

Earlier in the summer of 2004, Leon had done a piece consisting of two video cameras which choose to ignore the passing populace, instead turning their attention towards each other as if falling deeply in love. He and Brad installed the cameras on either side of a street corner, facing each other, lenses about four inches apart. To get hold of the cameras for the piece, Leon ordered a security catalog and researched the vast array of models on the market.

That's how he discovered that a recent trend in the video surveillance industry was the decoy model, a mock camera put up as a significantly cheaper deterrent than the more expensive – read functional – models. Leon ordered two. When they arrived, he realized that the majority of the video cameras they saw being used on private property were identical to the decoy models. These electronic red herrings all sported the trademark twin faux cables that ran from the rear to a false receiver; but they were powerless to put anything down on the tape, just fear out into the ether.

Walking around London one day, Leon spotted a corner building that had decoy camera after decoy, all pointing down at them, recording nothing. Twelve cameras in all, they gave the impression of angles overlapping, capturing every facet, every subtlety, even a bit of the camera stationed next to it. That is, if they had actually been working cameras. The constant surveillance, genuine or not, had been getting to both Brad and Leon, but neither had seen such a bold affront to date, especially an example of decoys used exclusively. It was one thing to be overly secured by an abundance of cameras, but to browbeat the locals with an excess of hollow boxes merely to give the impression of oppression. This was too much.

"We should take those down. That should be the next thing we do," declared Brad.

"What do you want to do to them?" Leon replied.

"Nothing. We should just take those down," said Brad.

"Well, where's the art?" said Leon.

"It's not about art, that shit's just terrible. It should go."

"We should leave something up there, like the arm," Leon said. "Just take the top part, so people that look up can see they're de-clawed and harmless."

Before they were able to complete the mission together, Leon was already on a plane back to the States. He was returning for good, leaving Brad alone with his thoughts on the subject and followed by cameras everywhere he went. The idea of redundancy, of these hollow objects seemingly making themselves more and more swollen and impregnated with images of Brad passing beneath, but in actuality barren all the while – it was insulting. Working with concepts of subtraction and exponential addition, everything began swirling around in Brad's head. He was slowly forming an idea.

It was the constant unblinking video feed that he felt weighed so heavily not only on himself, but the public as a whole. Like the all-knowing, all-seeing eye of God, this universal camera was invasive, but unlike a higher power, it was a physical presence. It wasn't just that Big Brother's eye was always watching, always judging and incriminating; it was the fact that the public was intended to know it was being watched, and was required to participate by behaving accordingly. Every person who spotted a camera would judge themselves as seen through its lens. It was creating a constant unease, a never-fail psychosis in the minds of the public. The content was the viewer, the tool of the medium was the message, and the result was inescapable guilt. Consensual, casual, or criminal, all was seen. Brad had never before been confronted by such an emotionally destructive force.

Video cameras suddenly became the haunting taboo of Brad's art. He figured that if there was one thing a governing force would not stand for, it was the manipulation or destruction of objects created to monitor its subjects. If this aspect of society operated as one big game of cops and robbers, then the thing that would invoke real punishment would be the dismantling of the tools of that game itself. The reaction that would follow such a move was a terrifying prospect.

Finally one day, months later, Brad bullied himself into stepping up. He decided to go back to the building that he had seen with Leon and to take down all of the video camera exteriors, exposing them as decoys. A friend of his named Jess, who had been filming Brad and Leon for a documentary, would join him and film the whole thing. Brad planned to be at the location at dawn on the approaching Sunday, before the subway was running, when the streets would be empty.[*] Luckily, because the lack of public transportation would also hinder Brad's getting around, Jess had a car.

Spending the night at Jess's, Brad woke around 4am, and the two started getting their materials together. Jess threw batteries into a wireless mic, which he would later attach to Brad, and loaded his camera while Brad got his backpack, which was empty except for a cordless electric screwdriver. Brad decided against bringing gloves, deciding they would only deprive him of the dexterity he would need to pull screw after countless screw out of the twelve cameras. They threw a large stepladder into the back of Jess's car and at around 4:45am they were off.

Showing up at the spot when the sky was just turning from black to dark blue, with the city at large still deep in REM sleep, Brad knew that even though they were right on time, he was under the shot clock. With

---

[*] Brad got the idea for his Sunday morning mission from the zombie film *28 Days Later*. Always wondering how the director managed to shoot famous London landmarks completely free of tourists during daylight on such a low budget, Brad saw an interview where Danny Boyle and Alex Garland explained that they shot those scenes at daybreak on Sunday mornings. The idea worked; it looked like the entire city had been evacuated.

every minute that passed now the sky would be getting brighter, people would be waking up, and the trains would soon be running. Jess was there to videotape, but he was no lookout. Brad rarely worked alone: to be one's own lookout was close to impossible, and to work blindly in the hopes that no one will notice is foolhardy at best.

Brad had decided early on that he wouldn't be using the construction worker costume on this mission. To remove these impotent objects, these decoys that were masquerading as intimidating official monitoring devices, he felt it was more genuine to dress normally. This time he was an ordinary citizen, taking back his rightful privacy, his uncatalogued innocence.

He set up the stepladder next to the first camera and began unscrewing the main housing. There were four screws holding the empty shell on. Once they were out, the entire thing slid off the metal arm that jutted out of the wall. The black lens, about the size of a bottle cap, wasn't attached to the box at all. Leaving this bizarre, black glass eye floating on the front end of the metal arm, Brad carried the housing down the steps, put it in his bag, and quickly moved the ladder to the next camera about five feet away.

By the third camera, Brad's hands were already freezing cold, and he was kicking himself for not bringing gloves. The dexterity that he was so worried about losing by covering his fingers with warm cloth was rapidly declining anyway, his hands getting noticeably number by the second. Watching his breath frost as he muttered curses to himself, he packed another camera in the bag, which was already filling up a little faster than planned, adding to his mounting list of problems.

At the top of the ladder at camera number six, his hands stopped working altogether. The screwdriver was slipping around the grooves of one screw, and suddenly caught, jerking it out of his fingers. As he saw it start sliding out of his grip, he panicked. He willed his fingers to close around it, but nothing happened. His hands tremored slightly, and then creaked. As the screwdriver began to roll back down his wrist, he pulled one of his arms back hard to pin it against his chest.

He pushed the screwdriver into his jacket and took a closer look at the last screw stuck in the camera. It was nearly out. He braced himself between the ladder and the wall and just ripped the camera clean loose with brute strength alone. Once back down he put the camera in the bag, filling it, and put both his hands in his armpits to warm.

He had taken down half the cameras; his bag was full and his hands had turned to wooden flippers that ached terribly with amateur's frost-bite. He was at a crossroads. He could take off now, job half done, but safe and sound, or he could go up and get back to work. He looked up and saw one of the cameras looking directly at him and for a second forgot that they were decoys. He felt a shot of panic that he had taken a breather and been caught in a moment of self-reflection.

As he recollected a split second later that the camera on the wall was fake, and registered that he had been assaulted yet again by these mechanical mental terrorists, his decision was made for him. He breathed warm air into his hands and set the ladder back up under the decoy camera that had spooked him.

The next three cameras came down like clockwork. Fast as anything he was up the ladder, four screws were pulled out and thrown to the ground, the camera was tucked under his arm, and the screwdriver placed back in his jacket. Then down to ground level, pick up the ladder and reposition it. He was setting it up and knocking them down.

Starting up again on the tenth camera, the thought of taking a moment to pause entered Brad's head. Halfway up the ladder, with the crisp air making his face hurt, he looked down the empty street and marveled. It had to have been for less than a second, but he thought how strange it was to see the streets empty. Not sparse, but really truly empty. Dead.

Then in the distance, there appeared a dot on the horizon. Far at the end of the street, a tiny, tiny car was speeding up. At that distance there were still options. He could cut and run or he could keep at it. The car could belong to a police officer; it could belong to the owner of the building. There was no way to tell. Brad stayed on top of the ladder and kept working.

As the car pulled up, Brad placed the screwdriver to another screw and continued his task. Then he looked down. Under the red traffic light was the car, and in the car was a middle-aged black woman staring directly up at Brad. She was taking the whole scene in, his bag on the ground, a growing pile of tan boxes that looked like exposed hard drives, a ladder set up next to a camera beside nine empty metal arms shooting out of a building with little camera lenses on the front of each. On top of the ladder was Brad, with a screwdriver, already pulling out another screw and tossing it aside, letting it hit the ground. Although Brad tried to hide himself entirely in the monotony of his work, their eyes found each other and locked. Brad counted slowly to three in his mind, momentarily hypnotized by her beady eyes and hard face. It seemed as if she was waiting for something, some tiny crack in his composure to come into focus, and she would come unhinged entirely, jump out of the car, run full speed to the ladder, and then Brad would have a real situation on his hands.

The light turned green and the car didn't move. The woman just sat there, neck craned directly at Brad's face, staring. Brad pulled the camera off the metal arm, routinely put it under his armpit, and came down. He stacked it with the rest of them, ignoring the woman, and placed the ladder under the next camera. Climbing the ladder, Brad could feel the woman's stare boring holes in the back of his head as he set the screwdriver to work on the next screw.

As his finger pulled down on the trigger to extract the screw, the engine of the car roared. The woman took off down the road. Brad thanked his luck and kept plugging on. As he came down with the second-to-last camera, he paused for a second to watch her disappear in the distance.

Swiftly climbing up the ladder to the last camera, Brad noticed the color of the sky had changed dramatically. The sun was now peeking out above the horizon and Brad knew his time was nearly up. Pulling that last camera out like an old pro, Brad slid down to the ground and quickly collapsed the ladder.

He threw his backpack on, tucked the pile of camera bodies under one arm, the ladder under the other, and finally spoke into the wireless mic, which he had completely forgotten about up to this point. The plan had been to narrate the short film live, with the very real fear audible in his voice.

"Ok Jess, I want to go now. Now," he said.

Rapidly walking around the opposite corner towards the agreed rendezvous point, Brad stopped suddenly and turned back. He had forgotten to view his handiwork. Seeing the naked arms, looking cheap, fragile, and not even slightly imposing, Brad was still too scared to smile, carrying all of the evidence of his crime, but he felt good for seeing it through. He wondered whether it would have been more helpful to the neighborhood to take down everything – arms, strange lenses, everything that made people feel watched. But that image of battered, skinned, and gutted cameras was a step in the right direction.

In what felt like twenty minutes, but was more like seconds, Jess pulled up and helped Brad load into the car. As they sped away, the sun was fully hanging in the air, and the clock read 5:55. The only video recording of the last two hours of Brad's life was entirely consensual, as it should have been.

BELISHA BEACON — DOWNEY

2005 | Visiting Miami to build a sculpture for the Art Basel fair, Brad gets a little turned around and has a full-blown revelation, inspiring art that will follow him back to London. There, on a mission that puts them in violence's way, he teams up with Matt Murphy to install a piece that keeps BBC radio abuzz for weeks.

While working in London, Brad was approached about a project by Tahu Deans, his friend and studio mate. Tahu had been commissioned to build a public sculpture for the Art Basel fair in Miami, and wanted to partner up. Brad was interested: he had never before had permission to do a public sculpture. Over the next few days, Brad tried to get Leon involved, but with his plane ticket already bought, his bags packed, his mind made up about London, and every sentimental bone in his body loving Brooklyn, the last thing Leon wanted was another detour before landing back in Brick City.

Brad and Tahu came up with the idea of creating a gigantic submarine surfacing in the middle of a local Miami park, miles away from water. Amidst American post-9/11 paranoia, the piece would represent all the ways, known and unknown, that the United States were vulnerable as a country and landmass, but more importantly socially and emotionally. A giant Iraqi submarine that could burrow through soft earth and rise in suburbia was a somewhat cartoonish expression of the fear of an enemy's penetration of virgin American soil, but the mood it represented was very authentic.

With only a week's room and board waiting for them in Miami before the sculpture would be presented, and a solid two weeks' worth of work to do it right, Brad flew down to Atlanta early to get a head-start. Brad and his father did the major construction of the big pieces, leaving it to him and Tahu to assemble once at the location in Miami. When everything was done, father and son loaded up the family truck and drove the thirteen hours to south Florida.

It was agreed that Brad could hold on to the truck while in Miami; his father would just hitch a ride with one of his pilot buddies at a nearby private airport. Clearly there were advantages to a career in aviation. When they pulled in to drop him off, the airport was already filling up with the personal Cessnas of returning Miami glitterati and international jetsetters visiting for the art fair.

On his way to give the park a once-over before picking up Tahu, Brad took a left, another left, and then ended up on an unmarked on-ramp which led immediately, thankfully, to an off-ramp. There was no question in his mind except for how it happened, but he was suddenly very lost in the complicated street/highway system of Miami. With cars whizzing by in all directions and having no idea where he should point the van, Brad sought help from the street signs all around the intersection. A giant sign on the pole before him read plain as day "Direct Route to Park Grounds," with an arrow pointing to his left. Brad breathed a sigh of relief until his eyes fell just beneath it, to a sign that was only slightly smaller reading "One Way Only" with an arrow pointing the opposite direction. Fantastic.

That's when it struck him. Not that he would have to stop and ask directions – that was obvious – but that he was face to face with something he had never seen before. If someone were to pay attention to these signs, they would actually be in worse shape than if they just followed their nose. It was staggering. It may have been the most idiotic thing he had ever seen. Redundancies that not only negated each other, but also actually acted as a subtractive force.

That chaos of signage would linger in his head through his stay in Miami. He assembled the submarine with Tahu Deans, without incident, and spent the remainder of his time there trying to get people to travel the two miles to the park. This was more difficult than it sounds, when every other piece of art was concentrated within the twenty most glamorous blocks in the state, while the park, though a mere two miles away, was frequented almost exclusively by crack addicts in the evenings.

One night, Brad and Tahu came across an art event featuring Brooklyn favorite Japanther, an art rock duo made up of Matt Reilly and Ian Vanek, two artists/musicians who had been at Pratt with Brad years before. Matt and Ian's art band was part of a performance piece that involved puppets, visible puppeteers, a projected film with puppets, and the musicians themselves on an extendable platform that intermittently came out of the wall and towards the audience. The work had been conceived by Dan Graham in the 1970s, and now, thirty years later, was fully funded and being presented to an eager audience. Hustling his way inside, Brad sat with Tahu in the backroom next to Dan Graham, and thought how this was one of the people who had helped Sonic Youth burst upon the scene. It was good to see Japanther doing so well.

The next day, while driving around, Brad came across one of the many city construction sites that litter the underpasses of the sloppy highway system. Pulling up to inspect it closer, he saw a stack of about fifty street and highway signs completely up for grabs. In a second he was loading sign after sign into the back of his truck. When he had twenty or so, he closed the tailgate and drove off, heavier and richer in raw materials than he had ever been so easily before.

Finishing up in Miami, and before heading back to London, Brad stopped off in Atlanta to drop off the truck and spend some time with his family. The ideas sparked by that intersection still fresh in his head, Brad began working on a sign to install during his visit. His parents had been asking recently if he could make a piece for them, something similar to his new work. With both the new concept and his parents in mind, Brad took one of the larger signs and picked a spot for it. Once he had the time to sit and focus, he completed it in an afternoon and put it up that evening. He installed it close to home, and waited for them to find it themselves.

On the side of the highway in Atlanta the next day, there was some important information being dispersed for the vehicular public. The sign was a full five feet across, eye-catching yellow, and succinct. It read "Ignore This Sign." It was impossible to miss. Brad's parents loved it.

The city didn't miss it, and neither did the local newspaper. Town Hall held in-house meeting after accusatory meeting, finally coming to the decision that they themselves did not install the sign. With their discovery of the obvious, they announced to the papers that the sign was incredibly dangerous and should be removed. A team was assembled and assigned with the task. Brad's parents laughed themselves silly over all of the attention.

Pushing the idea to the back burner as he returned to London, Brad, once in his studio, got busy on a clay sculpture he was working on at the time. As he worked he found himself repeatedly kicking around yellow Belisha beacon balls. Before he had gotten preoccupied with the submarine, Brad had been becoming more and more obsessed with the overabundance of Belisha beacons on the streets of London. Now he was finding them cluttering his studio as well.

When he first arrived in London he had found one such bright yellow ball and brought it to his studio as an ornament. After that it had become a habit of friends to swing by and drop off any that they came across. Quickly enough, he had three or four of the things, and they were getting in the way.

Brad had always been puzzled by the ever-present beacons, never getting a satisfactory explanation of their purpose, no matter how many locals he asked. Failing to uncover a clear rationale, he was left with the strong sense that they were primarily an antiquated relic held onto for reasons of aesthetic value and tradition.

The poles were painted with black and white stripes, and although the ball on top lit up yellow and blinked, it did little to light the surrounding area. The more he thought about them, the possible millions of these quaint objects throughout Britain, without any kind of real function, the more frustrated he got. When Matt, a friend who lived in a very upscale, almost suburban neighborhood in the middle of London, mentioned to Brad in passing the dozens of Belisha beacons he saw day in and out that were long burnt dead, Brad had had enough. The following day with a garbage bag and a stepladder, he began methodically removing them, taking them one by one so as not to be caught with a whole lot of stolen city property at once. He tossed them repeatedly into his studio, only to head out for more.

Now with an abundance of lights that lit nothing, Brad began stacking them in the corner of his studio, creating a collection that although initiated out of scorn, was growing into an image that was pleasing him more and more. There were seven yellow balls now, piled in a straight line to the heavens, duplicating itself higher and higher, a stack of functioning, yet non-functional objects atop each other. This was not simply quantity over quality, but replication and overlap almost to the point of meaninglessness.

With aid from a master craftsman and artist named Terry, who, over Brad's time in London, taught him a great deal and opened up a great many possibilities too, Brad found a way to construct the stack of balls, and how to light each ball from within as well. Unfortunately, time constraints and financial practicalities meant that the tower of lights was not to be, but in its place, Brad found a way to bleed the light from the base bulb through the whole of the sculpture, creating a pH-test strip of light gradients that he liked very much. The side effect of his experiments in filtering light was a slight sway and bow that would give life to the piece in high wind. Some found it phallic, which pleased Brad no end.

Quickly it became clear that others liked it as well. On a visit to his studio, Kay Saatchi, an ex-wife of Charles Saatchi, saw the piece and wanted very much to come back to photograph it. Unfortunately, Brad's timetable wasn't as flexible as he would have liked; he was scheduled to be heading to America soon and this would be his final installation during this stay in England.

Talking about the installation with his new girlfriend Julia, he decided to invite her along for her first mission. She invited a friend, a photographer from a London magazine, to come as well. Brad now had the makings of an entourage, something he didn't care for in the least, but wanting everything to be comfortable for his girlfriend, he didn't see the trouble with her bringing a friend, as long as she could control her.

The morning of the mission, Matt showed up at the studio. He was needed to help Brad carry the piece, which was just over six feet tall, as well as the two ladders they would need in order to get to eye level with the beacon itself. When he arrived, it was instantly clear to Brad that Matt had never done this before. He was Brad's near-doppelgänger, with identical hair color, haircut, and same length beard. But he arrived dressed conservatively in pressed slacks and a button-down shirt, not exactly common attire for a construction worker, no matter the continent. Brad, however, lent him a jacket very like the one he himself was wearing, and they were off.

Once at the location, meeting Julia with her friend in tow, Brad said a quick hello and got straight to work. They arranged the rickety aluminum ladders and began the ascent. Almost immediately, Julia's friend got on all fours and "set up shop" beneath the two ladders, getting every possible angle of the installation, while herself providing interesting angles in her miniskirt to passersby.

Ignoring the girl beneath them, Brad and Matt reached the top step of each ladder, the one clearly labeled "not a step," and from there, steadying themselves against the pole itself, stretched up on their toes, just as a dry run to see if they could do what they needed to without the weight of the piece yet in their hands. It was a balancing act, but it was possible. With the concrete sidewalk very much in their minds, they went back down a step or two and picked up the heavy stack of yellow balls. Although sturdily and strongly built, the stack had a great deal of sway to it, which meant lifting it was one thing, keeping it balanced another entirely.

Halfway up their respective ladders, holding the stack of balls between them, girl still beneath, unknowingly volunteering to break their fall should such occur, the men stopped. They were going to need help to steady the ladders. Brad was still doing his best to keep his girlfriend out of the criminal aspects of the installation; in his mind he was happy for her to be there to watch, but if she got arrested for helping, it might not be the best for the couple's future.

While Brad was adjusting himself to the necessity of putting Julia to work, a friend of Brad and Matt's named Rob walked past by chance. He was immediately recruited. Not thrilled to be involved, but having been promised that it would be over before he knew it, Rob was enlisted to steady the ladders while the two picked up the yellow column of balls and started the process of screwing in the four anchor screws at the base. In actuality, Rob only steadied one of the ladders with one of his hands, keeping the other in his pocket to look as nonchalant as possible. Brad and Matt were too busy sweating bullets to notice, standing on the tips of their toes, steadying the top-heavy stack so it didn't topple over and quickly turning down the four screws that would lock it in.

Suddenly, in the middle of the circus act that was being performed on the sidewalk, a man walked up and immediately started getting aggressive.

"Oy! What the fuck d'you think you're doing?" he said. "Fuck all, you work for the damn city, you twin bastards!"

He was in his early thirties, with a demeanor of intelligentsia that suggested he was connected with the nearby School of Oriental and African Studies, and he was already red in the face with anger.

Brad looked down at him and seeing he was a college student tried to appeal to his intellect. "We're installing a piece of art. To positively effect the public's environment."

"There isn't anything positive about what you're doing! This doesn't help the environment at all!" The man was incensed. He was furious, and worse than that, he was creating a scene.

Quietly, as the man hurled vulgar insults while screaming ways Brad and Matt could more positively interact with society, Rob started to dis-associate himself from the situation. Feeling his ladder go slack and almost falling backwards off of it, Matt looked down and saw that Rob's hand had let go of the ladder altogether. He had actually started to inch away step by step. Matt lost it.

"Rob! Hold the fucking ladders!" he screamed.

Rob quickly snapped back to reality, smiled up at Matt sheepishly and took hold of both ladders as Brad started tightening in the second screw.

With the man yelling at Brad full tilt, the girl on her back taking photographs, Brad and Matt on ladders, Julia on the sidelines taking more pictures, and Rob now firmly holding said ladders, it was quickly escalating from a scene to a spectacle. People who had been rushing by on the busy street stopped hurrying towards their important destinations, and started taking pictures with their camera phones of this piece of performance art they had stumbled across. A cab driver who was stuck in traffic started beeping his horn with excitement, perhaps trying to goad the two screaming young men into a fight. This was the perfect recipe for a sudden police presence.

With the honking and the crowd that was forming around them, and with only two screws in, Brad looked over at Matt.

"Hold tight for a second," Brad said.

Brad climbed down from the ladder and stepped about an inch from the man's angry face.

"Listen. You're done. Right now, you've got to go," Brad said, restraining every violent bone in his body.

The man simply looked at Brad and said nothing. Then Brad closed that inch between them and just touched his forehead to that of his adversary. If you blinked you would have missed it, but as soon as the man felt the contact, he snapped into the reality that he was about to be beaten in the street. Knees almost buckling, he stumbled backwards a few steps and looked at Brad and his friends. They were furious. The young intellectual got the hint, and without another word, quickly left.

With the possibility of a fight now nil, the cabbie sped off and the crowd dispersed, clearly more interested in a fistfight than a piece of public art. Brad got back up the ladder, and leaning even more against the pole now, screwed in the final two screws. Arms shaking, the two artists descended the ladders and dragged them across the street to look at their work from a distance, happy to have it up and their bodies done working for the day. He hadn't noticed it before, but when Brad saw the balls stacked atop the pole for the first time, making a symmetrical organic stem that connected the heavens to the earth, Brancusi's *The Endless Column* immediately came to mind. Brad decided on the spot that his piece would be called *Endless Column in Context*.

Brad didn't have time to go back the following day to get a fresh view of the work, but he was brought up to speed by an animated phone call late in the afternoon from one of his technical advisers, Gary Woodley. Apparently BBC Radio London had noticed the piece and had dedicated that day's show about "All Things Odd in London" solely to uncovering who or what was responsible for the sculpture.

The show's host Robert Elms declared that the work was seemingly too well crafted and smartly innocuous to be some kind of shock value prank. The BBC contacted the city department of public arts to see if they approved of the public sculpture as well as the nearby School of Oriental and African studies to see if it might represent some kind of social protest, hoping someone would be willing to come on the air to speak about it. Finding no answers, the BBC decided to cover the city's removal of the piece.

Only hearing about the broadcast after the fact, Brad tuned in the next day to hear what the program was like, and to his surprise they were still discussing the piece. During a phone-in segment Brad called in, explaining his involvement and his willingness to go on air. The woman who screened incoming callers asked a myriad of questions about the work, but when Brad answered them easily she called him a liar, explaining that his ability to answer the questions with such ease only supported her theory that the real artist would never call in. Clearly, she continued, he was nothing more than a well-researched imposter. If he had known less or, perhaps, been less forthcoming by not calling in at all, she might have believed he was the artist. With her theoretical Catch-22 proven irrefutably to her satisfaction, she promptly hung up.

Brad was frustrated that he was unable to discuss his piece on the air, but with the amount of attention it had gained, and seeing how popular the work was amongst the people of London, he felt a calm wash over him. He was finally communicating in the visual language of the London streets. His goal of becoming multilingual in his art was in sight, and Brad felt rejuvenated and even more driven. He was no longer limited by his past surroundings. The world was opening up to him. His art's language was becoming truly universal in its potential.

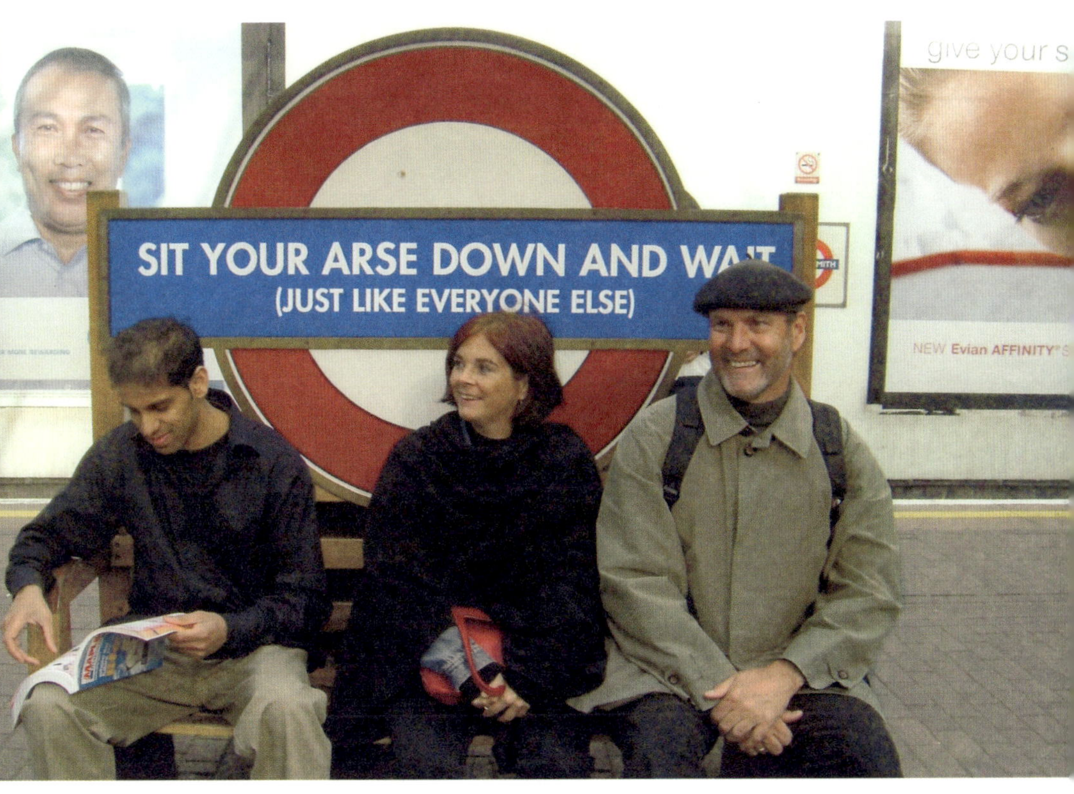

SIT YOUR ARSE DOWN AND WAIT
(JUST LIKE EVERYONE ELSE)
give your s
NEW Evian AFFINITY

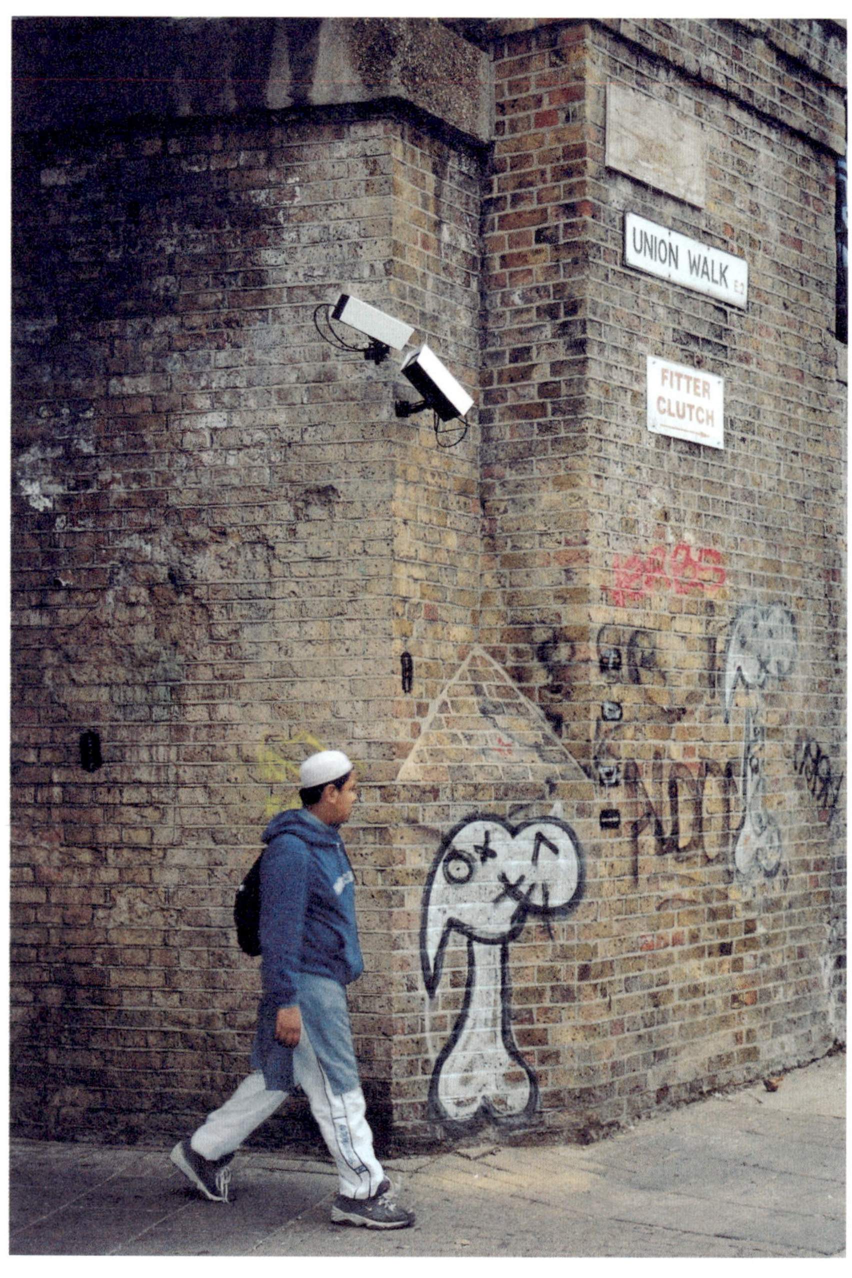

Eye To Eye/Big Brother Watching Himself, Darius Jones (Leon Reid IV), 2004.
London. Duration: 4 months.

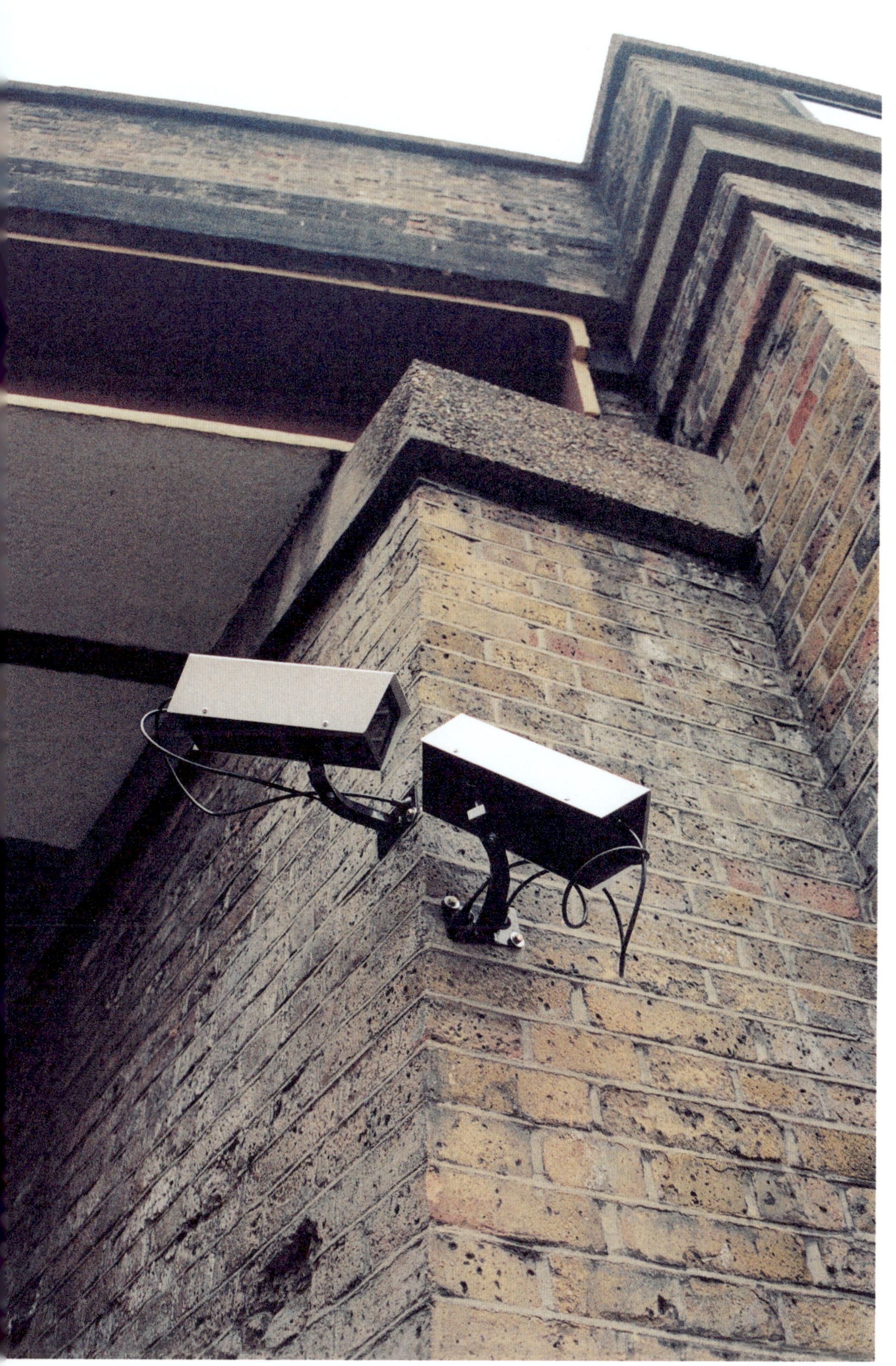

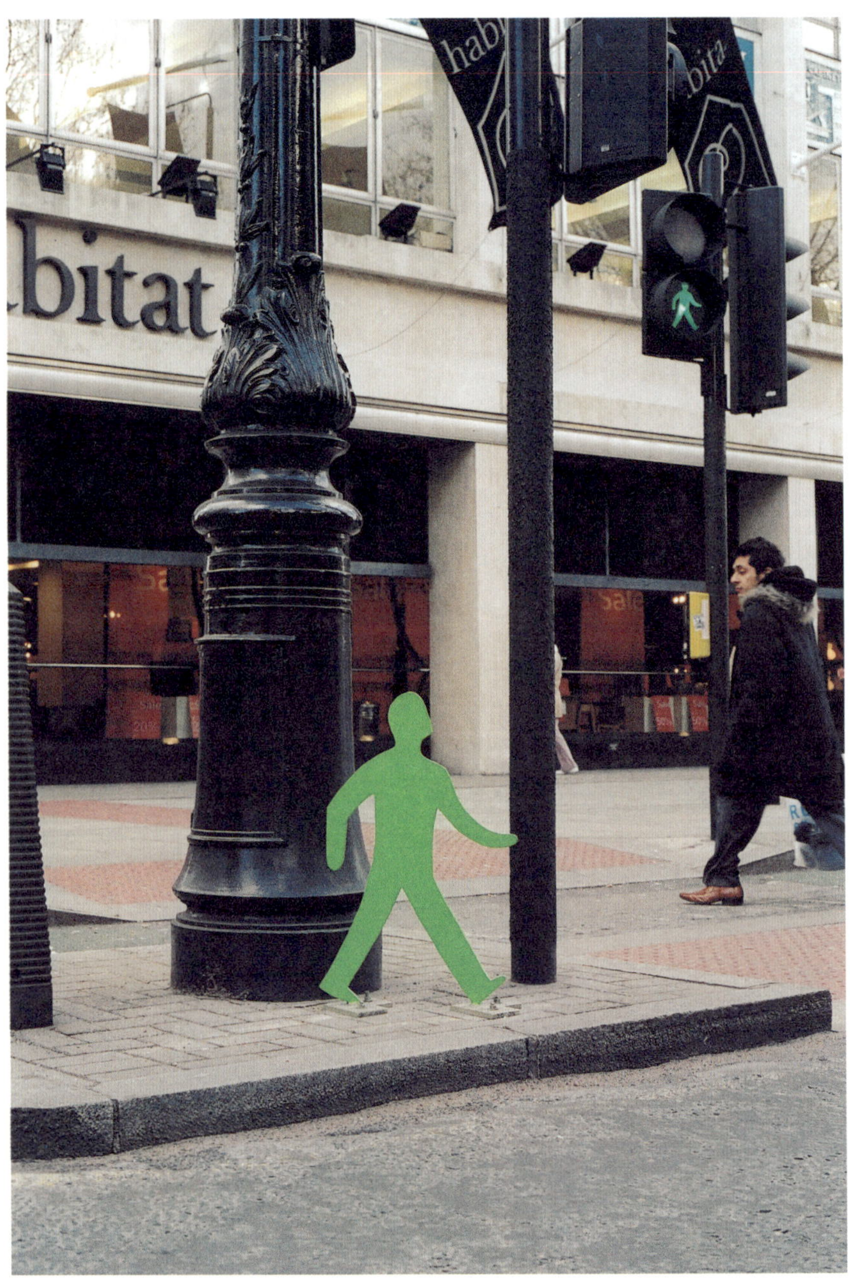

Walkin, Darius Jones (Leon Reid IV), 2004. London. Duration: 1 week.

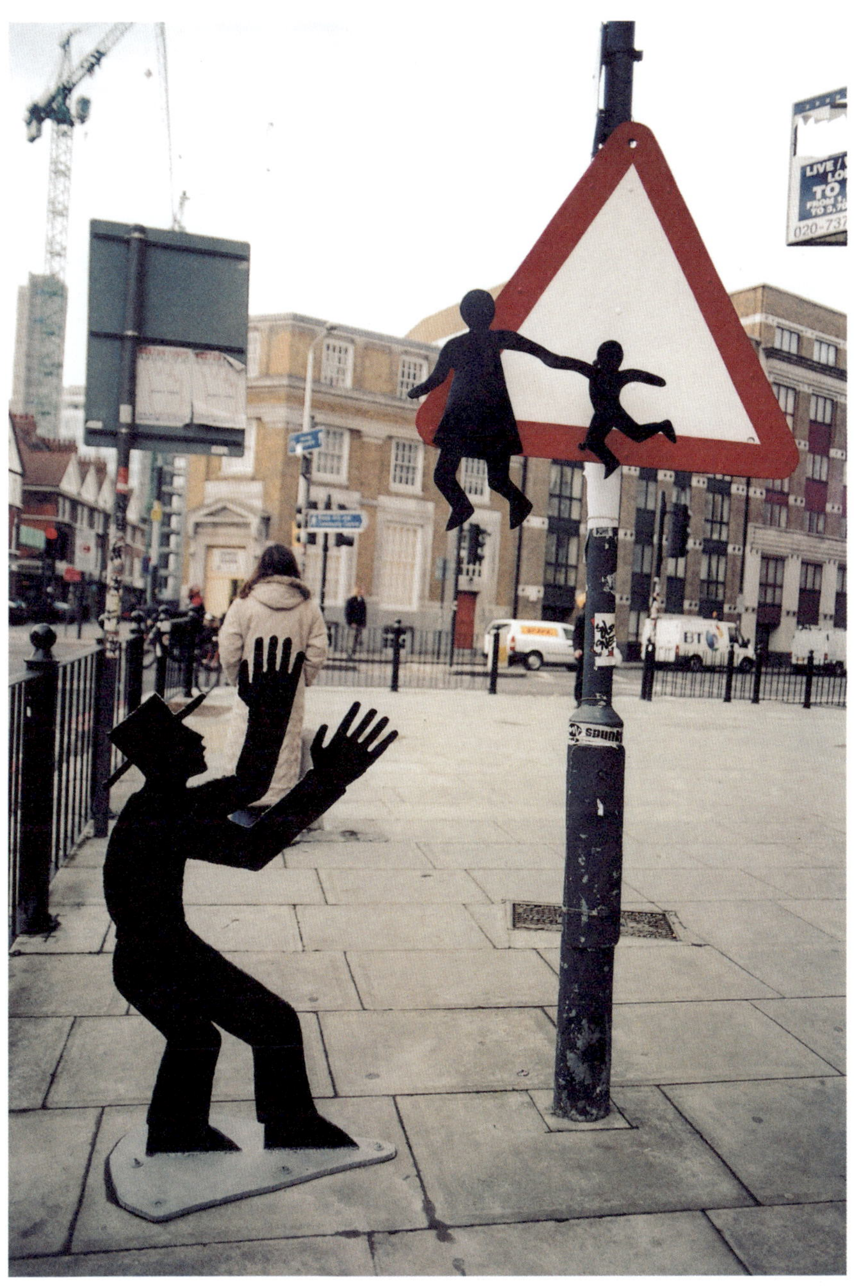

A Father's Duty, Brad Downey, 2003. London. Duration: father figure 6 days, sign 4 months.

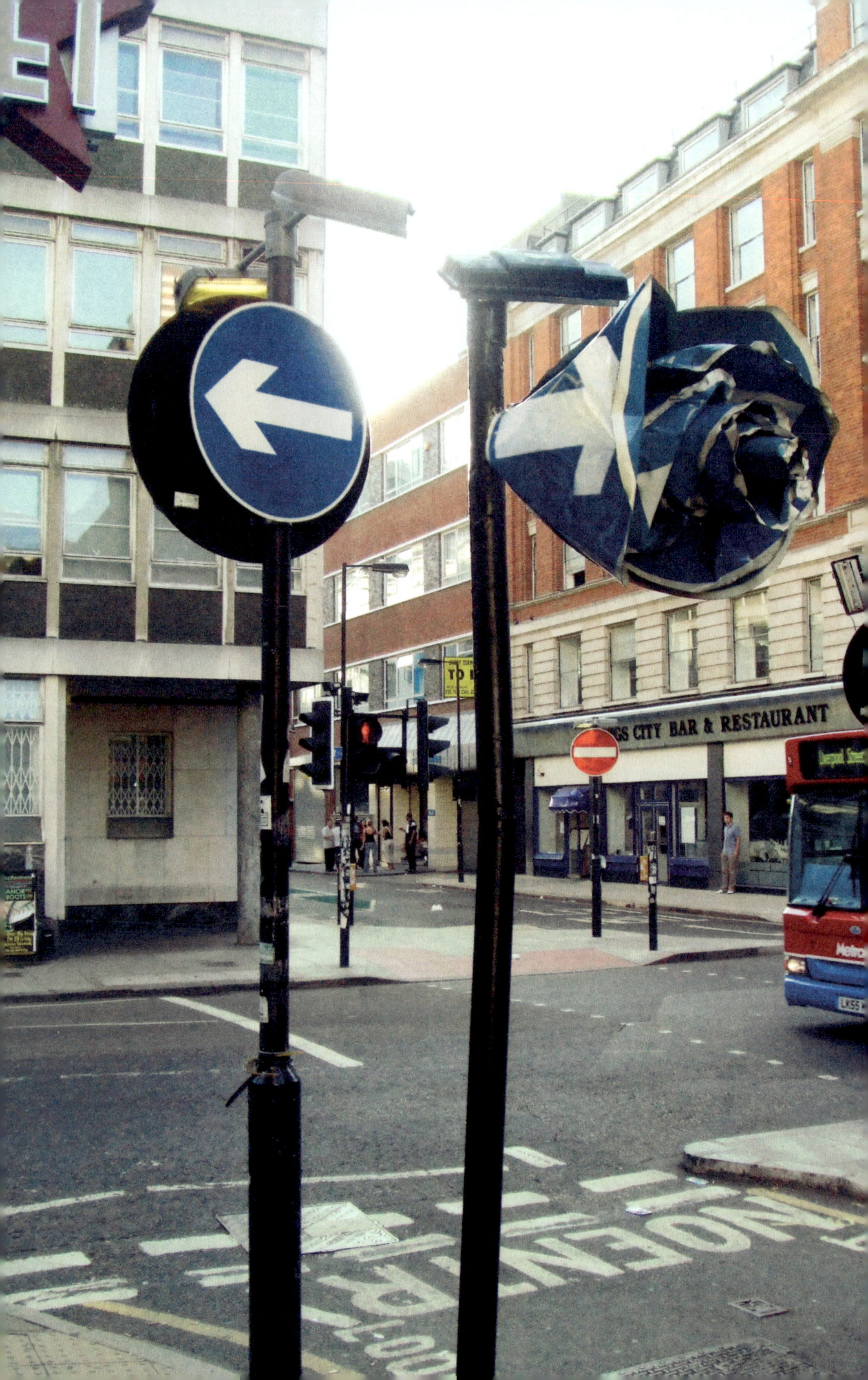
GS CITY BAR & RESTAURANT

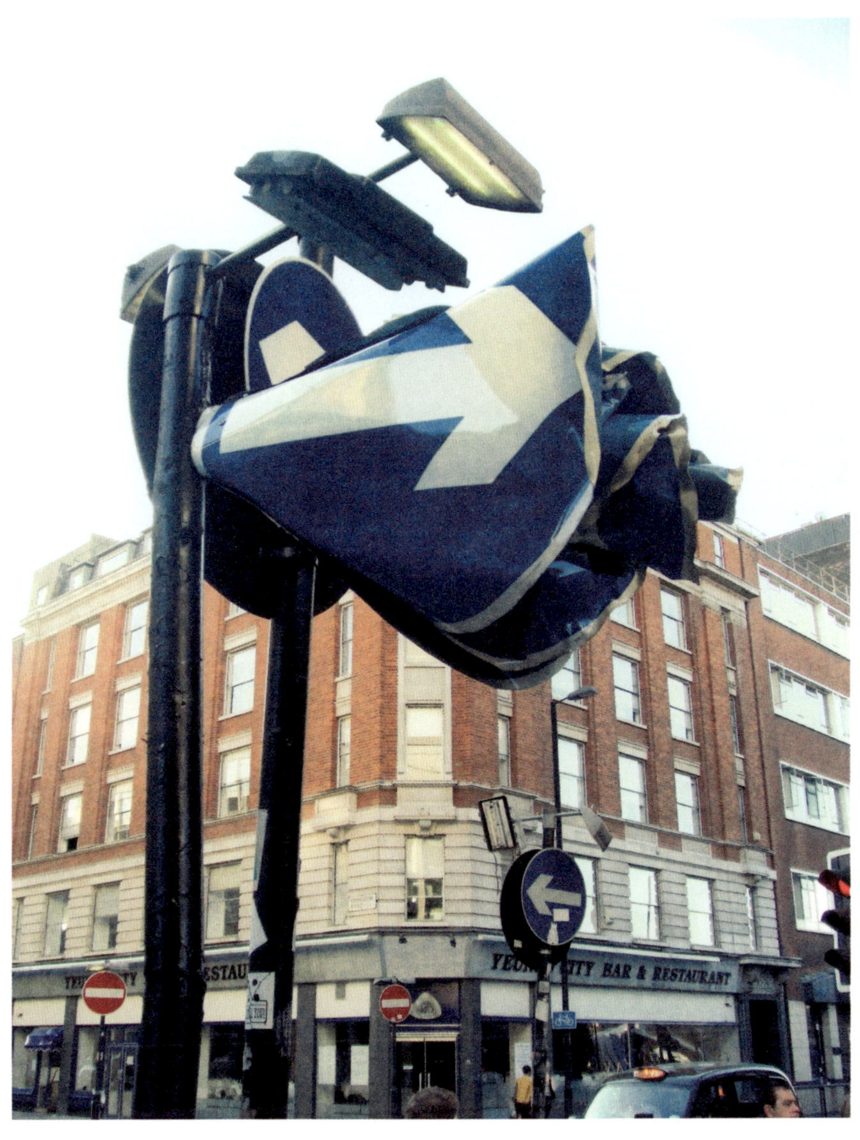

Wild at Heart, Brad Downey, 2006. London. Duration: 2 hours.

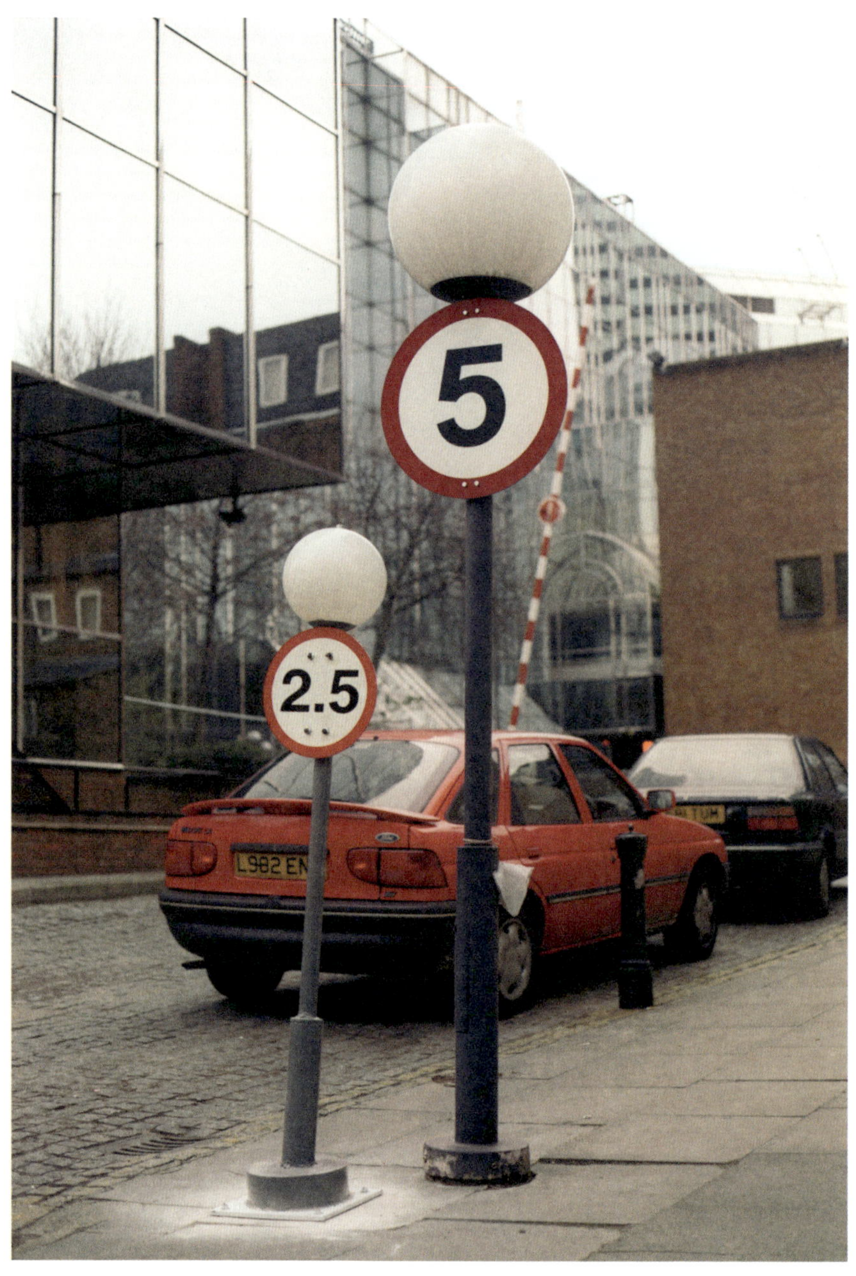

Madonna and Child, Brad Downey, 2003. London. Duration: 4 years.

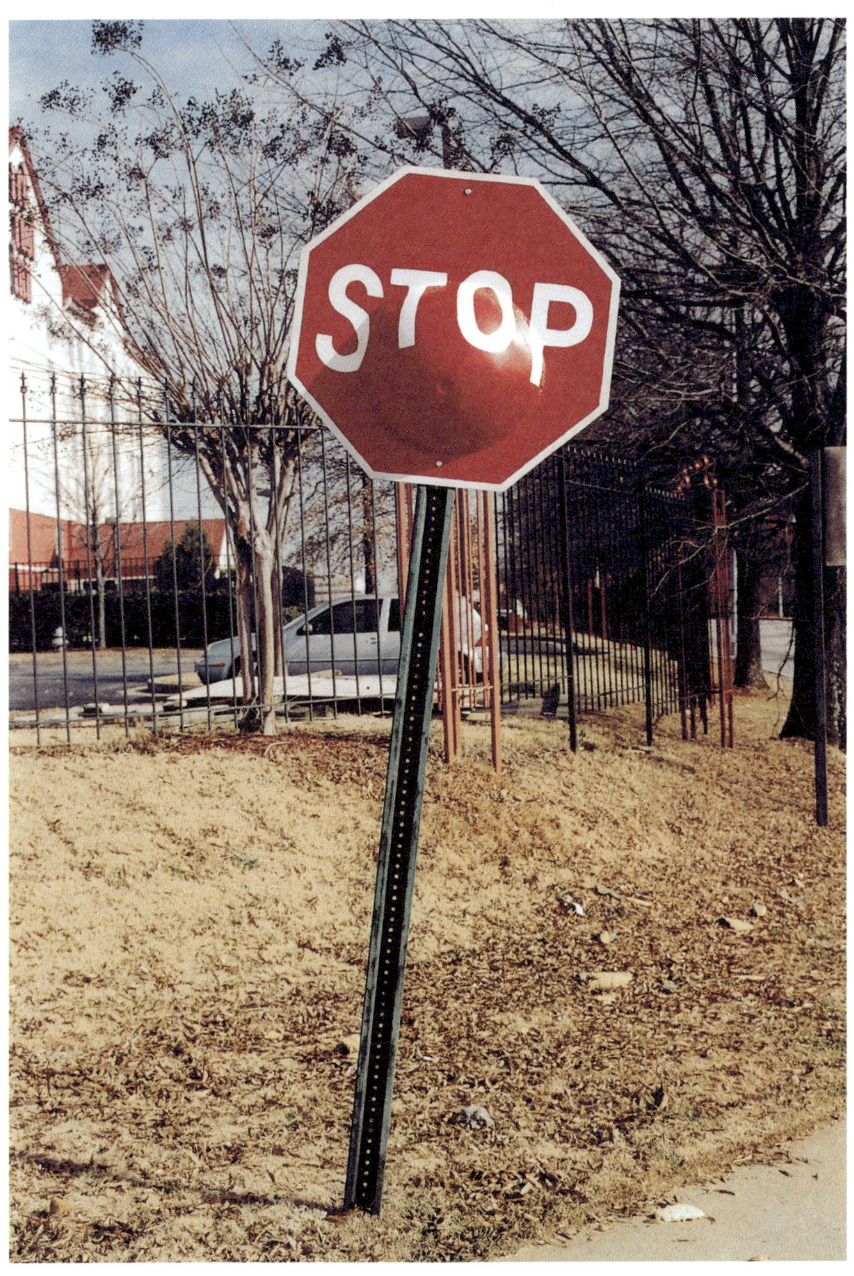

Pregnant Stop Sign, Brad Downey, 2004. Atlanta, GA. Duration: 6 weeks.

The Tree, Brad Downey, 2005. London. Duration: 2 weeks.
Photo by Jess Scott Hunter.

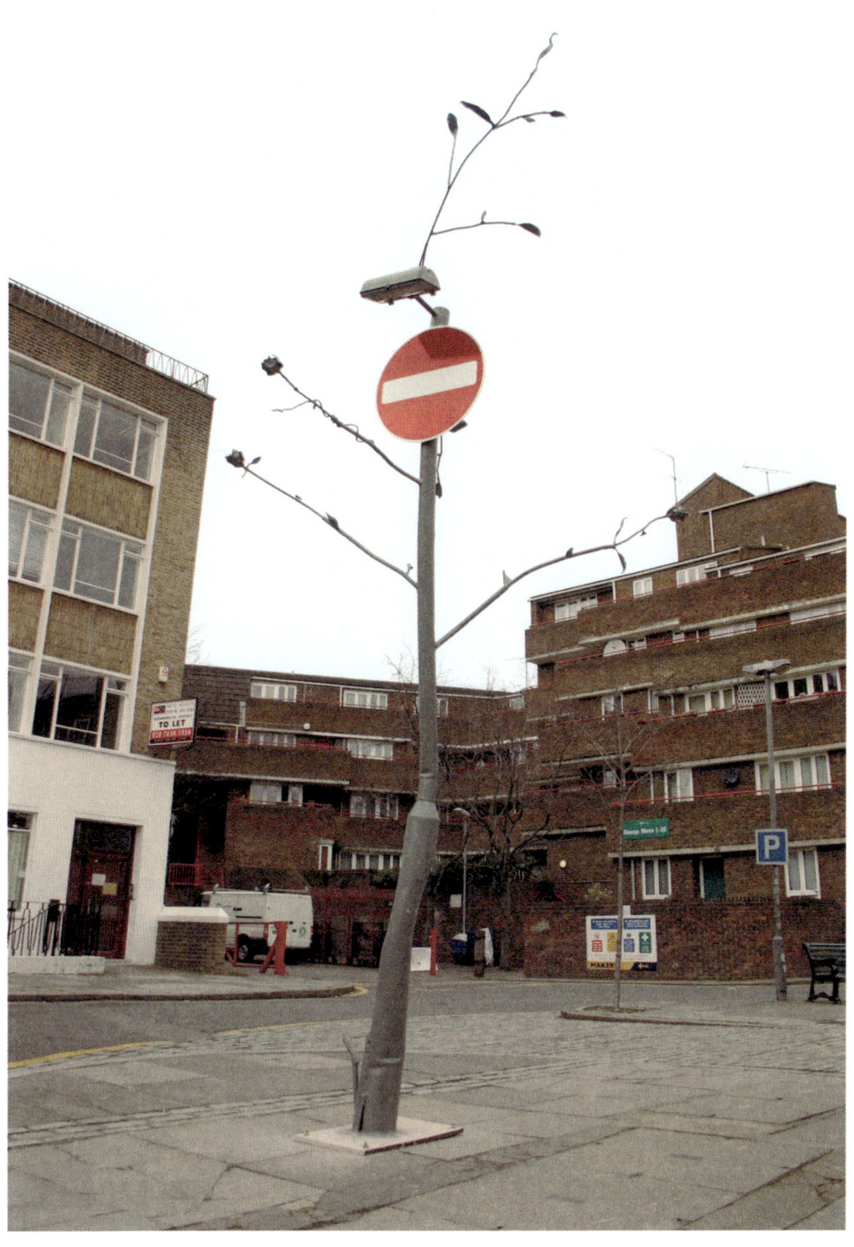

TO LET

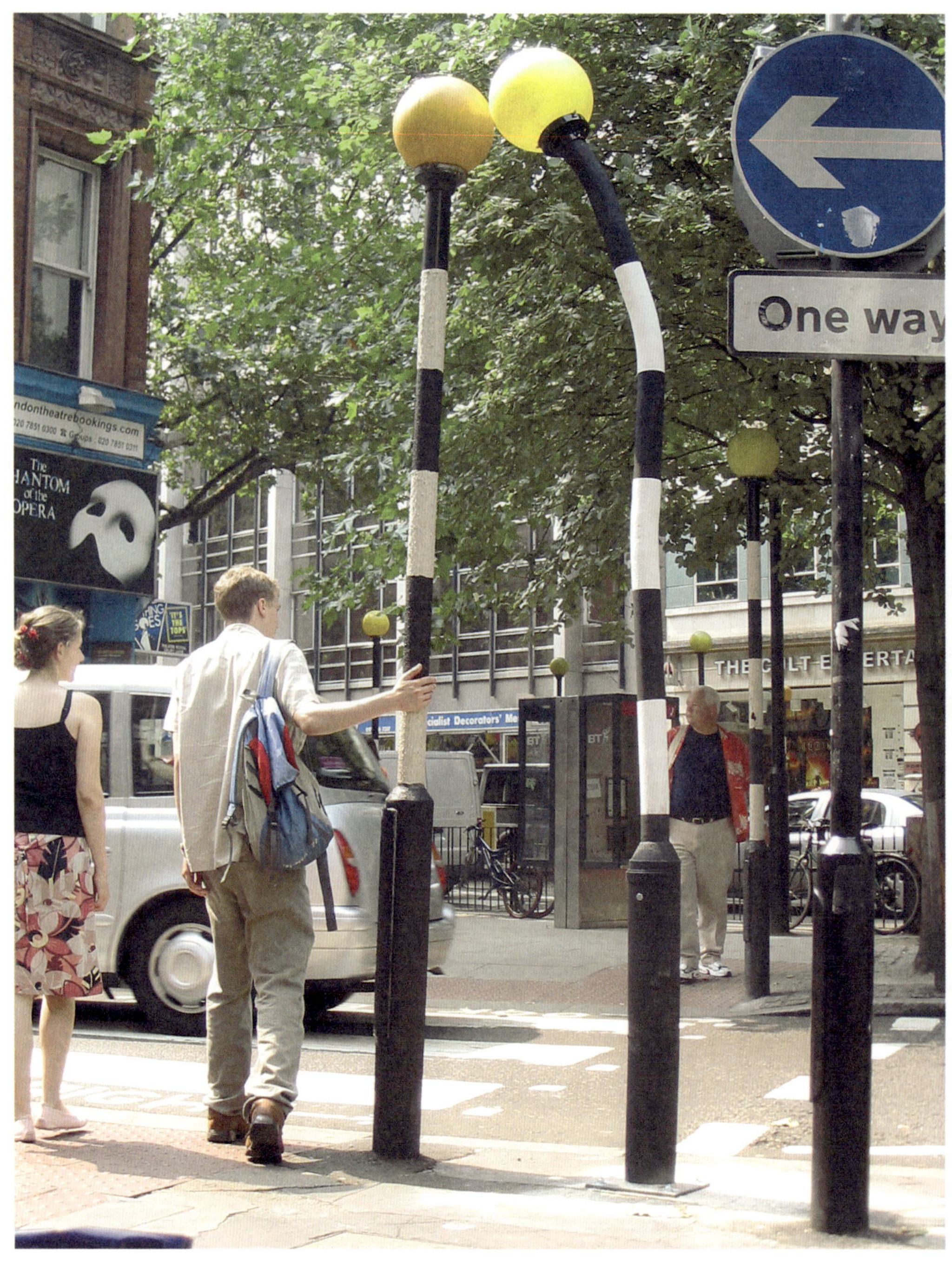

The Kiss, Darius Jones (Leon Reid IV), 2004. London. Duration: 1 hour. Photo by Ed Zipco.

OPPOSITE *The Break-up,* Brad Downey, 2004. London. Duration: 3 weeks.

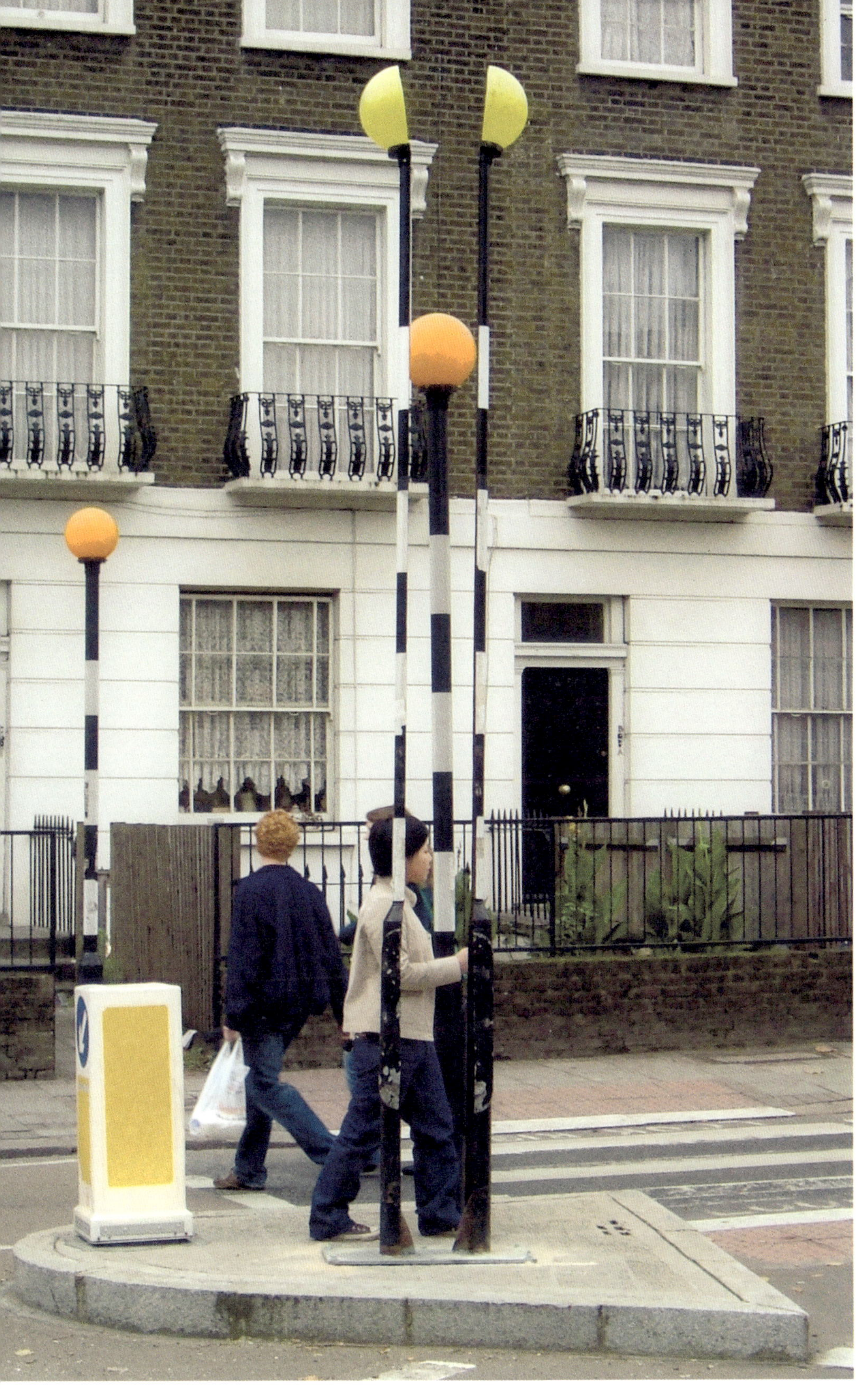

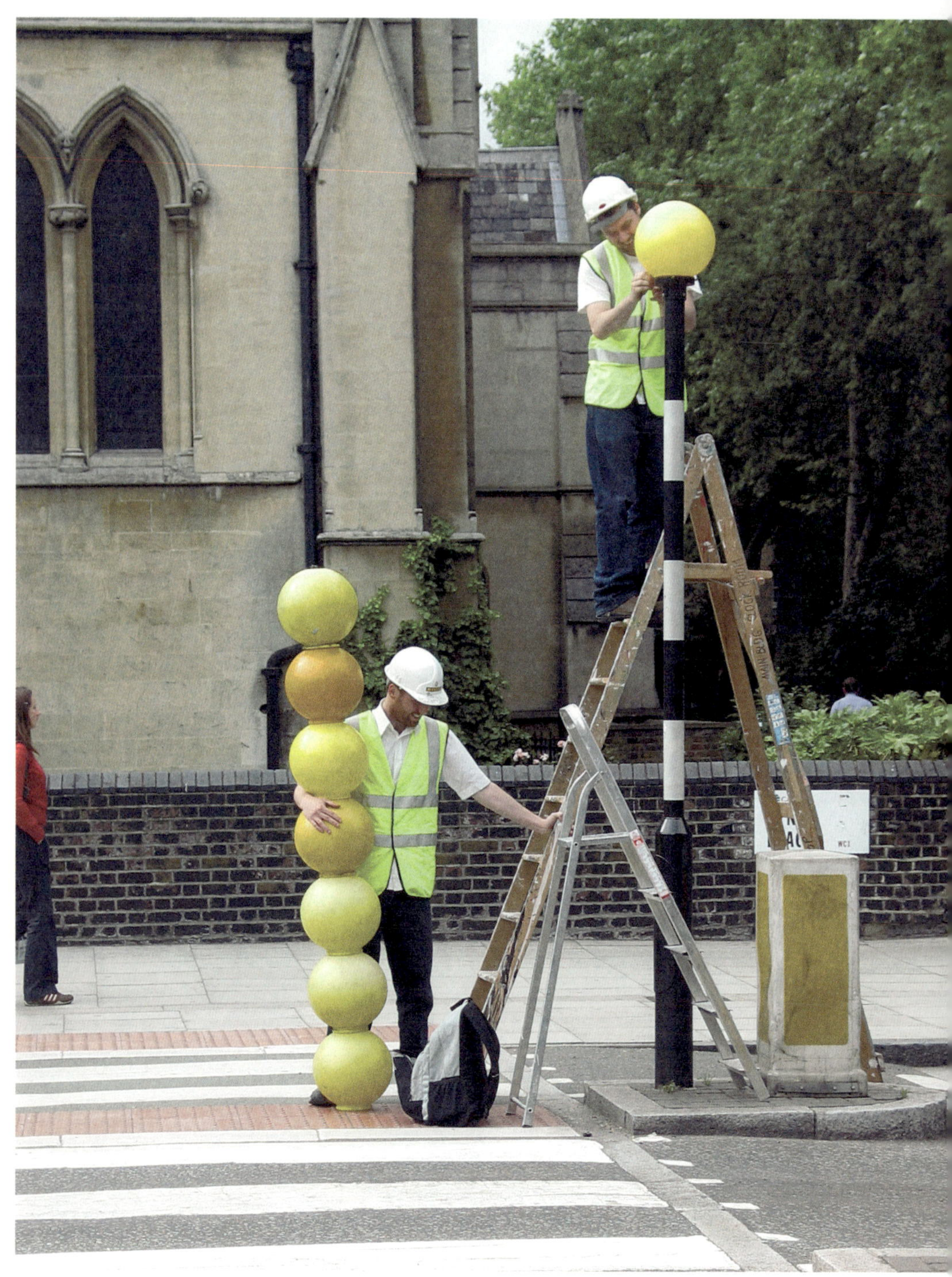

Matt Murphy suits up in London. Photo by Julia Tingulstad.

OPPOSITE *Endless Column in Context*, Brad Downey, 2005. London.
Duration: 1 week. Photo by Julia Tingulstad.

238

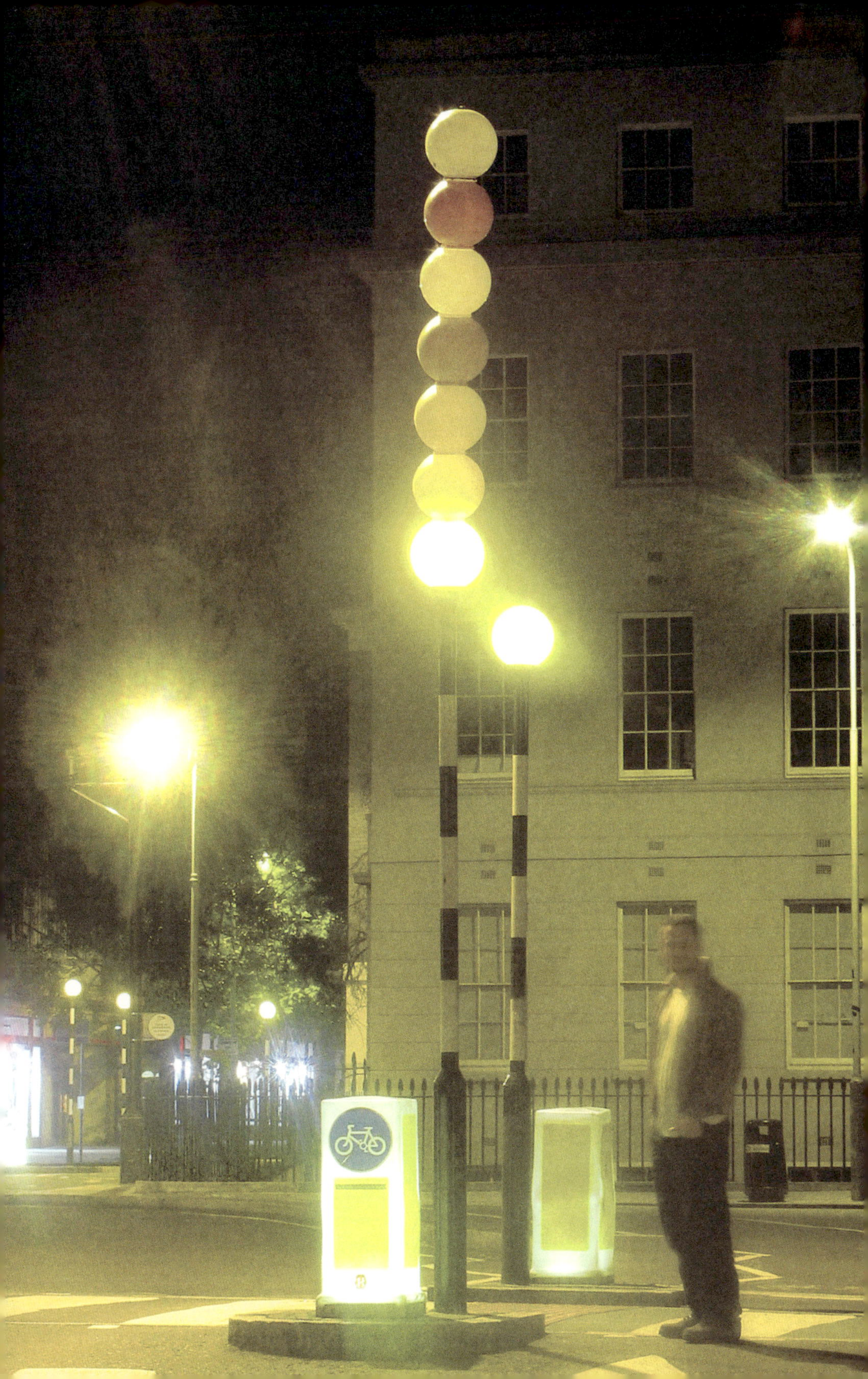

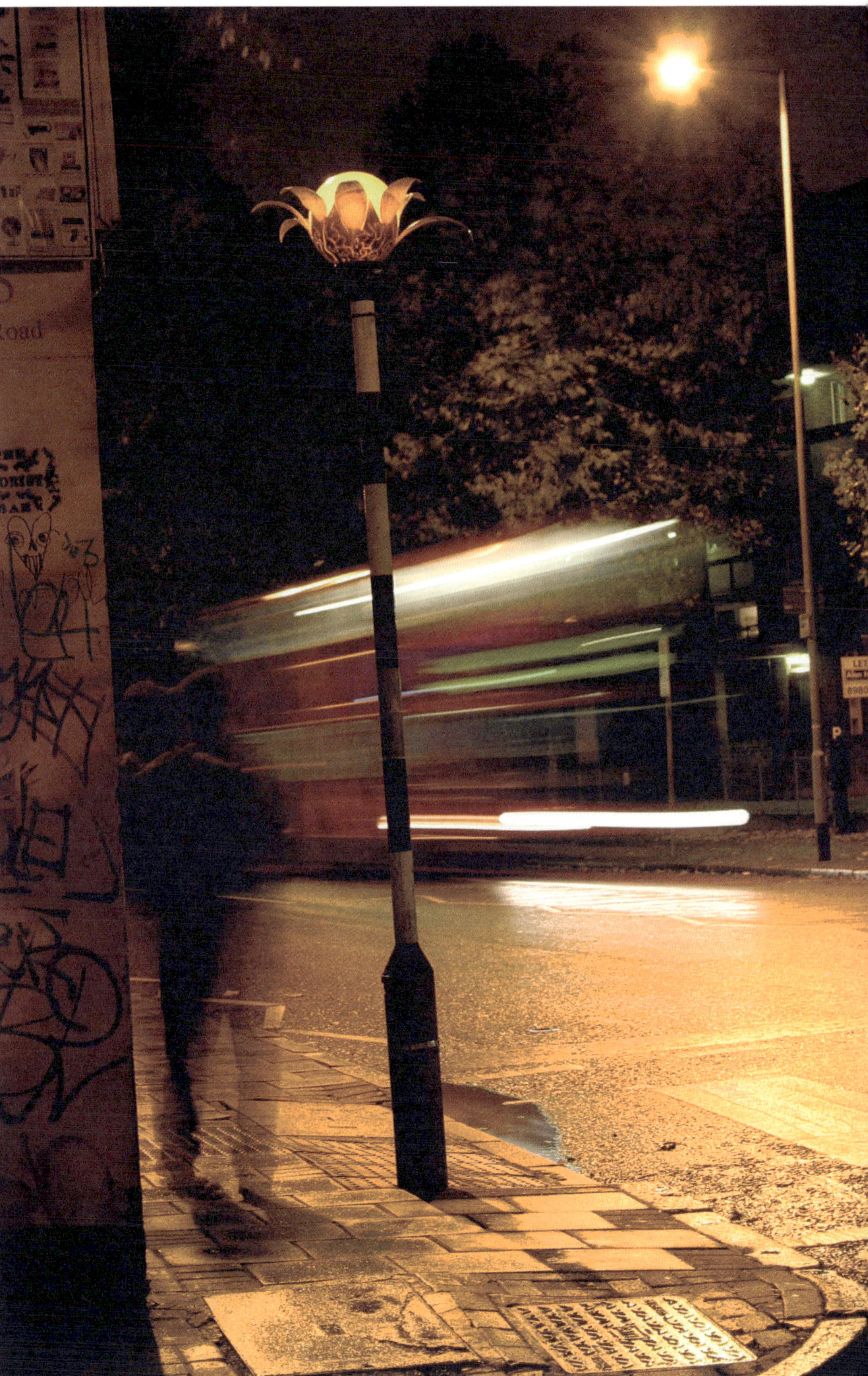

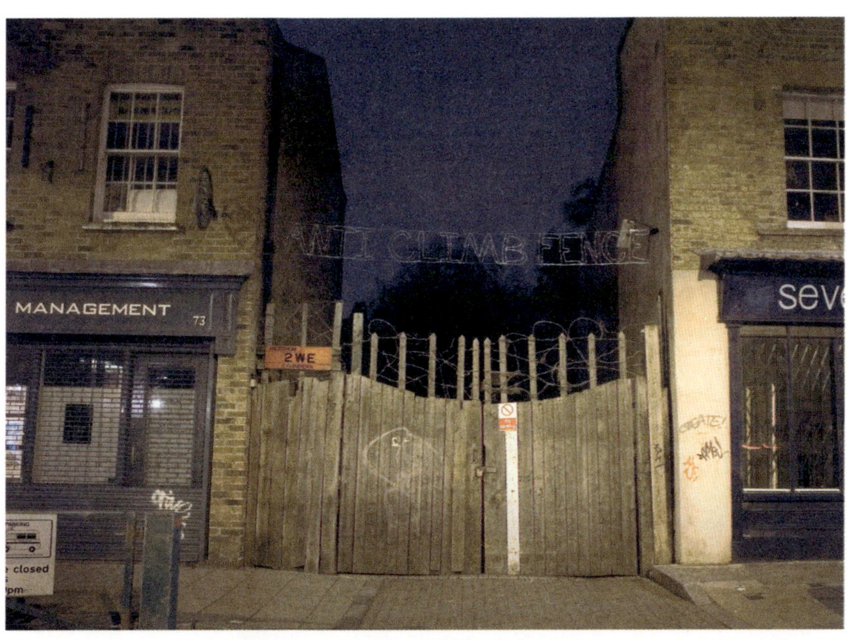

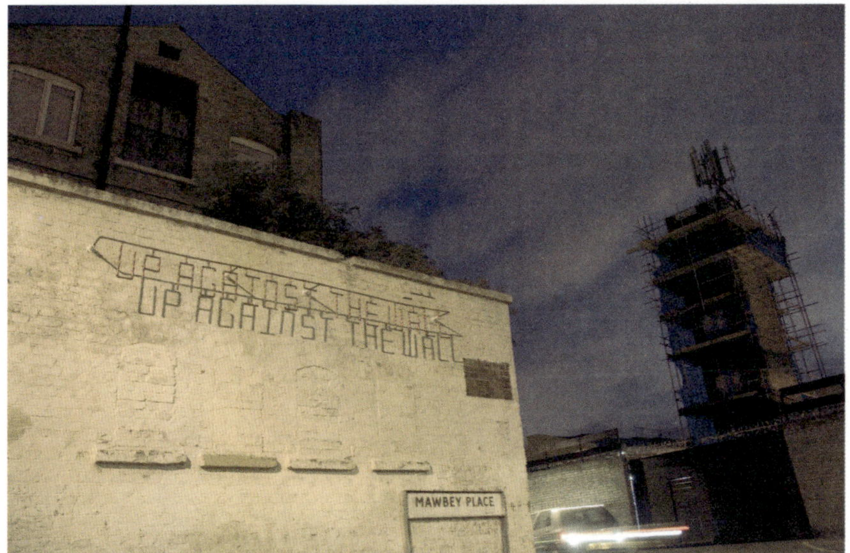

OPPOSITE *Fleur d'Plastique*, 2004. Darius Jones (Leon Reid IV). London. Duration: 5 months. Photo by Jess Scott Hunter.

TOP *Anti-Climb Fence*, 2006. Brad Downey. London. Duration: 1 year. Photo by Jasper Kidd.

ABOVE *Up Against the Wall*, 2006. Brad Downey. London. Duration: 4 months. Photo by Jasper Kidd.

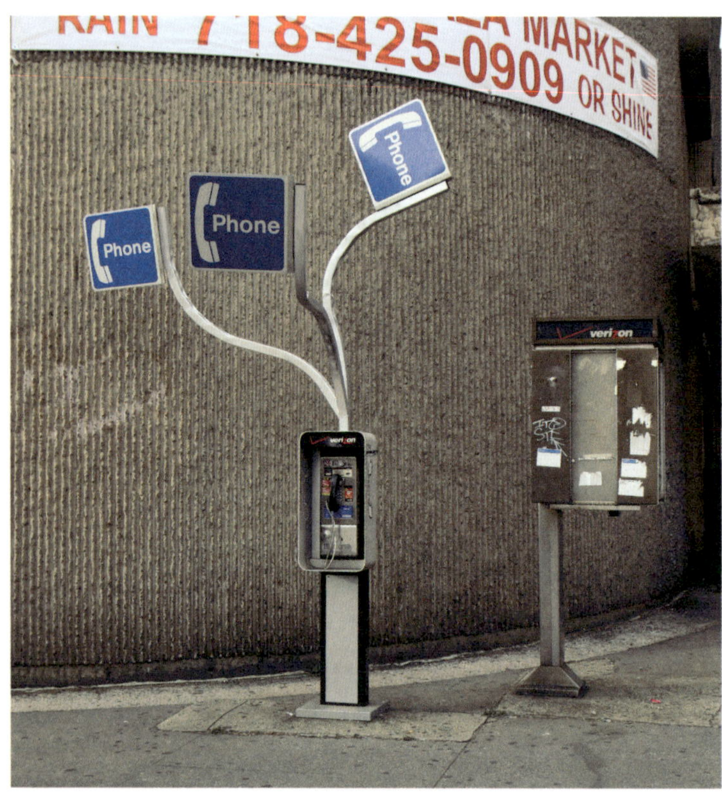

David vs. Goliath,
Brad Downey, 2006.
New York City, NY.
Duration: 6 months.
Photo by Tod Seelie.

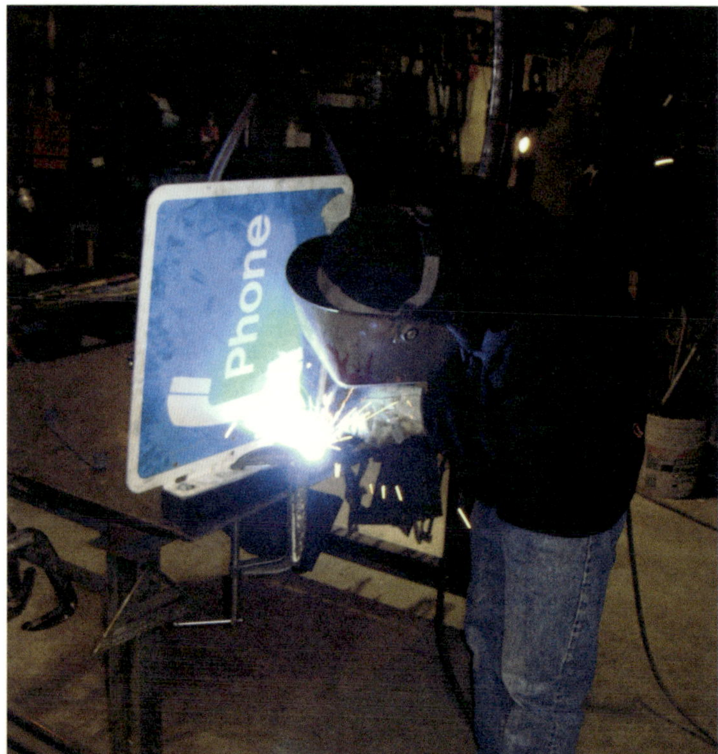

LEFT Leon Reid IV
at work in New York.
Photo by Albert Zuger,
2005.

OPPOSITE *It's All Right*,
Darius Jones (Leon Reid
IV), 2005. Brooklyn, NY.
Duration: 4 months.

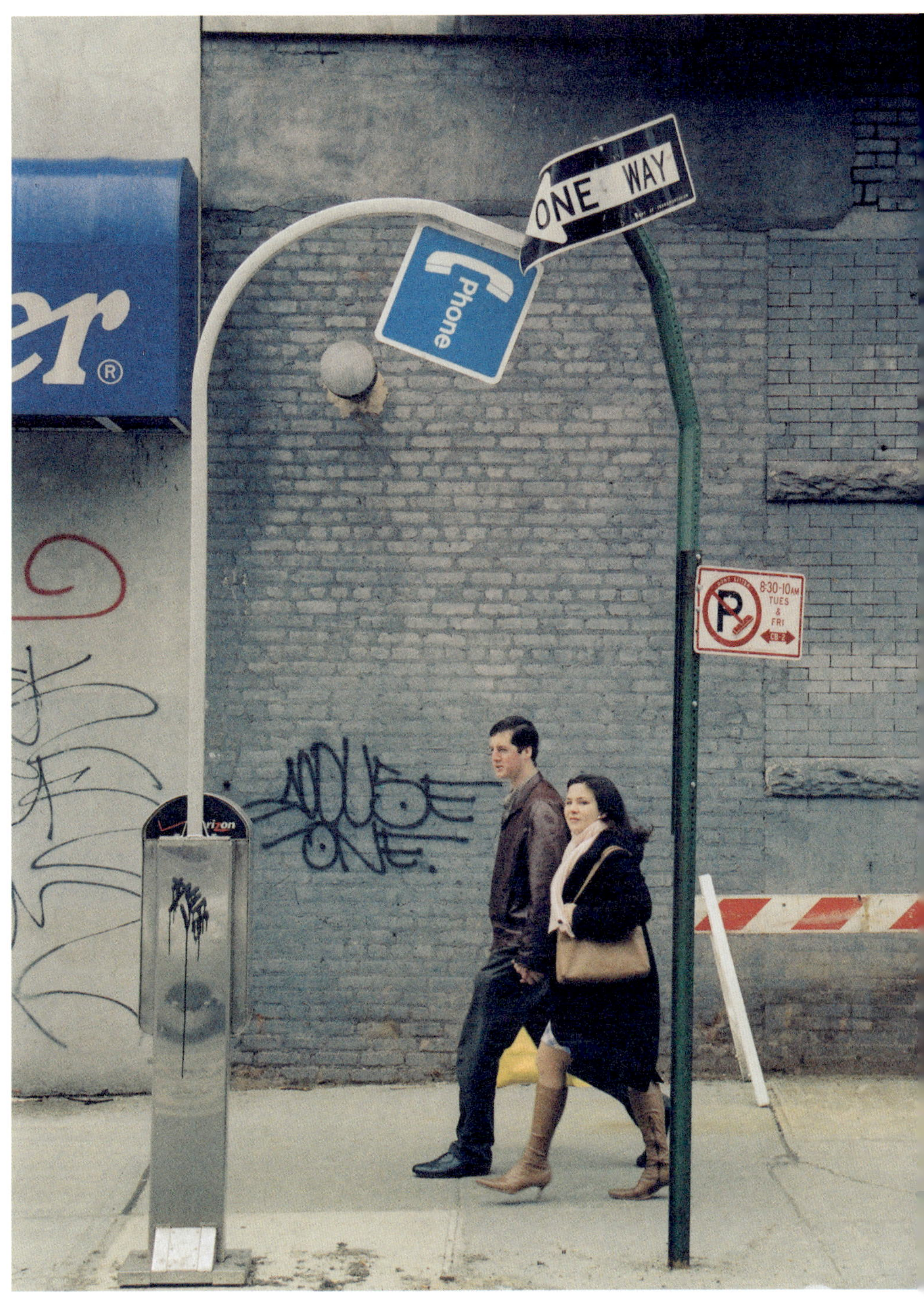

ONE WAY
Phone
er®
verizon
8:30-10 AM
TUES
&
FRI
CB 2
P

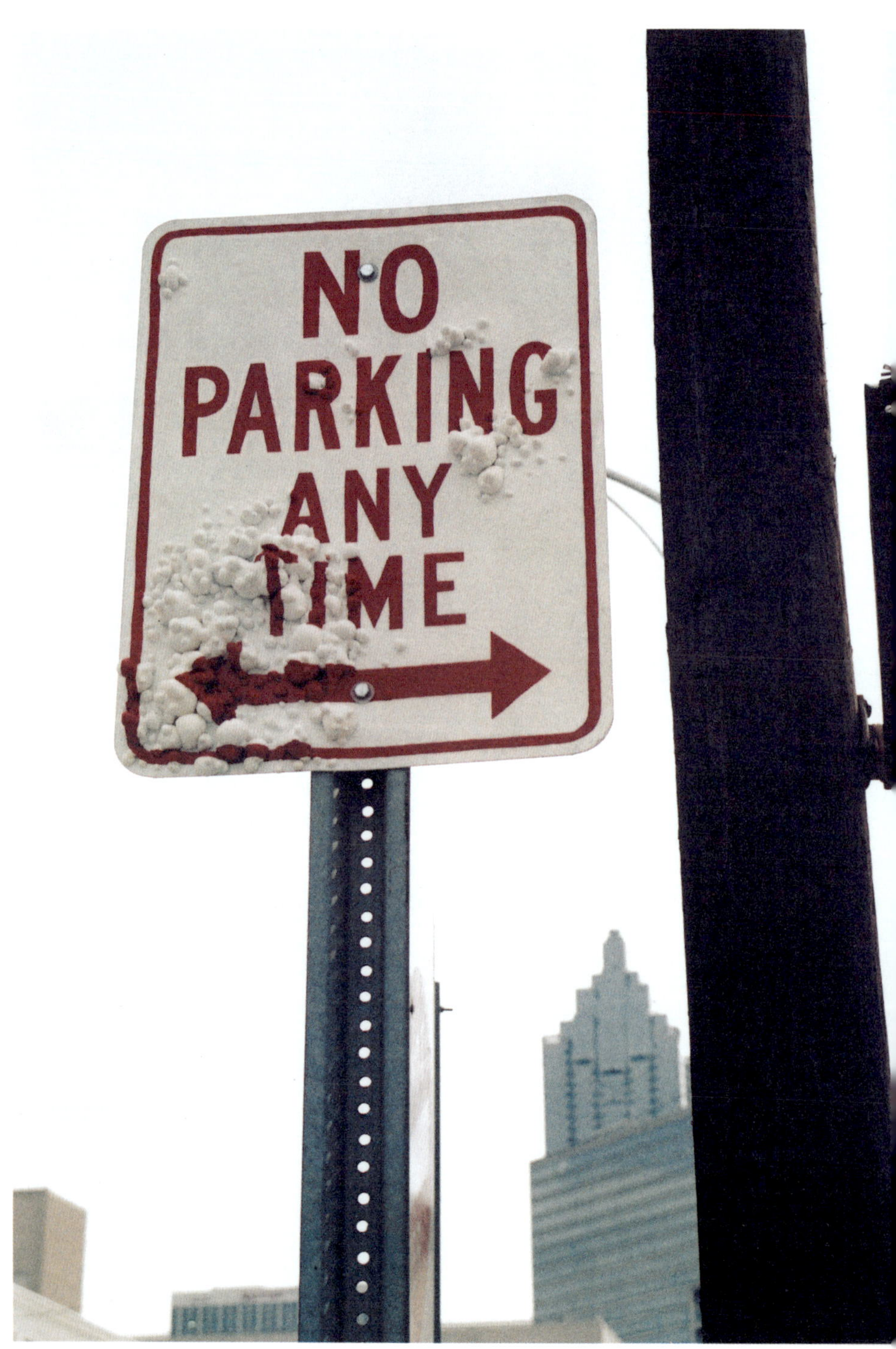

NO
PARKING
ANY
TIME

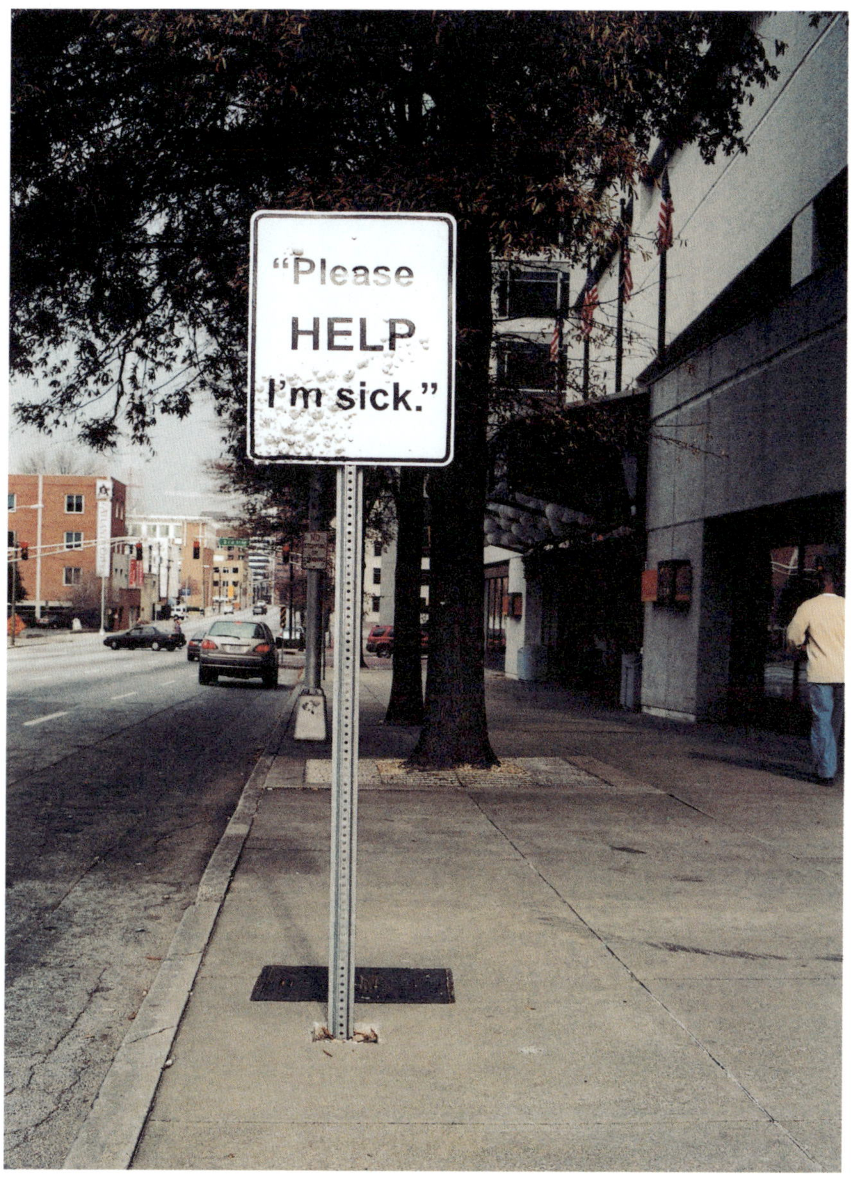

OPPOSITE *STD #1*, Brad Downey, 2004. Atlanta, GA. Duration: 3 years.

ABOVE *STD #2*, Brad Downey, 2004. Atlanta, GA. Duration: 5 days.

LUCKY CHAPTER THIRTEEN

2006 | After surviving all of their exploits and working collaboratively in Europe to great success, Leon and Brad take stock and brace themselves for new adventures.

Leon and Brad, in New York and Europe respectively, had finally come into their own. Individually and collaboratively they had evolved as artists, creating a language that they could work within, and finding ways to truly interact with the masses that walk the streets, their desired audience.

After Leon's departure from England in the fall of 2004, Brad remained in London to finish up his master's degree at the Slade. Divided by the Atlantic Ocean, the cheapest and easiest way to continue their ever-present dialogue was via email. The pair had separated once more as they had many times in the past, but this separation would see Darius and Downey's common wavelength become more successful than ever before.

Back in New York City, Leon at first found the American concrete beneath his feet soothing and reminiscent of the good days of street art. But then in an abrupt change of tack, he decided to dedicate his time to conceiving large public artworks to protest violence and conflict in Africa and the Middle East. This saw Leon master the rules and regulations of accessing official permission the same way he had absorbed the rules of the underground graffiti universe a decade before.

Brad, still curious to search the caverns of street art, continued creating installations in and beyond the Darius and Downey vein, incorporating the power of disguise in his operations and of context in his art. But at the same time he too began getting permission for larger public works. While in London, Brad also continued to pursue his parallel passion of filmmaking, shooting short films with a small creative team including Tahu Deans and Erik Tidemann, as well as collaborating with Quenell Jones on a documentary trailing the heritage of both their families through American history.

The work of Darius and Downey has not only revolutionized street art installation, but contributed to the reinvention of the urban landscape as a whole. Their partnership is a landmark in creative collaboration, one of those rare instances when two elements meet in a random occurrence but react and explode together in a perfect way, shape, and form.

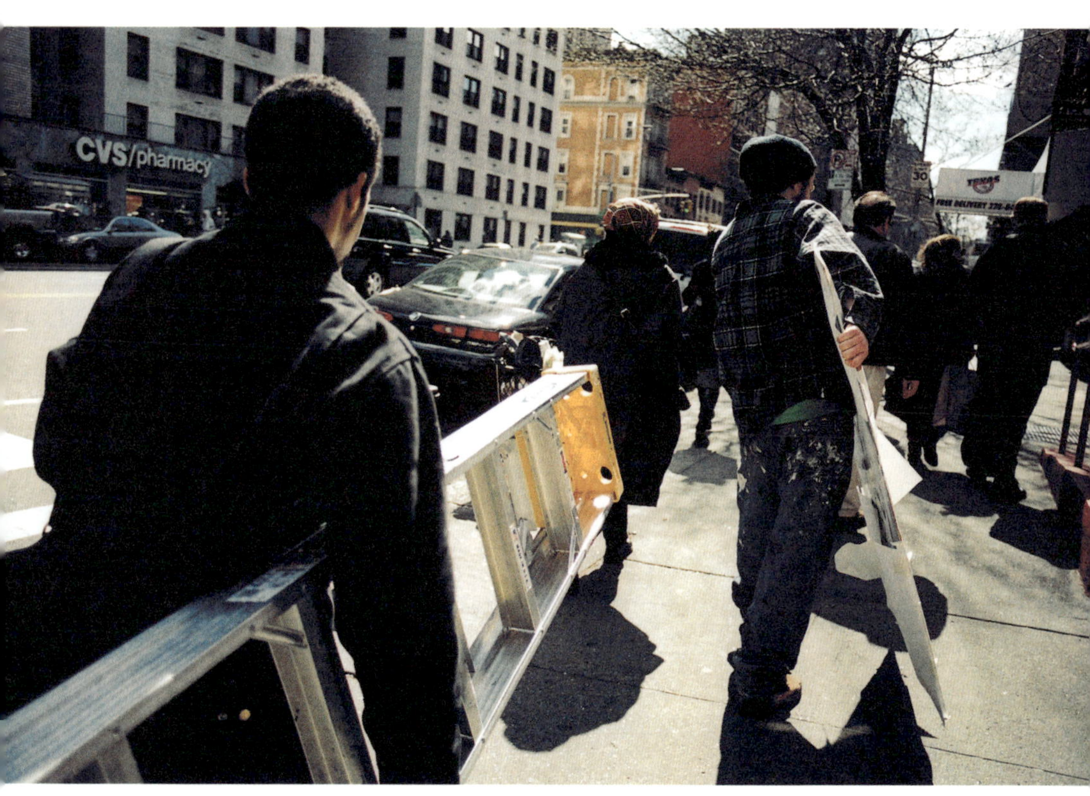

Darius and Downey go forth in New York, 2001. Photo by Leslie Stem.

AFTERWORD BY JENNIFER THATCHER

Among the fluffy pile of unremarkable '90s Hollywood romantic comedies, one film seemed particularly to capture the Zeitgeist. *LA Story* (1991) follows the plight of TV weatherman Harris Telemacher (Steve Martin), who is unexpectedly forced to confront his meaningless life by a talking sign on the Los Angeles Freeway. Against the cynical and superficial backdrop of LA – home of the "Have a nice day!" criminal and the "half double decaffeinated half-caf" coffee – the street sign stands as the only authentic and sympathetic voice in the film. This anarchic sign is the exception in the inhospitable urban cityscape of which it is a part, and can therefore be read as a glimmer of hope that humanity can be found in the most unexpected of places.

As in *LA Story*, Darius Jones (aka Leon Reid IV) and Brad Downey use their homemade street signs to speak to a disenfranchised urban population. "Please Help I'm Sick" pleads one of Downey's particularly bathetic signs on an urban American sidewalk. To an emotionally numb population, the startling context of this cry for help gives it a greater affective power than those similarly desperate messages held up by the dozens of homeless people we pass each day. But who is the "I" of Downey's sign? In a world where sick building syndrome is practically treated as a medical term, might we soon start legislating against sick city syndrome?

One of Darius and Downey's collaborative signs, this time on a London Tube platform, surprises by its exaggerated aggressiveness. "Sit Your Arse Down And Wait (Just Like Everyone Else)" commands the message, nestled neatly inside the iconic London Underground logo. It reminds me of the satirical '70s etiquette book, *The Unexpurgated Code* by J.P. Donleavy, in which the author translates social niceties into an un-PC "pukka" version for the benefit of common people. An installation shot of the piece shows a trio of commuters sitting on the bench below, grinning sheepishly like naughty schoolchildren.

For all their surface cynicism, Darius and Downey's pioneering approach to street art seems to share the underlying optimism of *LA Story*. Their street installations both mock the humourless and alienating bureaucracy of city planning, and pierce its apparent impenetrability through visibly human interventions. Darius's giant steel flower, *Fleur d'Acier*, suggests a world in which romance and urbanity might coexist – not through quick-fix attempts to jazz up deprived areas with gaudy shrubbery, but through a revaluing of the physical fabric of the city. For all its masculine industrial aesthetic, the welded steel maintains a rare delicacy among the urban jungle of lamp posts and street signs.

Brad Downey's oddly touching *Madonna and Child*, for which he added a baby speed-limit sign alongside a lone "parent" sign, defies our expectations about the functionality of "street furniture". Already three years old at the time of writing, the installation's resilience stands, as its biblical title ironically implies, as a protective symbol for all the unloved and defunct street furniture that governments are so keen to put up, but not to remove. And in the very intimacy of the title, the piece challenges the euphemistic cosiness and domesticity that the term "street furniture" suggests, all the while that these structures are designed to deter any loitering, or worse, corrode any sense of home for the homeless.

Belisha beacons – those black and white striped columns topped by a flashing amber globe that appear either side of pedestrian crossings – crop up in the large number of Darius and Downey's installations made while in the UK. As a series of eccentric permutations on a single unit, their Belisha

beacon works lend a gentle if ironic nod to the exhaustiveness
of Minimalist sculpture: a pair of beacons appear to kiss on
a busy London street, one leaning down to gently nuzzle the
other; one beacon is sliced vertically in half to encompass a
child-size beacon between the two "parent" halves; and in
another sculpture, seven orange lights are precariously
stacked on top of the striped pole.

Named after its inventor, the charismatic inter-war
Transport Minister Leslie Hore-Belisha, the Belisha beacon
is a curiously British phenomenon that harks back to a time
when the country was proud of its progressive social policies.
For two artists "classically" trained on the mean streets of
New York, London must have appeared quaintly parochial to
Darius and Downey. But it is their curiosity about their new
city – their enthusiasm for learning the semiotics of its street
signs – that lends their work a sensitivity to its environment
so lacking in British public art.

Sanctioned public art in the UK has in the recent past
tended to fall into two camps: bombastic pieces by a coterie
of well-known artists such as Rachel Whiteread and Antony
Gormley, which provoke months, if not years, of high-profile
public debate; and an increasing number of lesser-known,
locally commissioned pieces, much encouraged by the
New Labour government, which contribute to the goals
of regeneration and boosting cultural tourism. Official
public art in Britain today therefore has to meet exacting,
agenda-led criteria that require of the artist an enormous
degree of patience and flexibility, and a working method
that is anything but spontaneous. Since sites are usually
predetermined – that is, not selected by the artist – "site-
specific" public art tends to be contrived and heavily policed
in its political implications.

A few artists, mostly working outside the UK, do succeed

in producing more radical site-specific work, but ironically this often means fostering long-term relationships with councils and institutions (Thomas Hirshhorn spent a year and a half persuading the Pompidou Centre to lend him original works for his temporary museum in a working-class suburb of Paris) or colluding with art's traditional enemy – commercial enterprises – in order to secure their chosen site (the classic example being Jenny Holzer's *Truisms* on the electronic billboards of Times Square). No wonder that the ideals of site-specificity that postmodernist art theory encouraged – with its emphasis on a considered and sensitive understanding of local context and community – feel so compromised for public artists, and that non-sanctioned street art is receiving new respect, even envy, from the art world and, increasingly, the public.

It's become impossible to discuss the relationship between street art and sanctioned art without mentioning the so-called Banksy Effect, which has seen graffiti championed by the most unlikely of Hollywood celebrities. The most PR-friendly exponent of the new "stencil revolution" in graffiti, Banksy's sudden commercial success (£96,000 was paid for *Ballerina With Action Man Parts* at a Sotheby's auction in February 2007) has been received by some, not least the artist himself, with bitter contempt. Yet the criticism of "selling out" has become such an oxymoron in the fine art world – where previously uncompromising artists have found that working with private galleries has paradoxically proved less restrictive than with public institutions – that street art is in fact one of the few arenas in which this debate about hypocrisy can provoke any substantial controversy.

It would seem that, in judging street art by its own anachronistic and corrupt terms, some in the commercial art world are taking their revenge on an art form over which they have little control. Street artists can choose to go to art school or not, work with galleries or not, to make more art-market-friendly work or not, to sell work or not, and it unbalances the carefully managed hierarchy of the art world if artists want to have their cake and eat it. If there is any difference left between subcultural activities and the mainstream, then this is it: while the territory in which artists from both spheres work may indeed overlap, artists working within subcultures retain the right of veto over the rules by which either area is legally and arbitrarily subject.

One canonized artist who, nonetheless, seems particularly to have caught the imagination of street artists is Gordon Matta-Clark. The late American sculptor literally demolished the sanctity and integrity of the Western bourgeois home through his infamous "building cuts". With a certain equivalence, Darius and Downey challenge the naturalness of Western urban planning, albeit mostly through a strategy of additions and rearrangements rather than subtractions.

Their strategy might usefully be compared with French theorist Nicolas Bourriaud's concept of postproduction. The postproduction artist, according to Bourriaud, does not concern him or herself with the primary production of objects, of which there is already a surplus, but in operating on existing objects in order to make them function again. It may sound like the more familiar notion of recycling by a fancier name – Bourriaud prefers the DJ analogy of sampling – but the importance of his analysis lies in the attempt to find a more positive successor to the modernist project than postmodernism's obsession with relativism, and the banal, levelling effect of its indiscriminate appropriations.

If the Surrealists put Dada techniques to more constructive ends, Bourriaud's thesis runs, then postproduction is likewise the less nihilistic heir to the

Situationist art of the 1950s and '60s. Bourriaud argues for the continued validity of Situationist radical tactics – dérive and détournement – without "targeting the abolition of art", for the Situationist utopia was based on a "unitary urbanism" that had no need for a separate category of fine art.

In their concern for encouraging fresh perceptions of our tired cities, Darius and Downey certainly share the Situationist mission of reintroducing more playful and spontaneous possibilities into the urban environment. And, as with the Situationists, their work rewards the roving eye of the casual passerby, that rare figure with the leisure to interrupt, for even a brief moment, the patterns of learned behaviour to look beyond the expected motifs of urban iconography. But where the Situationists felt mostly disdain or pity for the poor commuter or privileged motorist, Darius and Downey's work lies in wait to try and catch their gaze. Like the *LA Story* we began with, coming across their work generates an unexpectedly private moment in a public space – a secret, shared moment with an anonymous creator who is trying to communicate with you, not in order to sell you something or stop you from doing something, but to remind you that the city belongs to you, however little it feels that way.

Jennifer Thatcher is a freelance art critic, contributing regularly to *Art Monthly* and *Art Review*. She is also Director of Talks at the Institute of Contemporary Arts, London, and teaches critical theory at the School of Photography, University College for the Creative Arts at Rochester.

Acknowledgments

Ed Zipco would like to thank: Lisa, for raising me right. Thank you for your unfathomable understanding, love and support. Anita Shapolsky for her surprising kindness, as well as Alex Smith, Daryl Clark, Bram Tihany, A'yen Tran, Andy Smith, Rip Torn, Quenell Jones, Swoon, Jesse, Matt, Mike Force, Amanda Vinnicombe and Arthur Nersesian.

Brad Downey would like to thank: Mom, Dad, Amber, and Stephanie for love, patience, and blind support, Rob Ponkos for design assistance, Ed Zipco for all the hard work and emotional support, Stephen Schuster, Tod Seelie, Albert Zuger, Michael Wrobel, JJ Veronis, Caledonia Dance Curry, Jennifer Thatcher, Anita Shapolsky, Tristan Manco, Julia Tingulstad, Akim, Matt Murphy, Jamie Camplin, Noah Sparks, Adrian Nabi, and Quenell Jones.

Leon Reid IV would like to thank: My Mother and Father, for unconditional love and support, Andre Hyland for lifelong friendship and creative advice, Rob Ponkos for design assistance, Stephen Schuster, Tod Seelie, Polina Soloveichik, Albert Zuger, Espo, JJ Veronis, Swoon, Quenell Jones, Jennifer Thatcher, Anita Shapolsky, and Tristan Manco.

www.edzipco.com
www.braddowney.com
www.leonthe4th.com